MOON

- BEST OF -
GLACIER, BANFF & JASPER

Becky Lomax & Andrew Hempstead

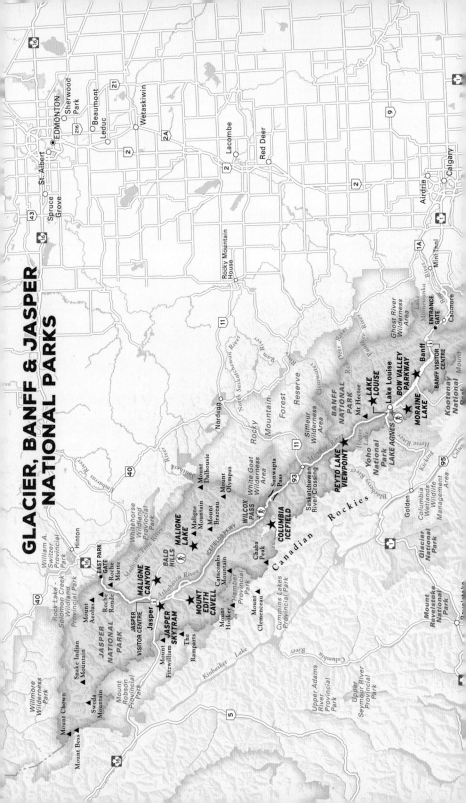

Scenic Drive

0   30 mi
0   30 km

CONTENTS

WELCOME TO GLACIER,
BANFF & JASPER 7
Best Days in Glacier, Banff & Jasper 9
Seasons of Glacier, Banff & Jasper 27
Need to Know: Glacier 30
Need to Know: Banff 30
Need to Know: Jasper 31

BEST OF THE BEST 33
Best Hikes 34
Best Views 36
Best Glacial Features 38
Indigenous Peoples of
 Glacier, Banff & Jasper 40
Best Scenic Drive 42
Practice Sustainable Travel in
 Glacier, Banff & Jasper 44

GLACIER NATIONAL PARK . . . 47
GLACIER NATIONAL PARK 3 WAYS . . . 53
HIGHLIGHTS AND SCENIC DRIVES 57
BEST HIKES 77
Backpacking 88
Biking 90
Paddling 93
Winter Sports 94
Food 96
Camping 100
Lodging 105
INFORMATION AND SERVICES | TRANSPORTATION 111

BANFF AND LAKE LOUISE . . . 117
BANFF AND LAKE LOUISE 3 WAYS . . .123
HIGHLIGHTS AND SCENIC DRIVES . . . 128
BEST HIKES 144
Backpacking 154
Biking 155
Paddling 158
Winter Sports 158
Food 160
Camping 164
Lodging 168
INFORMATION AND SERVICES | TRANSPORTATION . . . 174

ICEFIELDS PARKWAY 177
ICEFIELDS PARKWAY 3 WAYS 183
HIGHLIGHTS AND BEST HIKES 189
Backpacking 209
Biking 209
Food 209
Camping 211
Lodging 214
INFORMATION AND SERVICES | TRANSPORTATION . . . 218

JASPER NATIONAL PARK . . . 221
JASPER NATIONAL PARK 3 WAYS . . . 225
HIGHLIGHTS 229
SCENIC DRIVES 237
BEST HIKES 238
Backpacking 243
Biking 243
Rafting 244
Winter Sports 244
Food 246
Camping 249
Lodging 250
INFORMATION AND SERVICES | TRANSPORTATION . . . 257

WILDLIFE-WATCHING 259

WILDFLOWERS 269

ESSENTIALS 279

INDEX 298

LIST OF MAPS 305

242

263

275

Wilcox Pass

WELCOME TO
GLACIER, BANFF & JASPER

Snowcapped peaks, glaciers and ice fields, turquoise lakes, rushing rivers, wildflower meadows, and abundant wildlife make Glacier, Banff, and Jasper a trio of national parks that are rivaled by few places in the world.

Located in Montana just south of the U.S.-Canada border, Glacier preserves some of the wildest country in the United States. Captivating scenery, epic trails, and huge lakes fill this park's one million acres. While Glacier National Park is known as the Crown of the Continent, Banff National Park, located to the north in Alberta, Canada, is the crown jewel among all of Canada's national parks. Stunning lakes are backdropped by towering mountains that are enjoyed by skiers in the winter and hikers the rest of the year. Directly to the north, Jasper National Park is Banff's quieter, but still mountainous and beautiful, sibling. Connecting the two is one of the most scenic of scenic drives, the Icefields Parkway, which passes rushing rivers, breathtaking overlooks, and the largest and most accessible glacier field in the three parks, the Columbia Icefield.

Going-to-the-Sun Road

BEST DAYS IN
GLACIER, BANFF & JASPER

Day 1

1 Launch in Glacier National Park with a drive eastward on Going-to-the-Sun Road along **Lake McDonald.** Stop at one of the pullouts between 6 and 8 mi (9.7-13 km) up to drop to the shoreline for photos (page 57).

2 Climb higher and higher up the west side of Going-to-the-Sun Road with expansive views taking in glacier-carved peaks, deepening valleys, and waterfalls to **Logan Pass,** the highest point on the Continental Divide (page 61).

3 Hike the **Hidden Lake Overlook** trail, where you can spot glacial features, wildflowers, and perhaps mountain goats and bighorn sheep. On the return, enjoy the views of Going-to-the-Sun Mountain straight ahead (page 79).

4 Descend from Logan Pass eastward through a tunnel, curve around Going-to-the-Sun Mountain, and swing along St. Mary Lake to **Sun Point** to admire the view uplake (page 64).

5 Exit the park at St. Mary and drive north about 15 minutes to reenter the park via Many Glacier Road to catch the **tour boat** across Swiftcurrent and Josephine Lakes (page 70).

6 Spend the night at historic **Many Glacier Hotel** and catch the sunset over the Continental Divide (page 109).

Day 2

7 It's a 260-mi (420-km) drive from Glacier National Park to Banff. Plan for about 4.5 hours to make the trip. If you want to stretch your legs upon arrival, take a walk along the **Bow River** (page 128).

8 Afterward, ride the **Banff Gondola** to the top of Sulphur Mountain for sweeping views across the town and beyond. Plan on dining at the mountaintop restaurant or at a local favorite in town, like Park. Stay overnight in the town of Banff (page 132).

Day 3

9 This morning's itinerary includes two lakes. You'll need to make shuttle reservations well in advance to visit **Moraine Lake,** which is nestled among towering mountains (page 144).

10 **Lake Louise,** with its much-photographed turquoise water, is the next stop, and with that, you will have reached two world-famous lakes by lunchtime. Stroll along the lakeshore and take lots of photos (page 135).

11 Drive north along the Icefields Parkway. For stunning views and abundant wildflowers, stop near Bow Lake and make the trek to **Helen Lake,** one of the best hikes in Banff. Overnight at the historic Lodge at Bow Lake (page 190).

Day 4

12 In the morning, continue north to Jasper National Park and the **Columbia Icefield** to see a glacier up close (page 195).

13 Hike the trail to **Wilcox Pass,** taking in views of Mount Athabasca and Athabasca Glacier along the way (page 198).

14 Drive past the town of Jasper to **Maligne Canyon,** where the fast-flowing Maligne River has cut a deep canyon in the limestone bedrock. At the top end of the canyon, the Wilderness Kitchen is an ideal late lunch stop (page 234).

15 Continue along Maligne Lake Road, which ends at **Maligne Lake.** Jump aboard a tour boat for a cruise to Spirit Island (page 234).

16 You could begin your return trip to Glacier or Banff, or better still spend the evening in the town of Jasper, dining at the **Fairmont Jasper Park Lodge** and enjoying an evening stroll around Lac Beauvert (page 254).

ITINERARY DETAILS

- This itinerary works best **mid-June-August,** when most or all roads are usually open. This is also peak travel season.

- This itinerary starts in Glacier National Park and ends in Jasper. Allow **8 hours** for the 430-mi (690-km) drive back to your starting point.

- Plan to reach Glacier's Going-to-the-Sun Road **before 6am, after 3pm,** or **have a vehicle entry reservation** and make minimal stops to be able to get a parking spot at Logan Pass.

- **No RVs, trailers, or vehicles longer than 21 ft (6.4 m)** are permitted on Glacier's Going-to-the-Sun Road from Avalanche over Logan Pass to Rising Sun. You can take a guided bus tour or free shuttle to see Going-to-the-Sun Road instead.

- Make accommodations, camping, and shuttle **reservations,** such as the shuttle to **Moraine Lake,** as far in advance as possible.

Oberlin Bend on Going-to-the-Sun Road

SEASONS OF GLACIER, BANFF & JASPER

SPRING
(APR.-JUNE)

Although saddled with unpredictable weather, the spring off-season in all three parks offers less-hectic visits. April still clings to winter with snow. Low-elevation trails are usually snow-free in May, while higher elevations are still buried under snow into June. Toward June, **longer days** of sunlight (in late June it stays light until after 10pm) arrive along with a sense of optimism for the upcoming warm months.

In Glacier, **minimal commercial services are open.** Until about mid-June or so, **Going-to-the-Sun Road is closed to vehicles,** but bikers and hikers can tour it without cars. When Logan Pass opens in June, temperatures and weather can still be wintry at the pass despite warmer lower elevation conditions.

Late spring is a good time to visit Banff and Jasper: You'll **avoid the crowds,** and you'll **save money** with the hotels that stay open year-round. The Icefields Parkway may see snow and ice in April but remains open all spring.

Temperatures
Glacier: 50–69°F (10 to 21°C)
Banff and Jasper: 59 to 68°F (15 to 20°C)

SUMMER
(JULY-MID-SEPT., HIGH SEASON)

Summer attracts crowds in all three parks when the **weather is unbeatable**. It's peak visitation season. Mosquitoes descend in early summer, and snow buries some high trails into July. Wildflowers peak in late July and huckleberries ripen in August. Wildfire season is late July through September. The downside of summer travel is the difficulty in securing reservations.

In Glacier, all **lodges, campgrounds, and trails are open. Going-to-the-Sun Road** is generally open **mid-June to mid-October,** with vehicle ticket reservations required.

In Banff and Jasper, everything is open, and there's plenty to do and see, although the parks are **crowded** and **prices higher**.

Temperatures
Glacier: 67 to 79°F (19 to 26°C)
Banff and Jasper: 72 to 86°F (22 to 30°C)

FALL
(MID-SEPT.-NOV.)

Fall can be delightful, especially September, with lingering **warm temperatures** and a noticeable decrease in crowds immediately after the early part of the month. Warm bug-free days and cool nights usher in the **fall colors mid-late September:** the larch and aspen turn brilliant gold. Peak-tops often see snow by late September. October brings unpredictable weather: low-elevation trails are usually snow-free in October, while some higher ones have snow.

In Glacier, **minimal commercial services remain open.** In mid-October, **Going-to-the-Sun Road closes to vehicles,** but Logan Pass can see wintry weather by late September.

Fall is an excellent time to visit Banff and Jasper; you'll **avoid crowds** and **save money on lodging.** The **Icefields Parkway** remains open.

Temperatures
Glacier: 35 to 65°F (2 to 18°C)
Banff and Jasper: 59 to 77°F (15 to 25°C)

WINTER
(DEC.-MAR.)
Winters are cold, with Arctic fronts sometimes plunging temperatures below 0°F (-18°C). Be conscious of windchill factors that may make temperatures seem colder and can be life-threatening without appropriate winter clothing.

In Glacier, **minimal commercial services** are open in winter. Snow closes most park roads, which become quiet **snowshoeing and cross-country ski trails.**

In Banff and Jasper, **ski resorts** begin opening for the winter in mid-November. The best **powder snow** conditions are **January-February,** although for enthusiasts looking for a combination of good snow and warmer weather, **March** is an excellent time of year to visit. You can travel between the two parks on the **Icefields Parkway**.

Temperatures
Glacier: 14 to 32°F (-10 to 0°C)
Banff and Jasper: 14 to 32°F (-10 to 0°C)

Winter brings skiers to Sunshine Village and other Banff resorts.

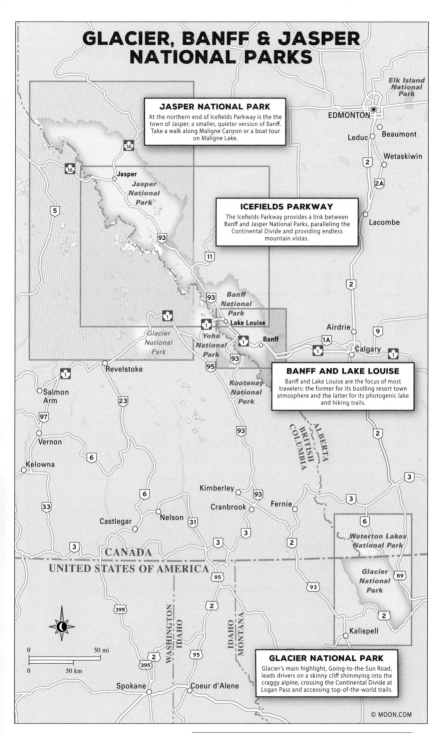

GLACIER, BANFF & JASPER NATIONAL PARKS

JASPER NATIONAL PARK
At the northern end of Icefields Parkway is the the town of Jasper, a smaller, quieter version of Banff. Take a walk along Maligne Canyon or a boat tour on Maligne Lake.

ICEFIELDS PARKWAY
The Icefields Parkway provides a link between Banff and Jasper National Parks, paralleling the Continental Divide and providing endless mountain vistas.

BANFF AND LAKE LOUISE
Banff and Lake Louise are the focus of most travelers: the former for its bustling resort town atmosphere and the latter for its photogenic lake and hiking trails.

GLACIER NATIONAL PARK
Glacier's main highlight, Going-to-the-Sun Road, leads drivers on a skinny cliff shimmying into the craggy alpine, crossing the Continental Divide at Logan Pass and accessing top-of-the-world trails.

Elk Island National Park

EDMONTON
Leduc
Beaumont
Wetaskiwin
Lacombe
Jasper National Park
Jasper
Airdrie
Calgary
Lake Louise
Banff
Banff National Park
Yoho National Park
Glacier National Park
Revelstoke
Kootenay National Park
Salmon Arm
Vernon
Kelowna
Kimberley
Cranbrook
Fernie
Castlegar
Nelson
ALBERTA
BRITISH COLUMBIA
Waterton Lakes National Park
Glacier National Park
Kalispell
CANADA
UNITED STATES OF AMERICA
WASHINGTON
IDAHO
IDAHO
MONTANA
Spokane
Coeur d'Alene

0   50 mi
0   50 km

© MOON.COM

NEED TO KNOW: GLACIER

- **Park website:** www.nps.gov/glac
- **Entrance fee:** $35 per vehicle ($25 winter)
- **Main entrance: West Glacier Entrance** (year-round}
- **Main visitor centers: Apgar Visitor Center** (year-round, weekends only in winter), **St. Mary Visitor Center** (late May-early Oct.), **Logan Pass Visitor Center** (mid-June-mid-Sept.)
- **In-park hotel and activity reservations:** www.glaciernationalparklodges.com
- **Campsite reservations:** www.recreation.gov
- **Vehicle entry reservations:** www.recreation.gov
- **Gas in the park:** None; closest in West Glacier, East Glacier, and St. Mary
- **Travel times:** 4.5 hours to Banff; 8 hours to Jasper

NEED TO KNOW: BANFF

- **Park website:** www.parks.canada.ca/banff
- **Entrance fees:** C$10 adult, C$8.40 senior, children free, up to a maximum of C$20 per vehicle
- **Main entrance: Banff East Gate** (Trans-Canada Highway; year-round)
- **Main visitor center: Banff Visitor Centre** (town of Banff; year-round)
- **In-park hotel and activity reservations:** www.banfflakelouise.com, www.banffjaspercollection.com
- **Campsite reservations:** www.reservation.pc.gc.ca
- **Gas in the park:** town of Banff, Lake Louise, Saskatchewan River Crossing
- **Travel times:** 4.5 hours to Glacier; 3.5 hours to Jasper

NEED TO KNOW: JASPER

- **Park Website:** www.parks.canada/jasper
- **Entrance fees:** C$10 adult, C$8.40 senior, children free, up to a maximum of $C20 per vehicle
- **Main entrance: Jasper East Gate** (Highway 16; year-round)
- **Main visitor center: Jasper Visitor Centre** (town of Jasper; year-round)
- **In-park hotel and activity reservations:** www.jasper.travel
- **Campsite reservations:** www.reservation.pc.gc.ca
- **Gas in the park:** town of Jasper
- **Travel times:** 8 hours to Glacier; 3.5 hours to Banff

spring biking on Going-to-the-Sun Road, Glacier

Lake Agnes, Banff National Park

BEST OF THE BEST
GLACIER, BANFF & JASPER

BEST HIKES

HIGHLINE TRAIL AND GRANITE PARK CHALET

Glacier National Park
STRENUOUS

From Logan Pass, this vertigo-inducing path tiptoes along the Continental Divide to Granite Park Chalet before dropping to The Loop. Hikers often spot bighorn sheep and mountain goats (page 82).

GRINNELL GLACIER

Glacier National Park
MODERATE-STRENUOUS

A boat ride clips mileage off the route to Grinnell Glacier. It's the shortest route to see a glacier up close (page 81).

hikers on the Highline Trail, Glacier

LAKE AGNES

Banff National Park
MODERATE

This walk is a good introduction to hiking in the Canadian Rockies, especially in fall when the larch trees have turned a brilliant gold (page 148).

GRIZZLY-LARIX LAKES LOOP

Banff National Park
EASY-MODERATE

Accessible by gondola from the valley floor, this hike in the flower-filled Sunshine Meadows high above the tree line leads to some of the most photogenic viewpoints in the region (page 146).

WILCOX PASS

Icefields Parkway, Jasper National Park
MODERATE

Views of the Columbia Icefield are unmatched along this trail. It climbs through a stunted forest of Engelmann spruce and subalpine fir to a ridge with panoramic views of Mount Athabasca and the Athabasca Glacier (page 198).

BALD HILLS

Jasper National Park
MODERATE-STRENUOUS

The sweeping views from this hike take in the jade-green waters of Maligne Lake, the Queen Elizabeth Ranges, and an alpine environment dotted with wildflowers in midsummer (page 240).

Grinnell Glacier Trail, Glacier

BEST VIEWS

HIDDEN LAKE OVERLOOK
Glacier National Park

Stand atop the Continental Divide at Hidden Lake Overlook on a 2.6-mi (4.2-km) round-trip adventure from Logan Pass, where you might spot baby mountain goats (page 79).

MANY GLACIER HOTEL DECK
Glacier National Park

Lounge on the large deck of this historic hotel, which overlooks Swiftcurrent Lake and a mountainous panorama. Bring a pair of binoculars so you can spot bears, mountain goats, and bighorn sheep (page 109).

SULPHUR MOUNTAIN
Banff National Park

Take the Banff Gondola 700 vertical m (2,300 vertical ft) to the summit of Sulphur Mountain. From the observation deck at the upper terminal,

view from Sulphur Mountain, Banff

a boardwalk leads to a breathtaking 360-degree view that includes the town, the Bow Valley, Cascade Mountain, Lake Minnewanka, and the Fairholme Range (page 132).

LAKE LOUISE SKI RESORT
Banff National Park

During summer, the main ski lift at the Lake Louise Resort whisks visitors up the face of Mount Whitehorn to Whitehorn Lodge. The view from the top—across the Bow Valley to Lake Louise and the Continental Divide—is among the most spectacular in the Canadian Rockies (page 142).

ATHABASCA GLACIER
Icefields Parkway, Jasper National Park

The Athabasca Glacier, an arm of the massive Columbia Icefield, fills a valley right beside the Icefields Parkway, making access easy—the best views are from the Icefield Centre and Toe of the Glacier trail (page 197).

MALIGNE LAKE
Jasper National Park

Maligne Lake is the second-largest glacier-fed lake in the world. Take a tour boat to Spirit Island or stroll along the lake's shoreline to take in the stunning vistas (page 234).

view from Hidden Lake Overlook, Glacier

BEST GLACIAL FEATURES

GLACIERS

Glaciers are slow-moving ice. Aided by gravity, the ice presses down, forming a thin elastic barrier that carries the mass toward the glacier's toe, where it may calve off in chunks. For a glacier to move, a certain amount of ice is needed—usually a surface of at least 25 acres (10 hectares) and a minimum depth of 100 ft (30 m). Glacier, Banff, and Jasper National Parks hold some must-see glaciers.

Grinnell Glacier
Glacier National Park

The shortest trail to an active glacier in Glacier National Park climbs to Grinnell Glacier, a small, thinning glacier melting into Upper Grinnell Lake. You can walk the entire trail round-trip or hop on the Many Glacier tour boat shuttle to chop the distance (page 81).

Saskatchewan Glacier
Icefields Parkway, Banff National Park

The short, steep hike up Parker's Ridge ends with sweeping views down to Saskatchewan Glacier, one of the largest glaciers connected to the Columbia Icefield (page 195).

Athabasca Glacier
Icefields Parkway, Jasper National Park

Nowhere in Banff or Jasper does a glacier come as close to a road as the Athabasca, with an interpretive center, bus tours, and hiking in the vicinity (page 197).

GLACIAL LAKES

Glacier, Banff, and Jasper National Parks are renowned for the turquoise color of many lakes. Finely ground particles of debris from melting glaciers are washed downstream and suspended in the water of local lakes. It is this "rock flour" reflecting the blue-green sector of the light

---

Saskatchewan Glacier, Icefields Parkway (left); Grinnell Glacier basin, Glacier (right)

spectrum that gives these lakes this unique color.

Grinnell Lake
Glacier National Park

Enjoy the turquoise hues in the middle of the lake, supplied via a multiledged waterfall fed by Grinnell Glacier. Looking down on the lake from the Grinnell Glacier Trail reveals a brighter turquoise backed by the steep walls of Angel Wing (page 84).

Lake Louise
Banff National Park

Lake Louise is Banff's best-known glacial lake, and with good reason—its turquoise color is mesmerizing; it is easily accessible by everyone; and the lakefront hotel is one of the world's grandest mountain resorts (page 135).

Lower Waterfowl Lake
Icefields Parkway, Banff National Park

Beside the Icefields Parkway, the intense turquoise color of Lower Waterfowl Lake is in stark contrast to the sheer cliffs of surrounding mountains (page 194).

Maligne Lake
Jasper National Park

Maligne Lake is the world's second-largest glacial-fed lake. Hike along the shoreline, go canoeing, or take a boat tour to Spirit Island (page 234).

CIRQUES

Glacier-carved hollows or bowls in the slopes of mountains are known as cirques.

Iceberg Lake, Glacier

Iceberg Lake
Glacier National Park

A trail ascends up to a lake tucked in a cirque below two peaks connected by two arêtes of serrated peaks. In late summer you may even see icebergs floating here below the tall surrounding walls (page 86).

Helen Lake
Icefields Parkway, Banff National Park

Helen Lake lies in a glacial cirque and is reached by a trail that boasts spectacular views and passes through extensive wildflower meadows (page 190).

INDIGENOUS PEOPLES OF GLACIER, BANFF & JASPER

Glacier, Banff, and Jasper National Parks and the surrounding lands are on the traditional land of the Blackfoot Confederacy, Salish, Kootenai (Kootenay in Canada), Shuswap, Stoney, and Gros Ventre People.

Spanning what became the U.S.-Canadian border, the **Blackfeet,** or Niitsitapi (original people), include several nomadic groups who based much of their livelihood on hunting bison in the vast prairies on the Continental Divide's east side. In Canada, the Siksika, or Blackfoot, were the first to meet European traders. (To refer to the group, *Blackfoot* is used in Canada, and *Blackfeet* is used in the United States.) Other groups include the Blood (or Kainai) and Piegan (or Piikuni). For thousands of years, according to legend, their lands ranged from the Saskatchewan to the Yellowstone River.

The land of the **Salish** and **Kootenai** are on the Continental Divide's west side, where they hunted, trapped, and fished. They ventured east over the mountains on annual bison hunts. Known as the Ktunaxa, the Kootenai (in Canada Kootenay) were the first human beings to enter the Canadian Rockies and comprise seven bands spanning the western Rockies from southern Alberta to Missoula, Montana. For the Kootenai, the Lake McDonald area was a place for sacred dances, hence its original name of Sacred Dancing Waters.

The Canadian Rockies are also the land of the **Shuswap,** who traveled into the mountains on and off for many thousands of years, hunting caribou and sheep. The descendants of the Shuswap people live on traditional land in the Columbia Valley, just south of Radium Hot Springs.

Around 1650, the mighty Sioux nation began splintering, with many thousands moving north into present-day Canada. Although these immigrants called themselves **Nakoda** (people), other tribes called them **Assiniboine** (people who cook with stones) because of their traditional cooking methods. Europeans translated *Assiniboine* as Stone People, or **Stoney** for short. Today, the Stoney people live on a sprawling reserve just outside Banff's eastern boundary.

NAMES

In Glacier, many of the Blackfeet names used for land features were replaced by other names, but the English form of some remain: Going-to-the-Sun Mountain, Two Medicine Lake, Pitamakin Pass, and Running Eagle Falls.

Although Europeans introduced their own terms for natural features throughout Banff and Jasper, Indigenous names such as Saskatchewan River and Lake Minnewanka have been preserved, and other traditional names are slowly being restored.

LEARNING MORE

North American Indian Days

The Blackfeet celebrate their culture during North American Indian Days in Browning, Montana. Dressed in regalia, the community dances and drums together. Traditional horse skills are part of the rodeo.

Sun Tours

406/732-9220 or 800/786-9220; www.glaciersuntours.com
Blackfeet-owned Sun Tours goes to Logan Pass and back in coaches with big windows for sightseeing. Blackfeet guides give insight into the park's rich Indigenous heritage, from the days of the buffalo to modern spirituality.

St. Mary Scenic Overlook and Blackfeet Interpretive Loop

Overlooking the St. Mary Valley and Glacier National Park, this self-guided interpretive site gives insight into the Blackfeet culture and history.

Native America Speaks

For more than three decades, Glacier has hosted the acclaimed Native America Speaks program in summer. Look for shows in park lodges, St. Mary Visitor Center, and at campground amphitheaters. Free 45-minute evening shows feature members of the Blackfeet, Sal-

St. Mary Scenic Overlook and Blackfeet Interpretive Loop

ish, and Kootenai people who share stories about their culture and heritage. Specialty programs include the **Two Medicine Lake Singers and Dancers** demonstrating Blackfeet dances in full traditional regalia and **Jack Gladstone**, a Grammy-nominated Blackfeet musician, who blends storytelling and music in multimedia walks through Glacier's history from the Blackfeet perspective. Check the park newspaper or online for current schedules and locations for all Native America Speaks programs.

Buffalo Nations Luxton Museum

1 Birch Ave. Banff; 403/762-2388; www.buffalonationsmuseum.com
This museum is dedicated to the heritage of the First Nations of Banff, Jasper, and adjacent lands. The collections contain memorabilia from local resident Norman Luxton, who had a lifelong relationship with the Stoney people.

BEST SCENIC DRIVE

ICEFIELDS PARKWAY – SOUTH SECTION

DRIVING DISTANCE: 77 km (48 mi)
DRIVING TIME: 1 hour
START: Lake Louise
END: Saskatchewan River Crossing

The Icefields Parkway, linking Banff and Jasper National Parks, is renowned for its mountain scenery, but the concentration of lakes, rivers, and glaciers along the southern section is especially memorable. If you are staying in Lake Louise (or Banff—add an extra 40 minutes to reach the Parkway), one hour of driving each way along the southern section of the Icefields Parkway to Saskatchewan River Crossing will be a highlight of your time in the Canadian Rockies. Although this section can be driven in one hour, you'll want to spend at least three hours stopping at viewpoints and watching wildlife, or even longer if you plan on a hike or two. Before heading out, check road conditions at local visitor centers and be aware that there is no cell reception along this stretch of highway. From Lake Louise, highlights for north-bound travelers include **Herbert Lake,** a small body of water famous for early-morning reflection shots, the **Crowfoot Glacier,** with its glacial claws clinging to the mountain's steep slopes, sparkling **Bow Lake,** the impossibly green **Peyto and Waterfowl Lakes,** and the rushing waters of **Mistaya Canyon.** For hikers, you only need to walk a short way along the **Bow Glacier Falls Trail** to see Bow Lake in all its glory, or strike out on a longer trek to **Helen Lake** (page 189).

Peyto Lake

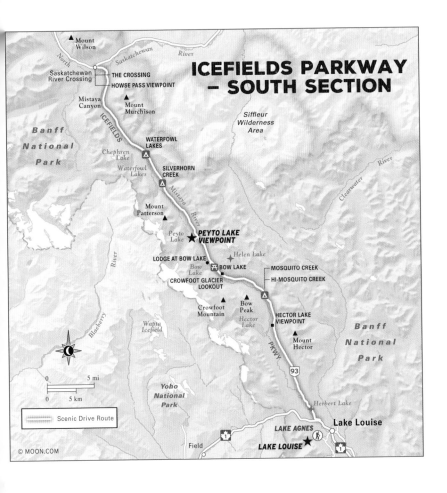

ICEFIELDS PARKWAY
– SOUTH SECTION

Mount Wilson

North

Saskatchewan River

Saskatchewan River Crossing
THE CROSSING
HOWSE PASS VIEWPOINT

Mistaya Canyon
Mount Murchison

Siffleur Wilderness Area

Banff

National

Park

ICEFIELDS

WATERFOWL LAKES

Chephren Lake

Waterfowl Lakes

SILVERHORN CREEK

Clearwater River

Mistaya River

Mount Patterson

Peyto Lake
PEYTO LAKE VIEWPOINT ★

LODGE AT BOW LAKE

Helen Lake

Bow Lake
BOW LAKE

MOSQUITO CREEK
HI-MOSQUITO CREEK

CROWFOOT GLACIER LOOKOUT

River

Crowfoot Mountain

Bow Peak

Hector Lake

HECTOR LAKE VIEWPOINT

Banff

Wapta Icefield

Mount Hector

National

Blaeberry River

Park

0   5 mi

0   5 km

Yoho National Park

PKWY

93

Scenic Drive Route

Herbert Lake

Herbert Lake

LAKE AGNES

Lake Louise

© MOON.COM

Field

LAKE LOUISE ★

1

1

PRACTICE SUSTAINABLE TRAVEL IN GLACIER, BANFF & JASPER

- Bring a refillable **water bottle** instead of disposable plastic bottles.
- Buy locally made products.
- Go with local park-approved guide companies.
- Bring **binoculars** to watch wildlife while maintaining a safe distance between you and the animals. **Drones** are prohibited in all U.S. and Canadian national parks so as not to disturb wildlife.
- Minimize driving by hiking, biking, paddling, and skiing to experience the parks, and ride shuttles where available.
- Turn off the car engine rather than idling when you use pullouts to watch wildlife.
- Use established paved or gravel pullouts for wildlife-watching and photography. Park in trailhead parking lots rather than on the roadside.
- Be a conscientious park visitor by following **Leave No Trace** guidelines at all times.
- Adjust your schedule to visit crowded sites at less popular times or seasons.
- Always have a Plan B in case crowds and full parking lots preclude your Plan A.

view from Standish Lookout over Sunshine Meadows, Banff

Hidden Lake Overlook

GLACIER NATIONAL PARK

The undisputed "Crown of the Continent," Glacier National Park preserves some of the nation's wildest country, where terrestrial forces have carved jagged mountain ridges, red pinnacles, and glacier-formed basins into the landscape. Waterfalls roar, ice cracks, and rockfalls echo in scenery still under the paintbrush of change. The park boasts a tremendous geological heritage, plus a cultural history as sacred Native American land.

Glacier also hosts a rich diversity of wildlife. Grizzly bears and wolves top the food chain. Mountain goats prance on precarious ledges. Wolverines romp in high glacial cirques. Bighorn sheep graze in alpine meadows while pikas shriek nearby.

Slicing through the center of the park, historic Going-to-the-Sun Road is an unforgettable experience, climbing up a narrow cliff through tight twists and hairpin turns. Tunnels, arches, and bridges lead sightseers over precipices where seemingly no road could go. Along the way, visitors can feast their eyes on ice-abraded valleys, thundering cascades, mammoth lakes, and serrated peaks.

Glacier National Park holds not only the imprints of glaciers past, but also those that are still present. The park's glaciers fuel North America's major rivers, with crystal-clear water tumbling to Hudson Bay, the Gulf of Mexico, and the Pacific. But those glaciers will soon meet their demise. That change will repaint the scenery once again.

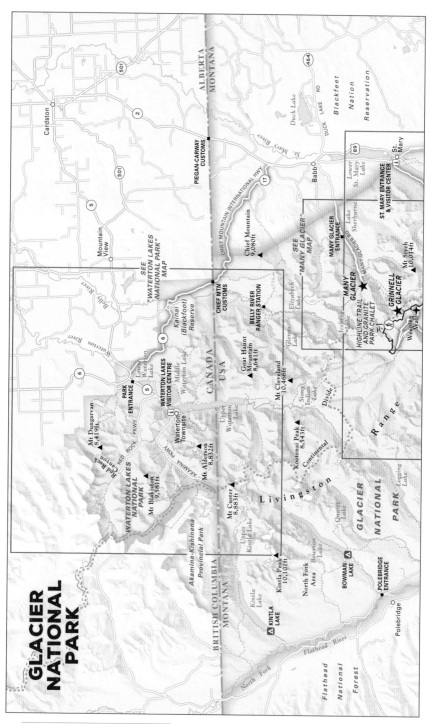

GLACIER NATIONAL PARK

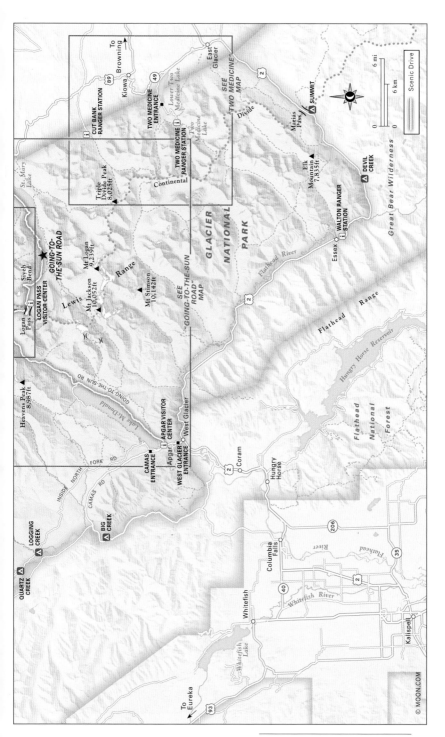

To Browning

89

49

Kiowa

East Glacier

2

SUMMIT

SEE TWO MEDICINE MAP

CUT BANK RANGER STATION

TWO MEDICINE ENTRANCE

Lower Two Medicine Lake

Divide

Marias Pass

Great Bear Wilderness

6 mi

6 km

Scenic Drive

TWO MEDICINE RANGER STATION

Two Medicine Lake

Continental

Triple Divide Peak 8,025ft

ELK Mountain 7,835ft

DEVIL CREEK

St. Mary Lake

GOING-TO-THE-SUN ROAD

Siyeh Bend

Mt Logan 9,239ft

Range

GLACIER NATIONAL PARK

WALTON RANGER STATION

Essex

Flathead River

Logan Pass

LOGAN PASS VISITOR CENTER

Lewis

Mt Jackson 10,052ft

Mt Stimson 10,142ft

SEE "GOING-TO-THE-SUN ROAD" MAP

2

Flathead Range

Hungry Horse Reservoir

Heavens Peak 8,987ft

GOING-TO-THE-SUN RD

Lake McDonald

APGAR VISITOR CENTER

West Glacier

Coram

Flathead National Forest

INSIDE NORTH FORK RD

CAMAS RD

CAMAS ENTRANCE

Apgar

WEST GLACIER ENTRANCE

2

Hungry Horse

206

LOGGING CREEK

BIG CREEK

35

QUARTZ CREEK

Columbia Falls

Flathead River

40

Whitefish River

Whitefish

93

Whitefish Lake

Kalispell

To Eureka

© MOON.COM

TOP 3

⭐ **1. GOING-TO-THE-SUN ROAD:** The 50-mi (81-km) road is a testament to human ingenuity and nature's wonders, with scenic surprises around each corner (page 60).

⭐ **2. MANY GLACIER:** Many Glacier is a setting of dreams: chiseled peaks, idyllic lakes, pastoral meadows (page 68).

⭐ **3. GRINNELL GLACIER:** See Grinnell Glacier before it melts completely. Hikers on the trail to the glacier often spot grizzly bears (page 81).

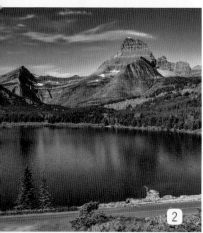

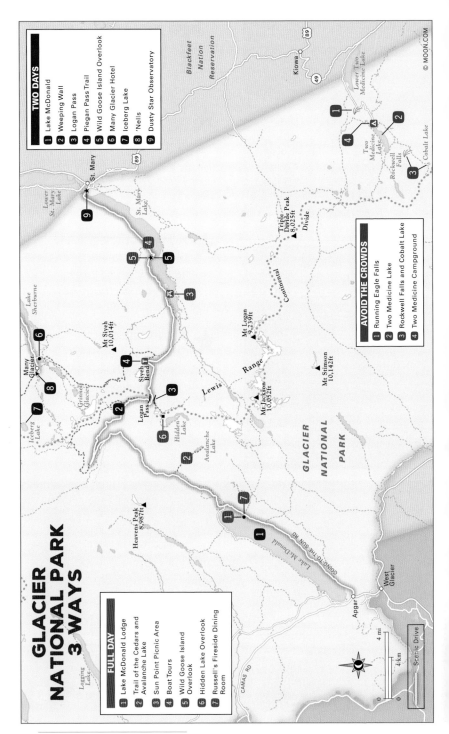

GLACIER NATIONAL PARK 3 WAYS

FULL DAY

1. Lake McDonald Lodge
2. Trail of the Cedars and Avalanche Lake
3. Sun Point Picnic Area
4. Boat Tours
5. Wild Goose Island Overlook
6. Hidden Lake Overlook
7. Russell's Fireside Dining Room

TWO DAYS

1. Lake McDonald
2. Weeping Wall
3. Logan Pass
4. Piegan Pass Trail
5. Wild Goose Island Overlook
6. Many Glacier Hotel
7. Iceberg Lake
8. 'Nells
9. Dusty Star Observatory

AVOID THE CROWDS

1. Running Eagle Falls
2. Two Medicine Lake
3. Rockwell Falls and Cobalt Lake
4. Two Medicine Campground

© MOON.COM

Blackfeet Nation Reservation

Kiowa

Lower Two Medicine Lake

Cobalt Lake

Rockwell Falls

Two Medicine Lake

St. Mary

Lower St. Mary Lake

St. Mary Lake

Triple Divide Peak 8,025ft

Continental Divide

Mt Logan 9,239ft

Mt Stimson 10,142ft

Lake Sherburne

Mt Siyeh 10,014ft

Siyeh Bend

Many Glacier

Grinnell Glacier

Iceberg Lake

Logan Pass

Hidden Lake

Lewis Range

Mt Jackson 10,052ft

Avalanche Lake

GLACIER NATIONAL PARK

Heavens Peak 8,987ft

GOING-TO-THE-SUN RD

Lake McDonald

West Glacier

Apgar

CAMAS RD

Logging Lake

Scenic Drive

Lake

4 mi

4 km

GLACIER NATIONAL PARK 3 WAYS

FULL DAY

Make reservations ahead of time for the boat tour (https://glacierparkboats.com) at Rising Sun, and start as early in the day as you can in order to beat the crowds. The boat tour reservation will give you access to Going-to-the-Sun Road in place of a vehicle reservation ticket.

1 Pack a picnic lunch and depart **Lake McDonald Lodge** by 7:30am to tour the west side of Going-to-the-Sun Road along McDonald Creek.

2 Wake up your legs by walking the boardwalk **Trail of the Cedars** to the Avalanche Trailhead. Then cut steeply uphill above Avalanche Gorge and continue hiking up to idyllic **Avalanche Lake.**

3 Continue your ascent of Going-to-the-Sun Road, climbing through the west-side tunnel around The Loop and over Haystack Falls to Logan Pass and the Continental Divide, where you will return later. Descend the east side to **Sun Point** and its **picnic area** to have lunch. After eating, walk to the windblown point for the panoramic view up St. Mary Lake.

4 Continue east to Rising Sun to catch an afternoon **boat tour** on St. Mary Lake. It will dock near the base of Baring Falls, and you'll have a few minutes to enjoy the falls and beach.

5 Retrace your route to head west on Going-to-the-Sun Road. Stop at **Wild Goose Island Overlook** and Jackson Glacier Overlook.

6 Continue climbing to Logan Pass, where you can tour the paved interpretive walk or go for a hike to **Hidden Lake Overlook.**

7 Descend the west side of Logan Pass back to Lake McDonald Lodge, and celebrate your day with dinner in **Russell's Fireside Dining Room** and sunset on the beach.

TWO DAYS

The best two-day adventure in Glacier hits two locales: Going-to-the-Sun Road and Many Glacier, combined with outstanding hikes. You will need a vehicle reservation ticket for Going-to-the-Sun Road and reservations at Many Glacier Hotel.

1 With a 6am start, drive westward along **Lake McDonald** on Going-to-the-Sun Road, stopping briefly at one of the pullouts for a quick photo.

2 You'll soon climb higher and higher on the west side of the Sun Road as the views get bigger and bigger. Admire Haystack Falls, Bird Woman Falls, and the **Weeping Wall** as you drive by.

3 The Continental Divide sign signals your arrival at **Logan Pass.** Hit the restrooms and take a selfie at the Continental Divide sign before descending eastward to your trailhead.

4 At Siyeh Bend, launch onto the **Piegan Pass Trail,** where an ascent through the forest reaches the wildflower meadows of Preston Park. Piegan Glacier comes into view in a hanging valley on Piegan Mountain. The trail sweeps along a steep hillside to the pass that faces the vertical jagged wall of the Continental Divide.

5 After returning the way you came back to the trailhead, drive down the east side of Going-to-the-Sun Road, stopping at **Wild Goose Island Overlook** for a view of St. Mary Lake.

6 Exit the park at St. Mary and swing north on US 89 to reenter the park on the Many Glacier Road. Watch for moose and bears en route to **Many Glacier Hotel** to dine, watch the sunset over Swiftcurrent Lake, and spend the night.

7 Grab your pack, lunch, and hiking boots for a full-day adventure to **Iceberg Lake.** Launch up a stiff, short climb to reach a gentler path that rounds Ptarmigan Falls and crawls below the Ptarmigan Wall to reach the partially frozen lake. (For a shorter hike instead, head up Swiftcurrent Valley to tour the waters of Fishercap Lake, Redrock Lake, and Bullhead Lake.)

8 After hiking, check in the Swiftcurrent parking lot for a ranger with a spotting scope for watching wildlife and grab a bite to eat at **'Nells.**

9 Return to St. Mary Visitor Center, timing your arrival around dusk, to enjoy a real-time star tour at the outdoor **Dusty Star Observatory.**

AVOID THE CROWDS

Located in the southeast corner of Glacier, Two Medicine is favored for its less-developed ambience, hiking trails, remote lakes, and campground with mountain and star views. Be sure to get a one-day vehicle reservation ticket if you are planning a day trip, or a Two Medicine Campground reservation for overnighting.

1 Enter the park before 8am through the Two Medicine Entrance station and stop to see **Running Eagle Falls** before driving up to Two Medicine Lake.

2 Shoot photos from the foot of **Two Medicine Lake** and admire the view of Mount Sinopah and Rising Wolf.

3 Hike the south shore trail to **Rockwell Falls** or farther up into the basin holding **Cobalt Lake.**

4 Back at your car, drive to **Two Medicine Campground** to set up camp. Enjoy scanning the slopes of Rising Wolf Mountain for bighorn sheep, mountain goats, and sometimes bears before counting the stars after dark.

More Ways to Avoid the Crowds

- Hiking early morning to Scenic Point
- Backpacking the Dawson-Pitamakin Loop

HIGHLIGHTS AND SCENIC DRIVES

LAKE MCDONALD

Catching water from Glacier's longest river, Lake McDonald is the largest lake in the park at 10 mi (16.1 km) long and 1.5 mi (2.4 km) wide. It is also the park's deepest lake at 472 ft (144 m). Squeezed between Howe and Snyder Ridges, both lateral moraines, the lake sits where an ancient glacier gouged out a trough. Larch forests that turn gold in fall rim the shores. On the lake, visitors fish, boat, paddle, and swim in its cold blue waters. Access the lakeshore at Fish Creek or Apgar Picnic Areas, Apgar boat ramp, or the many pullouts along Going-to-the-Sun Road.

Best Beaches

Smooth rounded rocks form Lake McDonald's beaches, which change size throughout the summer based on water level. Expect tiny beaches in June with high water and larger beaches for sitting, rock skipping, and swimming by August as the water level drops.

APGAR PICNIC AREA

Located on the southwest shore of Lake McDonald, this beach allows for swimming with a view uplake toward the Continental Divide.

FISH CREEK PICNIC AREA

On the northwest shore, the beach flanks Fish Creek with views across the lake to Snyder Ridge, Mount Edwards, and Mount Brown.

SPRAGUE CREEK PICNIC AREA

Near the southeast end of Lake McDonald, this beach forms a promontory that pushes out into the lake for views of Stanton Peak.

Boat Tour

Glacier Park Boat Company; 406/257-2426; www. glacierparkboats.com; several departures daily mid-May-late Sept.; adult $26, child $13

At the boat dock behind Lake McDonald Lodge, hop on the historic **DeSmet** for a one-hour tour. Tours depart at 11am, 1:30pm, 3pm, 5:30pm, and 7pm (7pm cruise ends on Labor Day). With a 90-passenger capacity, the 1930s-vintage wooden boat motors to the lake's core, where surrounding snow-clad peaks pop into sight. Go for a prime seat on the top deck; bring a jacket for marginal weather. Book in advance by phone or online; limited tickets remain at the boat docks on the day of tours.

TICKETED VEHICLE ENTRY
RESERVATIONS

In addition to entry fees, you'll need a reservation ticket for vehicle entry to several sections of Glacier National Park during peak season. The park may adjust this ticketing program; check online (www.nps. gov/glac) for the most recent updates.

WHERE AND WHEN DO I NEED A VEHICLE RESERVATION TICKET?

- **Going-to-the-Sun Road:** Tickets are valid for three days.
    - ○ **West entrances** (West Glacier and Camas): daily 6am–3pm, late May to mid-September
    - ○ **East entrance** (Rising Sun from St. Mary): daily 6am–3pm, July to mid-September
- **Polebridge Entrance to North Fork:** daily 6am–3pm, late May to mid-September, tickets valid for one day
- **Two Medicine:** daily 6am–3pm, July to mid-September, tickets valid for one day
- **Many Glacier:** daily 6am–3pm, July to mid-September, tickets valid for one day

HOW DO I GET VEHICLE TICKET RESERVATIONS?

- Purchase tickets online (877/444-6777; www.recreation.gov; $2 per vehicle). **Tickets are not sold at the park.**
- Some tickets are released **four months in advance** in four block releases:
    - ○ February 1 for all dates late May–June 30
    - ○ March 1 for all dates in July
    - ○ April 1 for all dates in August
    - ○ May 1 for September 1–mid-September
- Additional tickets are released **one day in advance** on a day-by-day basis.

- If you need entry for additional days, you will need to purchase additional tickets.

WHAT CAN I DO TO BE SUCCESSFUL IN GETTING A TICKET?

- Set up an account beforehand online with the reservation service.
- Plan to purchase tickets online. While you can call the reservation phone number, many tickets will be gone before you connect.
- Be aware that getting a ticket one day in advance from east-side locations is extremely difficult due to slow internet speeds.
- Get online and logged into your account before 8am mountain time on the day of the release for your desired tickets. Some reservation dates sell out within minutes.

HOW DO THE TICKETS WORK?

- Tickets are valid for any time during the 6am-3pm daily window.
- You may leave and reenter the park with your ticket on the same day.
- Tickets do not guarantee parking at specific trailheads or Logan Pass.

CAN I GET INTO THE PARK WITHOUT AN ENTRY RESERVATION TICKET?

- If you have reservations for lodging, camping, backpacking, horseback riding, licensed outfitters, boat tours, or bus tours **on the specific road** that requires reservations, you will not need a ticket; your service reservation will gain you entry.
- You do not need an entry reservation to go in before or after hours, nor in spring before late May or fall after mid-September.
- On the east side of Going-to-the-Sun Road, no tickets are needed to enter the park at St. Mary, go to St. Mary Campground, tour St. Mary Visitor Center, or park at the visitor center to catch the free Sun Road shuttles. The vehicle ticket checkpoint is at Rising Sun. Campers can enter Rising Sun Campground without a vehicle reservation but cannot go farther up the road without one.

★ GOING-TO-THE-SUN ROAD

406/888-7800 (road status); www.nps.gov/glac; approx. mid-June–mid-Oct.

Tunnels, switchbacks, arches, and a narrow two-lane highway cutting across precipitous slopes reveal feats of engineering. Cedar rainforests give way to windblown subalpine firs, broad lake valleys lead into glacial corridors, monstrous vertical cliff walls abut wildflower gardens, and waterfalls spew from every pore. Defying gravity, ragged peaks rake the sky, crowning all.

This National Historic Landmark and Historic Civil Engineering Landmark is a place to savor every nook and cranny. Oohs and aahs punctuate every sweep in the road as stunning scenery unfolds. Stopping at myriad pullouts along the road, many sightseers burn through scads of digital pixels. The sheer immensity of the glacier-chewed landscape leaves visitors gasping, "I can't fit it all in my photo."

To stretch your legs, well-signed short paths guide hikers through a dripping rainforest, along a glacial moraine, amid mountain goats, and beside a roaring waterfall. Those ready to put miles on their boots should tackle at least one of the longer high alpine trails, where you'll feel you've reached the apex of the world, sending your spirit soaring.

The Sun Road, as locals call it, is one place you won't want to miss. Its rugged beauty leaves a lasting impression.

Avalanche Gorge (top); Bird Woman Falls (middle); Weeping Wall (bottom)

Scenic Drive

DRIVING DISTANCE: 50 mi (81 km) one-way
DRIVING TIME: approx. 2 hours one-way (with no stops)
START: West Glacier
END: St. Mary

Going-to-the-Sun Road connects the towns of West Glacier and St. Mary via one of the most scenic highways in the United States. For some, scary tight curves that hug cliff walls produce white-knuckle driving. But for most, its beauty, diversity, color, flora, fauna, and raw wildness will leave an impression like no other. For that reason, many park visitors drive it more than once during their stay.

Going-to-the-Sun Road has **restrictions on vehicle sizes.** It does not permit any RVs or trailer combos over 21 ft (6.4 m) long between Avalanche on the west side and Rising Sun on the east side. Vehicles also must be under 10 ft (3.1 m) tall including rooftop gear, and 8 ft (2.4 m) wide including side mirrors.

WEST SIDE

From the west, the Going-to-the-Sun Road cruises along **Lake McDonald,** the largest lake in the park. The road follows McDonald Creek, the longest river in the park, with stops to see its tumbling rapids and waterfalls before reaching **Avalanche,** where the **Trail of the Cedars** tours through the easternmost Pacific rainforest in the country.

When the road swings north, its path climbs through engineering feats that garnered the road's designation as a National Civil Engineering Landmark. Its **West Side Tunnel** has two stunning alcoves framing **Heavens Peak.** Farther on, Going-to-the-Sun Road has one massive hairpin turn, known as **The Loop.**

Above The Loop, the road cuts through cliffs with views of the ribbonlike **Bird Woman Falls** and stairstep **Haystack Falls.** The **Weeping Wall** wails profusely in June, enough to douse cars driving the inside lane, but in August, drips slow to a trickle.

After **Big Bend,** drive slowly uphill to see **Triple Arches** (no pullout) at the very narrow S-turns. As the road arcs up the final mile to Logan Pass, a wheelchair-accessible path goes to **Oberlin Bend Overlook,** the best spot for photographing the road's west side and the knifelike **Garden Wall**—so named for the rainbow of white cow parsnip, pink spirea, yellow columbine, and blue gentian, among other flowers, that bloom in the meadows below its top cliffs—on the Continental Divide.

LOGAN PASS AND HIDDEN LAKE OVERLOOK

Located 32 mi (52 km) from the West Entrance, Logan Pass sits atop the **Continental Divide** at 6,646 ft (2,026 m) and rules an alpine wonderland of wildflower meadows and snowfields. Weather can be chilly and windy even in midsummer. Take a selfie at the Continental Divide sign. Explore the visitor center and scan surrounding slopes for mountain goats, bighorn sheep, and bears. In late July, the pink alpine laurel, paintbrush, and monkeyflower reach their prime. Meadows at this elevation are fragile, with short-lived flora, so stick to the paths. There are two must-do trails that depart from Logan Pass: **Hidden Lake Overlook** (page 79) and the **Highline Trail** (page 82). This is one of the most popular spots in the park; in midsummer, the parking lot fills by 7am. If the parking lot is full, forgo Logan Pass for

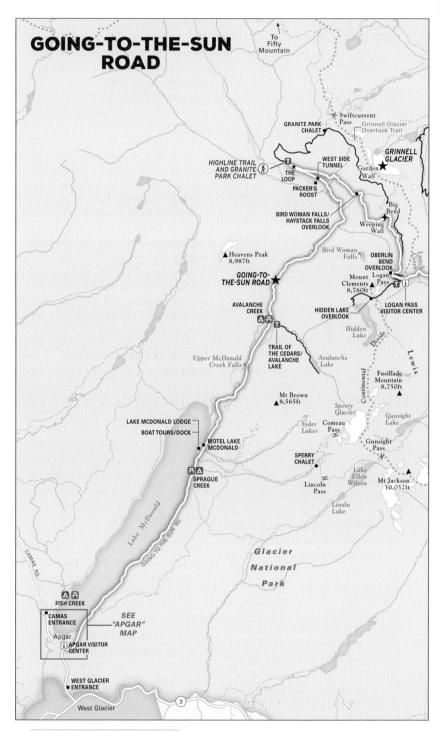

GOING-TO-THE-SUN ROAD

To Fifty Mountain

GRANITE PARK CHALET

Swiftcurrent Pass

Grinnell Glacier Overlook Trail

GRINNELL GLACIER

HIGHLINE TRAIL AND GRANITE PARK CHALET

THE LOOP

WEST SIDE TUNNEL

Garden Wall

PACKER'S ROOST

BIRD WOMAN FALLS/ HAYSTACK FALLS OVERLOOK

Big Bend

Weeping Wall

Bird Woman Falls

OBERLIN BEND OVERLOOK

▲ Heavens Peak 8,987ft

GOING-TO-THE-SUN ROAD

Mount Clements 8,760ft

Logan Pass

Lunch Creek

AVALANCHE CREEK

HIDDEN LAKE OVERLOOK

LOGAN PASS VISITOR CENTER

TRAIL OF THE CEDARS/ AVALANCHE LAKE

Hidden Lake

Divide

Lewis

Upper McDonald Creek Falls

Avalanche Lake

Fusillade Mountain 8,750ft ▲

Mt Brown ▲ 8,565ft

Sperry Glacier

Gunsight Lake

LAKE MCDONALD LODGE

BOAT TOURS/DOCK

MOTEL LAKE MCDONALD

Syder Lakes

Comeau Pass

Gunsight Pass

SPRAGUE CREEK

Continental

SPERRY CHALET

Lake Ellen Wilson

Mt Jackson 10,052ft ▲

Lake McDonald

Lincoln Pass

Linoln Lake

Glacier

GOING-TO-THE-SUN RD

National

Park

FISH CREEK

CAMAS RD

CAMAS ENTRANCE

Apgar

SEE "APGAR" MAP

APGAR VISITOR CENTER

WEST GLACIER ENTRANCE

2

West Glacier

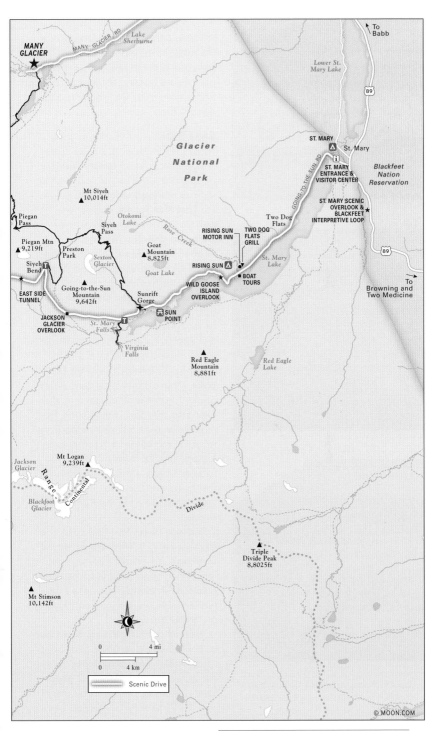

MANY GLACIER

MANY GLACIER RD

Lake Sherburne

To Babb

Lower St. Mary Lake

89

Glacier National Park

ST. MARY

St. Mary

ST. MARY ENTRANCE & VISITOR CENTER

Blackfeet Nation Reservation

ST. MARY SCENIC OVERLOOK & BLACKFEET INTERPRETIVE LOOP

89

Mt Siyeh 10,014ft

Otokomi Lake

Rose Creek

Two Dog Flats

RISING SUN MOTOR INN

TWO DOG FLATS GRILL

Piegan Pass

Siyeh Pass

Goat Mountain 8,825ft

St. Mary Lake

Piegan Mtn 9,219ft

Preston Park

Sexton Glacier

RISING SUN

GOING-TO-THE-SUN RD

To Browning and Two Medicine

Siyeh Bend

Going-to-the-Sun Mountain 9,642ft

Goat Lake

Sunrift Gorge

WILD GOOSE ISLAND OVERLOOK

BOAT TOURS

EAST SIDE TUNNEL

JACKSON GLACIER OVERLOOK

St. Mary Falls

SUN POINT

Virginia Falls

Red Eagle Mountain 8,881ft

Red Eagle Lake

Jackson Glacier

Mt Logan 9,239ft

Range

Continental

Divide

Blackfoot Glacier

Triple Divide Peak 8,8025ft

Mt Stimson 10,142ft

N

0   4 mi

0   4 km

Scenic Drive

© MOON.COM

the time being and return later in the day. Although there are pullouts 0.5 mi (0.8 km) east and west of the pass, the shoulderless road does not afford safe walking to the pass, and tromping across the fragile meadows is taboo.

EAST SIDE

From Logan Pass, the road drops by the cascades of **Lunch Creek,** a good place to sit on the rock wall to look up at **Piegan Mountain.** Below, the **East Side Tunnel,** dug out entirely by hand, pops with a downhill view of **Going-to-the-Sun Mountain.**

After **Siyeh Bend,** where a trailhead leads to **Piegan** and **Siyeh Passes,** the route drops into the trees to **Jackson Glacier Overlook,** the best view of a glacier (with the aid of binoculars) from Going-to-the-Sun Road. More views are available in the next several pullouts east.

The road follows along **St. Mary Lake.** The often-windy **Sun Point** marks the site of the park's former Going-to-the-Sun Chalets. Walk five minutes on the trail from the parking lot to the top of the rock promontory jutting into St. Mary Lake. Spectacular views from there take in Going-to-the-Sun Mountain, Fusillade Mountain, and the Continental Divide.

Midway down St. Mary Lake, the road arrives at **Wild Goose Island Overlook.** It's one of the most photographed spots, and you'll see tiny Wild Goose Island in the lake's blue waters, with the Continental Divide as the backdrop.

Around a bluff, **Rising Sun** has visitor services, including a boat tour, while **Two Dog Flats** lures elk, coyotes, and bears to grassland meadows bordered by aspen

boat tour dock on Lake McDonald (top); Garden Wall (middle); meadows above Logan Pass (bottom)

groves. Going-to-the-Sun Road terminates in the town of **St. Mary.**

Driving Tips

Although you can drive the Sun Road in two hours with no stops, most visitors take all day. Construction, sightseeing, and traffic slow travel. Don't be anxious about it; just sit back and enjoy the view.

- You will need a **vehicle reservation ticket** (www.recreation.gov; $2, valid for 3 days) for entry daily 6am-3pm late May to mid-September from west-side entrances, or July to mid-September from the east side.

- Follow posted **speed limits** (25-45 mph/40-72 kph), and turn on your headlights.

- Take **lunch, snacks, and drinks.** Between Lake McDonald Lodge and Rising Sun, no food or drinks are sold. Most restaurants around Glacier sell box or sack lunches.

- Watch for **bicyclists.** Although bicycle restrictions are in effect during July and August on the road's west side, the narrow roadway, lack of shoulders, and curves squeeze cyclists. Show them courtesy by slowing down to ease around them.

- Expect **construction delays.** Seasonal repair work can reduce traffic to a single lane.

- Check for **closures.** Heavy rain, snowstorms, fires, and accidents may close portions of the road. Entrance and ranger stations, as well as lodges, have current updates on the road status. You can also call 406/888-7800 for the Sun Road status recording, text 333-111 with the message "GNPROADS" to get alerts, or stop in at the Apgar or St. Mary Visitor Center to check on the status.

- Be prepared for all types of **weather.** Sunny skies may prevail in the valleys while visitors at Logan Pass creep along slowly in a dense fog on icy pavement.

- Passengers with a **fear of heights** should sit on the driver's side of the car for ascending the west side and descending the east. This will put you farthest from the cliff edges.

- **Cell phones** get little or no service on the Sun Road. Turn them off and enjoy the views.

- Bring **patience and flexibility.**

SEASONS

For big **waterfall** shows and snow left from winter, drive it in late June or early July. For alpine **wildflowers,** go in late July or early August. For **fewer crowds,** go mid-September-mid-October. From July through August, expect crowds around Avalanche, The Loop, Oberlin Bend, Logan Pass, Lunch Creek, Siyeh Bend, St. Mary Falls, and Sun Point. To avoid the hordes, drive in early morning or early evening, when lighting is better for photography and wildlife is more active. In midsummer, the Logan Pass parking lot fills 7am-5pm.

Both ends of Going-to-the-Sun Road have entrance stations, at **West Glacier** and **St. Mary.** Staffed during daylight hours in summer and on weekends only fall-spring, the stations hand out national park maps and the *Waterton-Glacier Guide*, the park's newspaper, updated twice annually.

Snow buries the Sun Road in **winter.** The usual vehicle closure runs from Lake McDonald Lodge to St. Mary late October-spring, but cross-country skiers and snowshoers trek the lowland corridors where avalanche danger is minimal.

FROM THE WEST OR EAST?

Many visitors drive Going-to-the-Sun Road both directions because of the different experiences they yield. Most will drive the Sun Road from the direction they approach the park. But if you have a choice, here's the considerations:

From the west, the uphill route between The Loop and Logan Pass follows the outer edge of the road along the guard wall for easy access to pullouts with big views. This outer lane also positions riders to nab frontal views of Haystack Falls and Triple Arches. But because West Glacier Entrance sees the most visitors entering the park, this climb up the Sun Road often feels like a big parade of vehicles.

Approaching **from the east** provides the shortest drive to Logan Pass, with the miles along St. Mary Lake yielding head-on views of the Continental Divide. Then, going up through the east-side tunnel emerges with a spectacular view of Logan Pass backed by Mount Clements. But driving down the west side means paying attention to the vertical cliff wall jutting up right outside the passenger side.

For the best of both worlds, drive down a portion of the opposite side from Logan Pass and climb back up. For coming from the west, drive down the east side to **Sun Point** before returning. For coming from

the east, drive down the west side to **The Loop** before ascending back to Logan Pass.

Bus Tours

Let someone else do the driving for the cliffy road over Logan Pass! Plus, buses are guaranteed parking at the pass. Your bus tour reservation gets you onto the Sun Road without needing a vehicle ticket reservation for that day. Make **advance reservations** for all bus tours. Meals, park entrance fees, and gratuities are not included. Both companies have tours originating on the west side and the east side.

SUN TOURS

406/732-9220 or 800/786-9220; www.glaciersuntours.com; late May-Sept.; adult $80-130, child 6-12 $45-70

A Blackfeet-led tour provides a different perspective, with emphasis on Indigenous cultural and natural history. Sun Tours drives air-conditioned 25-passenger coaches with extra-big windows for taking in the massive mountains on Going-to-the-Sun Road. Four-hour **Logan Pass tours** depart daily from St. Mary (9:30am), with a Rising Sun pickup shortly after. The tour goes up the east side of the Sun Road, explores Logan Pass, and drives down the west side to Big Bend to see the Weeping Wall before returning. You'll learn about original mountain names, geology, and Blackfeet history, cultural ceremonies, and traditions. **West-side tours** depart Apgar Visitor Center at 9am.

RED BUSES

855/733-4522; www. glaciernationalparklodges.com; full-day and half-day tours daily mid-June-mid-Oct.; adult $52-116, child half price, reservations required

Historic red buses tour visitors over

boat tour on St. Mary Lake

the Sun Road in vintage 1930s White Motor Company sedans operated by **Xanterra.** Drivers roll the canvas tops back for spectacular views of the Continental Divide on good weather days. Without a roof, it's one of the most scenic ways to feel the expanse of the glacier-carved terrain. Tours depart from Lake McDonald Lodge, Rising Sun Motor Inn, Apgar Visitor Center, and St. Mary Visitor Center. The Crown of the Continent tour takes a full day, but half-day Logan Pass tours have multiple departures. Evening tours go in July-August.

ST. MARY
St. Mary Lake
The second-largest lake in the park, St. Mary Lake fills a much narrower valley than its larger counterpart, Lake McDonald. At 9 mi (14.5 km) long and 292 ft (89 m) deep, it forms a blue platform out of which several stunning red argillite peaks rise. Its width shrinks in The Narrows to less than 0.5 mi (0.8 km), where buff-colored Altyn limestone resisted erosion. These strata contain the most ancient exposed rock

Blackfeet Interpretive Loop at St. Mary Scenic Overlook

in the park. Going-to-the-Sun Road follows the lake on its eastern shore for a few miles.

BOAT TOUR
Glacier Park Boat Company; 406/257-2426; www. glacierparkboats.com; daily early June-early Sept.; adult $39, child $20
At the Rising Sun boat dock, catch a 90-minute cruise on **Joy II** or **Little Chief** to brave St. Mary Lake's choppy waters. Views of Sexton Glacier and Wild Goose Island can't be beat, but be ready for some healthy wind. Walk to Baring Falls at a stop on tours departing on the hour 9am-5pm. A 6:30pm tour (1 hr; adult $26, child $13) does not include the falls stop. Book in advance by phone or online; limited tickets remain at the boat docks on the day of tours.

St. Mary Scenic Overlook and Blackfeet Interpretive Loop
Outside the park 2 mi (3.2 km) south of St. Mary on US 89, the St. Mary Scenic Overlook has an impressive panoramic view into the park. Far below is St. Mary Lake backed by Glacier's peaks. The 0.2-mi (0.3-km) paved, wheelchair-accessible Blackfeet Interpretive Loop begins from the overlook's parking area at a sculpture of a woman and a travois. The route tours metal tepee sculptures at overlooks, while interpretive signage tells stories of the Blackfeet. On the highway, look for signs that say "Turnout ½ mile."

★ MANY GLACIER
On Glacier's east side, Many Glacier is idyllic, filled with rugged scenery. Mountains graze the sky and drop abruptly to wide-open grassland prairies. Below sheer cliffs, elk

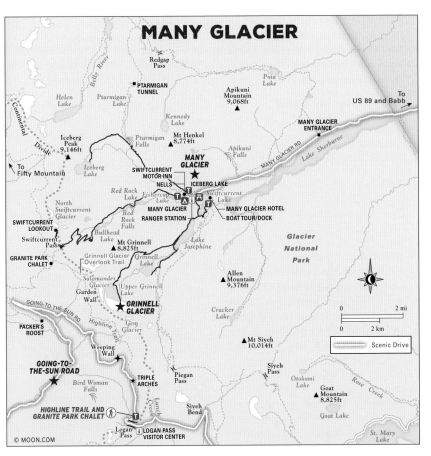

MANY GLACIER

Scenic Drive

browse. Aspen leaves chatter in only a hint of breeze.

From the valley floor, a wild panorama of Glacier's peaks runs across the western skyline, dominated by red sediments and milky sapphire lakes. Ice fields cling for dear life to cliffs as the summer sun shrinks them each year. It's a place of extravagant color, where tumbling waterfalls and pink, purple, white, and yellow wildflowers intoxicate the eyes.

The morning sunrise gleams gold across the rampart of peaks. Loons call across glassy lakes. Grizzly bears forage on hillsides, clawing at the ground for glacier lily bulbs. By evening, when the trails vacate, the

sunset paints royal hues above the Continental Divide. Dark descends, with a multitude of stars. And if you're lucky, the **northern lights** dance across the sky.

Officially called the Swiftcurrent Valley, Many Glacier is the nickname long given the area due to the string of small glaciers that populate its peaks: Grinnell, Salamander, Gem, North Swiftcurrent, and South Swiftcurrent. **Grinnell Glacier** is the closest trail-accessible glacier in the park, reached via an 11-mi (17.7-km) round-trip hike (page 81).

An easy walking trail circles **Swiftcurrent Lake,** a mountain-rimmed pool sometimes inhabited by moose. Paddlers can rent kayaks and rowboats or ride a tour boat on Swiftcurrent and Josephine Lakes, which shortens the walk to milky turquoise **Grinnell Lake.**

Many Glacier Road
DRIVING DISTANCE: 12 mi (19.3 km) one-way
DRIVING TIME: 25 minutes one-way
START: Babb, east of Many Glacier Entrance
END: Swiftcurrent Motor Inn

The 12-mi-long (19.3-km) Many Glacier Road (Glacier Rte. 3; open May-Oct.) is a stunning drive into **Swiftcurrent Valley.** From Babb, the road follows Swiftcurrent Creek upstream across Blackfeet Nation lands. Watch for **bears,** particularly around dusk. If you spot a bear, drive by slowly to watch rather than stop and create a bear jam, which conditions them to be comfortable around cars. Above all, stay in the car for safety.

After the road rises to reach Sherburne Dam (mi 4.8/km 7.7), it follows the reservoir's north shore, crossing into the park, but you won't reach the park entrance station for another 3 mi (4.8 km). As of 2022, the road from the Sherburne Dam to the entrance station was still gravel. Check the shoreline for deer, bears, and sometimes errant cows. Wildflower meadows with early July's pink sticky geraniums and lupine line the road. Scenic stops have views of **Sherburne Reservoir** and up the valley to **Grinnell Glacier.**

After the reservoir, you'll reach **Many Glacier Hotel** (mi 11.5/km 18.5), the picnic area (mi 12.1/km 19.5), and the ranger station and campground (mi 12.3/km 19.8). The road terminates at Swiftcurrent Motor Inn and trailheads.

Boat Tour
Glacier Park Boat Company; 406/257-2426; www. glacierparkboats.com; several departures daily mid-June-mid-Sept.; round-trip adult $39, child $20
In Many Glacier, jump on a pair of historic wooden boats for a two-lake tour. Catch the 1961-vintage *Chief Two Guns* at Swiftcurrent Lake's boat dock behind Many Glacier Hotel. In 75 minutes, you'll cruise across the lake, hike five minutes over a hill, hop aboard the 1945 *Morning Eagle* for a cruise on Lake Josephine, and return. Don't forget your camera, although you may have difficulty cramming the view into the lens. Tours depart at 9am, 11am, 2pm, and 4:30pm, with additional launches at 8:30am, 1pm, and 3pm starting in July. The 2pm launch offers a guided walk to **Grinnell Lake** (2.2 mi/3.5 km round-trip), and the 8:30am boat has a ranger-led hike to **Grinnell Glacier.** Tours sell out; make reservations in advance online or in person at the dock.

With reservations, hikers can use the boats as **shuttles** (round-trip or one-way return only) to cut down trail mileage. For one-way return boats (half price) from the Lake Josephine upper dock, reserve tickets in advance online or purchase, if available, at the boat dock before hiking.

TWO MEDICINE
Quiet and removed, Glacier's southeast corner harbors a less-traveled wonderland. It's a favorite part of the park for many locals.

It's away from the harried corridor of Going-to-the-Sun Road with its endless line of cars. With no hotel in Two Medicine, you'll find trails far less clogged on day hikes than at Many Glacier. Just because it sees

Swiftcurrent Creek and Lake in Many Glacier

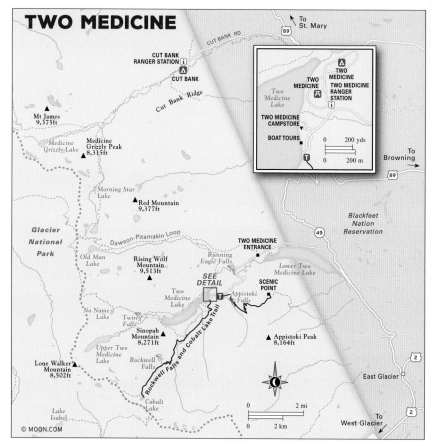

TWO MEDICINE

Map labels:
CUT BANK RD
To St. Mary
89

CUT BANK RANGER STATION
CUT BANK

TWO MEDICINE
TWO MEDICINE RANGER STATION
Two Medicine Lake
TWO MEDICINE CAMPSTORE
BOAT TOURS
0 200 yds
0 200 m
To Browning
89

Cut Bank Ridge

Mt James 9,375ft

Medicine Grizzly Lake
Medicine Grizzly Peak 8,315ft

Morning Star Lake

Red Mountain 9,377ft

Glacier National Park

Dawson-Pitamakin Loop

Blackfeet Nation Reservation
49

Old Man Lake

Rising Wolf Mountain 9,513ft

Running Eagle Falls

TWO MEDICINE ENTRANCE

Lower Two Medicine Lake

SEE DETAIL

Two Medicine Lake

Appistoki Falls

SCENIC POINT

No Name Lake

Twin Falls

Sinopah Mountain 8,271ft

Rockwell Falls and Cobalt Lake Trail

Appistoki Peak 8,164ft

Upper Two Medicine Lake

Rockwell Falls

Lone Walker Mountain 8,502ft

Cobalt Lake

Lake Isabel

East Glacier

2

To West Glacier

2

0 2 mi
0 2 km

© MOON.COM

fewer people, however, does not make it less dramatic.

A string of three lakes curves through the Two Medicine Valley, the middle one dominated by **Rising Wolf Mountain,** a red hulking monolith to the north. Even though glaciers vacated this area within the past 150 years, their footprints are left in swooping valleys, cirques with blue lakes, and toothy spires. **Two Medicine Lake** shimmers in a valley strewn with hiking trails.

Running Eagle Falls

Shortly after the park entrance at Two Medicine, a short nature trail (0.6 mi/1 km round-trip) leads to Running Eagle Falls, formerly known as Trick Falls. In high runoff, water gushes over the top of the falls, spraying those standing nearby. But in lower flows, you can see the trick. Part of the falls runs underground and spits out through a cavern halfway down the cliff face. Running Eagle, the Blackfeet name for the falls, honors a female warrior named Pitamakin who had her vision quest here. She gained renown for stealing horses from the Kootenai but was eventually killed during a raid.

Two Medicine Lake

The largest of three lakes in the Two Medicine area, Two Medicine Lake is the highest road-accessible lake in Glacier, sitting almost 1 mi (1.6 km) high and flanked by peaks rich in Blackfeet history. Its waters collect snowmelt from peaks of over 8,000 ft (2,438 m) but devoid of glaciers. The lakes are all that remain of the 1,000-ft-thick (305-m) ice field that filled the valley and flowed out onto the prairie to the east, past the town of Browning. To explore Two Medicine Lake, jump on the historic *Sinopah* tour boat, or if the waters are calm, paddle its shoreline or swim in its chilly temperature.

Mount Sinopah

BOAT TOUR

Glacier Park Boat Company; 406/257-2426; www. glacierparkboats.com; June-mid-Sept.; adult $20 round-trip, child $10
The **Sinopah** started service on Two Medicine Lake in 1927 and has never left its waters. The 45-ft (14-m), 49-passenger wooden boat cruises uplake six times daily for 45-minute tours (9am, 10am, 11am, 1pm, 3pm, and 5pm) while the captain narrates history, trivia, and natural phenomena. The 1pm and 3pm tours also incorporate an optional guided hike to **Twin Falls** (0.9 mi/1.4 km one-way). An 8am trip starts up in July, geared as a shuttle for early hikers. Make reservations online or by phone at least one day in advance; if available, you can buy tickets at the office near the dock.

Hikers use the tour boat as a **shuttle** to shorten mileages on trails. You can buy one-way return rides online in advance or at the ticket office, if available, before you depart on your hike.

Blackfeet Peaks

From the beach at Two Medicine Lake, you can see a trio of mountains: **Sinopah** across the lake, **Lone Walker** in the distance behind the lake's head, and the most prominent feature in Two Medicine Valley, **Rising Wolf** (9,513 ft/2,900 m), on the north shore. Rising Wolf's sheer mass is larger than any other peak in the park.

Lone Walker is named after a chief of the Small Robes band of Piegans, a tribe of the Blackfeet. He befriended Hugh Monroe, the first person of European descent to meet the Blackfeet. Lone Walker's daughter, Sinopah, married Monroe, who was eventually officially admitted to the band and given the name Rising Wolf. Many of Sinopah and Rising Wolf's descendants still live on the Blackfeet Reservation.

NORTH FORK

Home to scenic lakes for paddling, hiking, and camping, this remote area in the northwest of the park is accessible only by rough potholed and washboard dirt roads. This is rugged country with no services, no cell reception, and mostly vault toilets, but it's prized for those same reasons. The area can only be reached by driving north of

WATERTON LAKES NATIONAL PARK

Bordering Glacier in Canada, Waterton Lakes National Park serves as the entrance to Glacier's remote north country. Together, the two national parks are the world's first International Peace Park and International Dark Sky Park. They are also a Biosphere Reserve and World Heritage Site. In summer 2017, the Kenow Fire burned 19,394 ha (47,700 acres) of the park, which included many trails, a campground, backcountry campsites, picnic areas, and roads, but not Waterton Townsite, which houses motels, restaurants, a campground, boat tours, and visitor services.

The **Waterton Lakes Visitor Centre** (404 Cameron Falls Dr., Waterton Townsite; 403/859-5133; www.pc.gc.ca/en/pn-np/ab/waterton; 9am-5pm daily year-round) provides information, maps, and permits. The entrance gate is open 24/7 year-round (staffed early May-early Oct.). To enter, purchase a **Parks Canada day pass** (C$9-11 per person over 17 years, or up to 7 people in one vehicle C$21; May-Oct.).

HIGHLIGHTS
Chief Mountain International Highway
This two-nation scenic road circles Chief Mountain, sacred to the Blackfeet, and crosses through Glacier and Waterton.

Waterton Shoreline Cruises
marina, junction of Mount View Rd. and Waterton Ave.; 403/859-2362; www.watertoncruise.com; daily early May-early Oct.; from adult C$61-85 round-trip, child C$31-42
Hop aboard the historic *MV International* for a ride on the deepest lake in the Canadian Rockies to the international border or to Goat Haunt, USA.

MV International boat tour on Waterton Lake

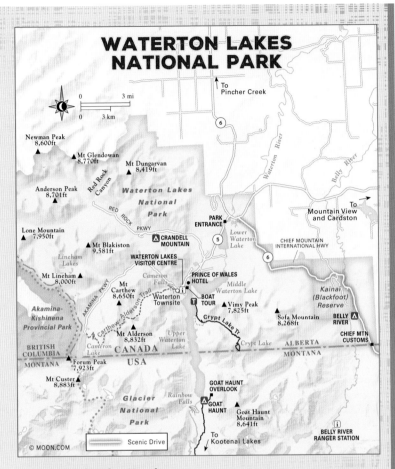

WATERTON LAKES NATIONAL PARK

Prince of Wales Hotel

844/868-7474 or 403/859-2231; www.glacierparkcollection.com; daily early June-mid-Sept.

This 1927 hotel maintains British ambience thanks to kilt-wearing bellhops and afternoon high tea.

Cameron Falls

near the junction of Cameron Falls Dr. and Evergreen Ave.

This roadside falls on Cameron Creek splits several directions in its plunge to the valley floor.

BEST HIKES

Crypt Lake

17 km (10.6 mi) round-trip

A boat ride on Waterton Shoreline Cruises leads to the trailhead, where switchbacks ascend to what looks like impassable cliffs. A hid-

Prince of Wales Hotel

den tunnel curls into a hanging valley holding an alpine lake cowering below peaks in Glacier.

Goat Haunt, USA

Accessible only by Waterton Shoreline Cruises, Goat Haunt is a launchpad onto Glacier's remote northern trails. Destinations include Rainbow Falls (2.3 km/1.4 mi round-trip), Goat Haunt Overlook (3.1 km/1.9 mi round-trip), and Kootenai Lakes (9 km/5.6 mi round-trip).

TRANSPORTATION

From St. Mary, take US 89 north through Babb, Montana. North of Babb, turn left onto **Chief Mountain International Highway** (Hwy 17), which leads to the Canadian border, where the road becomes AB 6. At the north terminus, turn west onto Highway 5 and south to the **Waterton Entrance Station.** The drive is 48 km (30 mi) total and takes one hour.

The road's season and hours are linked to the Canadian and U.S. immigration and **customs stations** at the border (daily, 9am-6pm May 15-30, 7am-10pm, June 1-Sept. 4, 9am-6pm Sept. 5-30, closed Oct.-May 15). Passports are required for crossing.

From Banff National Park, the fastest route heads east on the Trans-Canada Highway from the town of Banff to Calgary (129 km/80 mi, 90 minutes). From Calgary, head south on Hwy 2 toward Fort Macleod for 182 km (113 mi). Then turn west onto Hwy 3 to Pincher Creek, and turn south onto Hwy 6 to the park entrance. The drive from Calgary to Waterton is 240 km (149 mi) and takes about 3.5 hours.

Apgar outside the park and entering through the remote **Polebridge Entrance** (27 mi/43 km, 1 hour on mostly dirt road). In addition to entry fees, you'll need a **vehicle reservation ticket** (6am-3pm daily, late May-mid-Sept.; www.recreation.gov; $2 per vehicle; valid for 1 day) for the Polebridge Entrance. From the Polebridge Entrance, rough roads of very slow driving reach **Kintla Lake** (12 mi/19.3 km, 1 hour) or **Bowman Lake** (6 mi/9.7 km, 35 minutes). Outside of the reservation hours and season, access roads can close due to congested traffic. Quiet primitive campgrounds are at Bowman Lake, Kintla Lake, Logging Creek, and Quartz Creek. Trailers and vehicles longer than 21 ft (6.4 m) are not permitted on any North Fork roads in Glacier.

BEST HIKES

GOING-TO-THE-SUN ROAD
Trail of the Cedars and Avalanche Lake
DISTANCE: 0.9-mi (1.4-km) loop to 5.9 mi (9.5 km) round-trip
DURATION: 0.5-3 hours
ELEVATION GAIN: 0-730 ft (0-223 m)
EFFORT: easy-moderate
TRAIL SURFACE: accessible boardwalk and hard surface on the Trail of the Cedars; dirt, roots, mud, and rocks for Avalanche Lake
TRAILHEAD: across the Sun Road from Avalanche Picnic Area and shuttle stop

As the second-busiest trail in the park, Avalanche can see around 1,500 people per day in summer. The parking lots crowd with cars by sunrise, and the path shows the steady stream of hikers with widening and social trails trampling vegetation on the edges. Come prepared with drinking water and appropriate footwear.

With interpretive signs, the Trail of the Cedars boardwalk guides walkers and wheelchairs on a loop that crosses two footbridges over Avalanche Creek. The route tours the lush rainforest, where fallen trees become nurse logs, fertile habitat for hemlocks and tiny foamflowers. Immense black cottonwoods furrowed with deep-cut bark and huge 500-year-old western red cedars dominate the forest. At **Avalanche Gorge,** the creek slices through red rocks. To finish the 0.9-mi (1.4-km) loop, continue on the hard-surface walkway past large burled cedars to return to the trailhead.

The trail to Avalanche Lake departs from about halfway around Trail of the Cedars Loop. Turn uphill for the short grunt to the top of the water-carved Avalanche Gorge. Be extremely careful: Too many fatal accidents have occurred from slipping here. From the gorge, the trail climbs steadily through woods littered with glacial erratics. Some of these large boulders strewn when the glacier receded still retain scratch marks left from the ice. At the top, 1.9 mi (3.1 km) from the trailhead, a cirque with steep cliffs and tumbling waterfalls cradles the lake. An additional 0.7-mi (1.1-km) path goes to the lake's less-crowded head, where anglers find better fishing.

Avalanche Gorge on Trail of the Cedars

Hidden Lake Overlook

DISTANCE: 2.6 mi (4.2 km) round-trip to overlook, 5 mi (8 km) round-trip to lake
DURATION: 2-4 hours round-trip
ELEVATION GAIN: 482 ft (147 m)
EFFORT: moderate
TRAIL SURFACE: wide boardwalk with stairs and rocky dirt
TRAILHEAD: behind Logan Pass Visitor Center and shuttle stop

Regardless of daily hiker numbers in summer topping 1,500 people, Hidden Lake Overlook is a spectacular hike and the most popular in the park. Avoid long lines of hikers by going shortly after sunrise or in the evening. The trail is often buried under feet of snow (which can get icy overnight) until mid-July or later, but tall poles mark the route. Once the trail melts out, a boardwalk climbs the first half through alpine meadows where fragile shooting stars and alpine laurel dot the landscape with pink. The trail ascends through argillite: Look for evidence of mud-cracked and ripple-marked rocks from the ancient Belt Sea. Above, **Mount Clements** reveals various sea sediments in colorful layers.

The upper trail climbs past moraines, waterfalls, mountain goats, and bighorn sheep. At Hidden Pass on the Continental Divide, the trail reaches the platform overlooking Hidden Lake's blue waters. For ambitious hikers or anglers, the trail continues 1.2 mi (1.9 km) down to the lake. This portion is often closed in July for bears feeding on spawning fish at the lake's outlet. The return climb (776 ft/237 m) back up to the pass is demanding, followed by the descent back to the visitor center. After late September, you may need ice cleats.

Piegan Pass and Siyeh Pass

DISTANCE: 8.8 mi (14.2 km) round-trip, 11.5 mi (18.5 km) to Many Glacier, or 10 mi (16.1 km) point to point
DURATION: 4-6 hours
ELEVATION GAIN: 1,739 ft (530 m)/2,278 ft (694 m)
EFFORT: moderate-strenuous
TRAIL SURFACE: dirt path with roots and rocks
TRAILHEAD: Piegan Pass Trailhead at Siyeh Bend and Siyeh Bend shuttle stop

Piegan Pass, named for the Piikani or Piegan people of the Blackfeet Nation, sneaks a close look at the Continental Divide. This trail is often snowbound until early July and can retain steep snow patches along the base of Siyeh Peak. After climbing 2 mi (3.2 km) through subalpine forest and turning north at the first trail junction, the trail breaks out into **Preston Park,** bursting with purple fleabane, blue gentians, white valerian, and fuchsia paintbrush. During the climb, spy four glaciers: **Piegan, Jackson, Blackfoot,** and **Sperry,** the last seen through trees. As the trail waltzes through the wildflower meadows of Preston Park, a signed

steps leading to Hidden Lake Overlook Trail

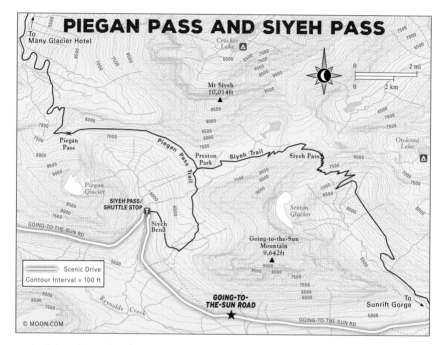

PIEGAN PASS AND SIYEH PASS

To Many Glacier Hotel

Cracker Lake

Mt Siyeh 10,014ft

Piegan Pass

Piegan Pass Trail

Preston Park

Siyeh Trail

Siyeh Pass

Otokomi Lake

Piegan Glacier

SIYEH PASS/ SHUTTLE STOP

Siyeh Bend

Sexton Glacier

Going-to-the-Sun Mountain 9,642ft

GOING-TO-THE-SUN RD

Scenic Drive
Contour Interval = 100 ft

Reynolds Creek

GOING-TO-THE-SUN ROAD

To Sunrift Gorge

GOING-TO-THE-SUN RD

0   2 mi
0   2 km

© MOON.COM

trail junction splits the Piegan Pass Trail (left) from the Siyeh Pass Trail (right).

Shortly after the junction, the **Piegan Pass Trail** heads into the seemingly barren alpine zone as it crosses the base of Siyeh Peak. But miniature flowers bloom and serve as food for pikas. The trail sweeps around a large bowl where two steep snowfields often linger through July. At **Piegan Pass,** you'll face the jagged Continental Divide. Rather than returning to **Siyeh Bend** (8.8 mi/14.2 km round-trip), some hikers opt for continuing on to **Many Glacier Hotel** (11.5 mi/18.5 km from Piegan Pass Trailhead) to link with shuttles to return.

An alternative route is to take the **Siyeh Pass Trail** from Preston Park. When switchbacks ascend above the tree line, the elevation gain provides a look back at the hanging valley in which Preston Park sits. The switchbacks appear to lead to a saddle, which is **Siyeh Pass.** But eight more turns climb above the pass before swinging through a cliff to the divide between Boulder and Baring Creeks. Snow can bury the steep switchbacks south of the divide until mid-July. **Sexton Glacier** hunkers protected from the afternoon sun by Going-to-the-Sun Mountain (accessible via a 1-mi/1.6-km spur trail). The trail descends in 3,446 ft (1,050 m) of elevation past bighorn sheep and a multicolored cliff band before traversing the flanks of Goat Mountain and dropping a couple hot miles through the 2015 Reynolds Creek Fire to the lower trailhead and shuttle stop at the **Sunrift Gorge** on Going-to-the-Sun Road. From Piegan Pass Trailhead to Sunrift Gorge is 10 mi (16.1 km) total.

St. Mary and Virginia Falls
DISTANCE: 2-3.4 mi (3.2-5.5 km) round-trip
DURATION: 1-2 hours round-trip
ELEVATION GAIN: 216 ft (66 m)
EFFORT: easy
TRAIL SURFACE: dirt path with roots and rocks
TRAILHEAD: St. Mary Falls Trailhead or St. Mary Falls shuttle stop

In midsummer, this trail sees a constant stream of people. Two trailheads depart from Going-to-the-Sun Road. The west trailhead descends from the shuttle stop. The east trailhead launches from the vehicle parking lot. Both trails connect with the St. Mary Lake Trail leading to the falls. Between the trailheads and St. Mary Falls, the 2015 Reynolds Creek Fire burned the forest, opening up views of surrounding mountains and the St. Mary River. On hot days, hike it in the morning.

The trail drops 1 mi (1.6 km) through several well-signed junctions en route to St. Mary Falls, a multidrop falls that cascade through a mini-gorge into blue-green pools. After crossing the wooden bridge at St. Mary Falls, the trail switchbacks up 0.7 mi (1.1 km) to Virginia Falls, a broad veil-type waterfall spewing mist. A short spur climbs to the base of Virginia Falls. Be wary of slippery rocks and strong, cold currents at both falls. Nesting near both waterfalls, water ouzels (American dippers) are dark gray birds easily recognized by their dipping action, up to 40 bends per minute.

MANY GLACIER
★ Grinnell Glacier
DISTANCE: 11 mi (17.7 km) round-trip
DURATION: 6 hours round-trip
ELEVATION GAIN: 1,619 ft (493 m)
EFFORT: moderate-strenuous
TRAIL SURFACE: narrow, dirt, rocks, rock steps
TRAILHEADS: on the south side of Many Glacier Hotel, at Swiftcurrent Picnic Area, or via the tour boat

In early summer, a large steep snowdrift frequently bars the path into the upper basin until early July; check the status before hiking. The closest trail-accessible glacier in the park, Grinnell Glacier requires stamina because most of its elevation gain is packed into 2 mi (3.2 km). Many hikers make reservations

view north from Piegan Pass (left); Virginia Falls (right)

TOP HIKE
HIGHLINE TRAIL AND GRANITE PARK CHALET

DISTANCE: 7.4 mi (11.9 km) to Granite Park Chalet, 11.4 mi (18.3 km) to The Loop
DURATION: 5-6 hours to The Loop
ELEVATION GAIN: 975 ft (297 m) up; 3,395 ft (1,035 m) down
EFFORT: strenuous
TRAIL SURFACE: narrow, dirt, rocks
TRAILHEAD: across Going-to-the-Sun Road from Logan Pass parking lot and shuttle stop

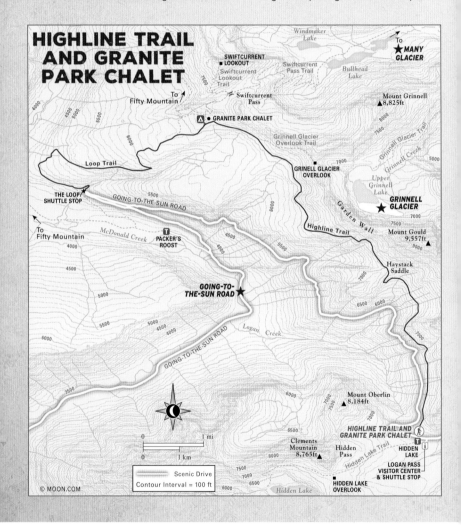

Many first-time hikers stop every 10 steps to take photos on this hike, which scares severe acrophobes with its exposed thousand-foot drop-offs. The trail drops from **Logan Pass** through a cliff walk above the Sun Road before crossing a flower land that gave the Garden Wall arête its name. At 3 mi (4.8 km), nearly all the elevation gain is packed into one climb: **Haystack Saddle** appears to be the top, but it is only halfway. After the high point, the trail drops and swings through several large bowls before passing **Bear Valley** to reach **Granite Park Chalet** atop a knoll at 6,680 ft (2,036 m). Due to steep snow-filled avalanche paths, this trail is closed from Logan Pass usually into early July or later. After the trail dries out, dust billows around hikers' legs due to the crowds of nearly 900 hikers per day. **Do not underestimate this trail:** Hikers have high incidents of dehydration and hypothermia here due to exposure to the sun, wind, rain, and snow. Carry two quarts of water and extra layers for surprise changes in weather.

Stronger Highline hikers can add on side trails to **Grinnell Glacier Overlook** (a steep 1.6 mi/2.6 km round-trip) and **Swiftcurrent Lookout** (4.2 mi/6.8 km round-trip). To exit the area, some hikers opt to hike out over Swiftcurrent Pass to **Many Glacier** (7.6 mi/12.2 km) and catch shuttles; backpackers continue on to **Fifty Mountain** (11.9 mi/19.2 km farther) and **Goat Haunt** (22.5 mi/36.2 km farther). Most day hikers head down **The Loop Trail** (4 mi/6.4 km) to catch the shuttle.

Granite Park Chalet (July-early Sept.) does not have running water. Carry your own, filter water from the campground stream below the chalet, or purchase bottled water (cash only). Snacks are also sold. Day hikers may also use the outdoor picnic tables at the chalet.

Grinnell Lake

Lake Josephine and Grinnell Lake

DISTANCE: 2.2-7.8 mi (3.5-12.6 km) round-trip
DURATION: 1-4 hours round-trip
ELEVATION GAIN: 75 ft (23 m)
EFFORT: easy
TRAIL SURFACE: dirt and rocks
TRAILHEADS: on the south side of Many Glacier Hotel, at Swiftcurrent Picnic Area, or via the tour boat

For a 2.2-mi (3.5-km) round-trip walk, make reservations for the tour boat across Swiftcurrent Lake and Lake Josephine to hike to Grinnell Lake. From the upper boat dock on Lake Josephine, a level, well-signed trail goes over a swinging bridge and uphill to a junction. Continue straight to reach the milky turquoise waters of Grinnell Lake and the giant multitiered waterfall across the lake. Return to the same dock.

For a longer hike (7.8 mi/12.6 km rt), begin at Many Glacier Hotel, following the trail winding around Swiftcurrent Lake to the west boat dock opposite the hotel. Another starting point begins at Many Glacier picnic area (7.6 mi/12.2 km rt), where the trail follows Swiftcurrent Lake to that same boat dock.

From the west boat dock, pop over the hill to Josephine Lake, where the trail hugs the north shore. Take the left route at the two junctions that split off to Grinnell Glacier. Round Josephine's west end to the Grinnell Lake junction. Turn right and follow the trail over a swinging bridge. After climbing a hill, continue straight at the junction to drop to the lakeshore to enjoy Grinnell's milky turquoise waters and the giant falls across the lake. Although you can return to the trailheads via the south lakeshore trail, it is not as scenic due to deep

for the boat shuttle, cutting the length to 7.8 mi (12.6 km) round-trip, or just trimming 2.5 mi (4 km) off the return. To hike from the picnic area, follow Swiftcurrent Lake's shore to the west boat dock. From Many Glacier Hotel, round the southern shore to the same west dock. Bop over the short hill and hike around Lake Josephine's north shore.

Toward Josephine's west end, the Grinnell Glacier Trail diverges uphill. As the trail climbs through multicolored rock strata, Grinnell Lake's milky turquoise waters come into view below. Above, you'll spot Gem Glacier and Salamander Glacier, both shrunken to static snowfields, long before Grinnell Glacier appears. The trail ascends on a cliff stairway where a waterfall douses hikers. The path skirts cliffs and steep ravines to reach a rest stop with outhouses. A steep grunt up the moraine leads to a stunning view. Trot through the maze of paths crossing the bedrock to Upper Grinnell Lake's shore, but do not walk out on the glacier's ice, as it harbors deadly hidden crevasses.

forest. Shorten this hike by reserving return tour boat tickets for the ride back.

Swiftcurrent Pass and Lookout

DISTANCE: 3.6–16.2 mi (5.8–26 km) round-trip
DURATION: 2–8 hours
ELEVATION GAIN: 100–3,496 ft (30–1,066 m)
EFFORT: easy–strenuous
TRAIL SURFACE: narrow dirt path with roots and rocks
TRAILHEAD: Swiftcurrent parking lot

This trail leads to various destinations along a scenic path dotted with lakes, waterfalls, moose, bears, glaciers, and wildflowers. Expect crowds along the valley floor, but they will thin the farther you go. The trail winds through pine trees and aspen groves, with a spur to **Fishercap Lake** to spot moose. Then, it rolls gently up to **Redrock Lake and Falls** at 1.8 mi (2.9 km), with Redrock Falls at the inlet. The trail continues through meadows rampant with Sitka valerian in July to **Bullhead Lake** at 3.9 mi (6.3 km). Scan scree slopes for bighorn sheep.

Departing the valley floor, the views improve on the uphill switchbacks to a waterfall before cutting around a cliff face. A bit more climbing leads to **Swiftcurrent Pass** at 6.6 mi (10.6 km). At the signed junction, go north 1.4 more mi (2.3 km) of switchbacks (you'll lose count of them) to **Swiftcurrent Lookout** to survey almost the entire park: glaciers, peaks, wild panoramas, and the plains. Many Glacier Hotel looks minuscule. Enjoy the one-of-a-kind view from the outhouse. Return by retracing your steps, or from Swiftcurrent Pass, drop downhill 0.9 mi (1.4 km) to Granite Park Chalet, which connects with the Loop Trail and the Highline Trail.

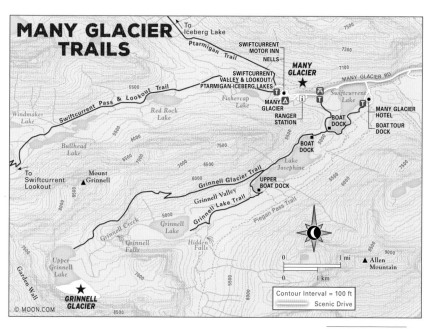

Iceberg Lake

DISTANCE: 9.8 mi (15.8 km) round-trip
DURATION: 5 hours round-trip
ELEVATION GAIN: 1,193 ft (364 m)
EFFORT: moderate
TRAIL SURFACE: narrow, dirt, roots, rocks
TRAILHEAD: behind Swiftcurrent Motor Inn cabins in Many Glacier

One of the top hikes in Glacier, the trail to Iceberg Lake begins with a steep jaunt uphill with no time to warm up muscles gradually. Within 0.4 mi (0.6 km) you reach a junction. Take note of the directional sign here, and watch for it when you come down. On the return, some hikers zombie-walk right on past it.

Scenic Point in Two Medicine

At the junction, go left; the trail maintains an easy railroad grade to the lake. Make noise on this trail, known for frequent bear sightings. Wildflowers line the trail in July: bear grass, bog orchids, penstemon, and thimbleberry. Forests alternate with brushy meadows and intermittent views that take in the splendor of Swiftcurrent Valley, Grinnell Peak, and Mount Wilbur. Soon, the trail arcs northward at a red argillite outcropping to enter a pine and fir forest broken by Ptarmigan Falls at 2.6 mi (4.2 km), a good break spot where aggressive ground squirrels will steal your snacks. Do not feed them; feeding only trains them to be more forceful. Just beyond the falls, the Ptarmigan Tunnel Trail veers right. Stay straight to swing west through multiple brush and wildflower avalanche paths below the jagged Ptarmigan Wall. After crossing a creek, the trail climbs the final bluff, where a view of stark icebergs against blue water unfolds. Drop to the beach for lunch. Brave hikers dive into the lake, but be prepared to have the frigid water suck the air from your lungs.

TWO MEDICINE
Scenic Point

DISTANCE: 7.4 mi (11.9 km) round-trip
DURATION: 4 hours round-trip
ELEVATION GAIN: 2,124 ft (647 m)
EFFORT: moderate-strenuous
TRAIL SURFACE: narrow, dirt, roots, rocks
TRAILHEAD: milepost 6.9 up Two Medicine Road

Scenic Point is one short climb with big scenery. The trail launches up through a thick subalpine fir forest. A short side jaunt en route allows a peek at Appistoki Falls. As

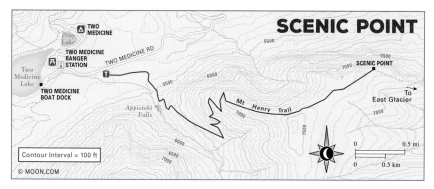

SCENIC POINT

TWO MEDICINE

Pray Lake

TWO MEDICINE RANGER STATION

TWO MEDICINE RD

5500

Two Medicine Lake

TWO MEDICINE BOAT DOCK

Appistoki Falls

5500

6000

6500

7000

6000

Mt Henry Trail

7000

7500

6500

7000

7000

SCENIC POINT

To East Glacier

7000

Contour Interval = 100 ft

© MOON.COM

0   0.5 mi

0   0.5 km

switchbacks line up like dominoes, stunted firs give way to silvery dead and twisted limber pines. Broaching the ridge, the trail enters seemingly barren alpine tundra. Only alpine bluebells and pink mats of several-hundred-year-old moss campion cower in crags.

On the ridge, the trail traverses a north-facing slope; avoid the early summer steep snowfield by climbing a worn path that goes above it before descending to Scenic Point. To reach the actual Scenic Point above the trail, cut off at the sign, stepping on rocks to avoid crushing fragile alpine plants. At the top, views plunge several thousand feet straight down to Lower Two Medicine Lake and across the plains. Return the way you came.

Rockwell Falls and Cobalt Lake

DISTANCE: 6.8-15.8 mi (10.9-25.4 km) round-trip
DURATION: 4-8 hours round-trip
ELEVATION GAIN: minimal-2,518 ft (minimal-767 m)
EFFORT: easy-strenuous
TRAIL SURFACE: narrow, dirt, roots, rocks
TRAILHEAD: adjacent to Two Medicine boat dock

Follow the gentle South Shore Trail along Two Medicine Lake past beaver ponds and bear-scratched trees to Paradise Creek, crossing on a swinging bridge. At 2.3 mi (3.7 km), turn left at the signed junction. The trail wanders through avalanche paths with uprooted trees shredded like toothpicks. At 3.4 mi (5.5 km), you reach Rockwell Falls. Spur trails explore the falls.

Continuing on to Cobalt Lake, the trail climbs up several switchbacks into an upper basin, crossing the creek. It ascends at a moderate pitch for the last 2 mi (3.2 km). Tucked in the uppermost corner of the basin, Cobalt Lake sits below mountain goat cliffs.

Rockwell Falls

GUIDED HIKES
Glacier Guides
11970 US 2 E., West Glacier; 406/387-5555; https://glacierguides.com; mid-May-Sept.

Glacier Guides runs the trail-guiding concession in the park. They lead day hikes, backpacking, and overnight chalet trips. For day hiking, reservations are required, and rates include the guide service, a deli lunch, and transportation to the trailhead. Solo travelers can hook up with the daily group day hikes (July-early Sept.; $170 pp), scheduled to a different destination each day. Backpacking trips depart every week for 3- to 6-day adventures; rates run from $290 per day and include the guide service, transportation to and from the trailhead, meals, and snacks.

National Park Service Hikes
National Park Service naturalists lead free hikes during summer in Glacier. Consult current schedules online (www.nps.gov/glac), in the park newspaper, or in visitor centers.

BACKPACKING

Glacier National Park's backpacking is unrivaled, with miles of well-marked scenic trails. Sixty-six designated backcountry campgrounds spread campers out to avoid crowds. Long-distance trekkers can tackle more than 100 mi (161 km) of Continental Divide Trail in 7-10 days.

For backpacking, secure an advance reservation (www.recreation.gov, $10) for a **wilderness permit** starting mid-March.

Permits (adults $7 pp/night) for backpacking trips are in high demand, available by advance reservation for mid-June through September trips or walk-in 24 hours in advance during and outside the reservation season. Pick them up 24 hours in advance in person at the **Apgar Backcountry Permit Office** (406/888-7859 May-Oct.; 406/888-7800 Nov.-Apr.; 7:30am-5pm daily June-Sept., 8am-4pm daily May and Oct.), **St. Mary Visitor Center** (406/888-7800; backcountry permit desk 7:30am-5pm daily late May-late Sept.), or **Many Glacier Ranger Station** (406/888-7800; 7:30am-5pm daily late May-late Sept.). Lines begin forming an hour or more before opening. All permits must be picked up by 4:30pm. For trip planning, reservations, and the permits, three-letter codes are used to designate assigned wilderness camps, but the specific sites are first-come, first-served.

Outside the reservation season (mid-June-Sept.), permits are only issued in person. During winter, permits are available at park headquarters by appointment (406/888-7800; Nov.-Apr.).

For guided backpacking trips, contact **Glacier Guides** (406/387-5555; https://glacierguides.com).

DAWSON-PITAMAKIN LOOP
18.4-25 mi (29.6-40 km)

Although this route can be done as a day hike, you can also stretch it out to make a backpacking trip of it. The Dawson-Pitamakin Loop takes a top-of-the-world Continental Divide traverse between high passes through bighorn sheep summering habitat and alpine tundra. Hike this loop in either direction, starting from the trailhead at **Two Medicine Campground.** For an 18.4-mi (29.6-km), three-day trip, camp a night at **Old Man Lake** (OLD) and a night at **No Name Lake** (NON). For four days and 25 mi (40 km), add a night at **Morning Star Lake** (MOR) in the middle, but be prepared for the plunge to the lake and a 2,000-ft (610-m) climb back up the next day. The route is snow-free some summers by early July and walk-in permits are available, but starting a trip reserved in advance is not available until July 15.

GUNSIGHT PASS
28 mi (45 km)
This four-day trek is best hiked from **Jackson Glacier Overlook** (on Going-to-the-Sun Road) west over Gunsight Pass to finish at Lake McDonald Lodge, but you can do it in reverse or shorten it to three days by skipping one overnight. Spend the first night at **Gunsight Lake** (GUN). Then, climb above the lake, crossing a steep snowfield or two in July, to

Gunsight Pass (beware of ticks and habituated goats around the hiker cabin) and descend to the boulder camp at **Lake Ellen Wilson** (ELL) for the second night. For the third night, a short ascent pops over Lincoln Pass to **Sperry Chalet** campground (SPE). Set up camp, store your food properly, and hike up through Comeau Pass to Sperry Glacier and back. On the final day, descend to **Lake McDonald Lodge.** This trail affords little shade due to recent fires.

FIFTY MOUNTAIN
32 mi (52 km)
This four-day trek has miles of sun-exposed high-elevation trekking along the Continental Divide. While you can do the loop either direction, most people choose to start at **Logan Pass** to gain the elevation by shuttle rather than on foot. Traipse along the Garden Wall to reach the wilderness campsites below **Granite Park Chalet** (GRN). Get an early start for the second day for 12 mi (19.3 km) of climbs and descents through Ahern Pass, Cattle Queen, and Mineral Creek basins. Snowfields can be tricky in July: A steep one bars the trail in the cliffs before Ahern, and Cattle Queen melts into a dangerous snow

Dawson-Pitamakin Loop (left); Gunsight Pass Trail (right)

bridge. Climb around to be safe. The day finishes with a long climb over Kootenai Pass before dropping through gorgeous wildflower meadows to camp at **Fifty Mountain** (FIF). In the morning, take a side trip to Sue Lake Overlook (2.7 mi/4.3 km roundtrip) before packing up to cross West Flattop to the **Flattop Camp** (FLA). On the last day, finish with a downhill hike to **Packer's Roost.** To catch the shuttle, hike 1.4 mi (2.3 km) uphill to reach The Loop on the Sun Road.

NORTHERN CIRCLE
52 mi (84 km)

Hike the Northern Circle in either direction to take in prime fishing lakes and high passes. The loop makes logistics easy. The classic route starts from **Many Glacier** at the Iceberg-Ptarmigan Tunnel Trailhead and ends at the Swiftcurrent Trailhead. The route crosses through Ptarmigan Tunnel into the Belly River Area to stay at **Elizabeth** and **Glenns Lakes.** Then, it climbs over Stoney Indian Pass to **Stony Indian Lake** for a night before dropping and ascending to the Continental Divide to camp at **Fifty Mountain** and **Granite Park Chalet.** Complete the loop by popping over Swiftcurrent Pass, exiting at the Swiftcurrent Trailhead. The trek takes 5-7 days; choose between 12 backcountry campgrounds on or near the route; the best are at the foot of Elizabeth Lake (ELF), Cosley Lake (COS), Stoney Indian Lake (STO), Fifty Mountain (FIF), and Granite Park (GRN). Ptarmigan Tunnel usually opens mid-July, and the steep snowfields between Fifty Mountain and Granite Park by late July. Get walk-in permits for July, but advance reservations for Fifty Mountain and Stoney Indian Lake can only be made for August 1 and beyond. Prepare for high-elevation snow in September.

BIKING

Glacier is a tough place to cycle. There are no shoulders, roads are narrow and curvy, and drivers gawk at scenery instead of the road, all putting cyclists in precarious positions. With that caveat, for a dedicated cyclist, nothing compares with bicycling Going-to-the-Sun Road, one of the premier routes in the United States.

GOING-TO-THE-SUN ROAD

Going-to-the-Sun Road is an unforgettable bicycle trip. While the 3,500-ft (1,067-m) climb up the west side seems intimidating, it's not steep, just a constant uphill grind amid stunning scenery. The road maintains a 6 percent grade because cars of the 1920s required rigorous shifting at a steeper grade.

Bicyclists pedal as much of the road as possible, starting in spring when plowing begins and finishing in late fall when snow closes the lower elevations. Because the Sun Road is so narrow, **it is not the place for a family ride, except when the road is closed to cars.**

While laws do not mandate helmets, wear one anyway, considering most drivers are gaping at the views rather than paying attention to the road. Wear bright colors for visibility, and consider tacking reflectors or flags on your bike. Be sure to carry plenty of water: exertion, wind, and altitude can lead to a fast case of dehydration. Before heading out, check your brake pads, as the screaming downhill off the Continental Divide can wear them down to nubbins. Mountain, hybrid, and road bikes are appropriate here, but with skinny tires, be wary of obstacles: debris, grates, rockfall, and ice.

Spring

Bikers relish spring riding when the Sun Road is **closed to cars.** Cycling begins in early April as soon as snowplows clear the pavement beyond Lake McDonald Lodge or Avalanche on the west side and Rising Sun on the east side; spring riding goes until the road opens to vehicles for the season. Riders climb up as far as permitted by the bike closures for road crews working or avalanche hazards; do not ride beyond these signs. By May, it is such a popular activity that free bicycle-carrying **shuttles** (9am-5pm weekends only) run from Apgar

Visitor Center and Lake McDonald Lodge to the Avalanche road closure to expand parking options. Mother's Day often brings out wee ones on tricycles, training wheels, tagalongs, and trailers.

Stay on the **right side of the road,** as downhill riders often come at high speed. Alert riders in front of you when you are passing by saying "on your left" as you approach and go around. Slow down around walkers, who need to be facing bike traffic for safety. Call or consult the park website (406/888-7800; www.nps.gov/glac) to check on biking access: how far you can ride and the locations of work crew or avalanche hazard closures.

SPRING BIKING PROGRAMS

- **Glacier Outfitters** (196 Apgar Loop Rd., Apgar; 406/219-7466; www.goglacieroutfitters.com): Make reservations with Glacier Outfitters at least 48 hours in advance. They rent hybrids, e-bikes, and car racks ($45-140) and run a bike shuttle from West

bicycling Going-to-the-Sun Road

Glacier ($35), both which are service reservations so you won't need a vehicle ticket reservation after late May.

- **Glacier Guides** (11970 US 2 E., West Glacier; 406/387-5555; https://glacierguides.com): This company leads bicycle tours ($199-290 pp), rents hybrid and e-bikes ($55-135), and runs bike shuttles ($40) from their office for four hours of Sun Road riding. Their tours and shuttle (but not rentals) negate the need for a vehicle ticket reservation after late May.

Summer

When the Sun Road opens to vehicles, strong riders who are comfortable being pinched between cliffs and cars head for Logan Pass. Some riders return the way they came; others continue on to the other side. Local racers make a 142-mi (229-km) loop (Going-to-the-Sun Road, US 89, MT 49, and US 2) in one day; tourers take two days.

Cyclists must be prepared to ride the narrow, shoulderless Sun Road with a constant stream of cars. Due to heavy midday traffic, **bicycles are not permitted on two sections of the west side** (11am-4pm daily June 15-Labor Day): along Lake McDonald between Apgar Junction and Sprague Creek, and climbing uphill between Avalanche Campground and Logan Pass. If starting from the west side, head out from Lake McDonald by 6am for adequate time to pedal to Logan Pass. In early summer, long daylight hours allow for riding after 4pm, when traffic lessens. The east side has no restrictions, but it is still easier to ride early or late in the day with fewer cars on the road. Most free shuttle buses are equipped with bicycle racks in case you need a lift. Catch the shuttles only at official stops.

Locals also celebrate the full moon with a bone-chilling night ride. It's dangerous (injuries and one fatality have occurred), but an otherworldly experience. At dusk or night, tail reflectors and front lights are mandatory.

APGAR BIKE TRAIL

Especially good for families, a level, paved bicycle trail connects West Glacier with Apgar. Approximately 2 mi (3.2 km) long, the Apgar Bike Trail begins in Apgar, near the Apgar Backcountry Permit Office. An extension connects the village, visitor center, and campground. Use caution at two road crossings that interrupt the path. In the park employee housing area, follow bike signs for a couple blocks. Walkers and dogs on leashes share this path.

RENTALS
GLACIER OUTFITTERS

196 Apgar Loop Rd., Apgar; 406/219-7466; www.goglacieroutfitters.com; 9am-5pm daily Going-to-the-Sun Road opening-late Sept., 7am-6pm daily late Apr.-Going-to-the-Sun Road opening

PADDLING

Glacier has instituted strict boating and paddling guidelines in order to protect its pristine waters from invasive aquatic species. The lakes are only open in summer and only available by **permit** to boaters and paddlers who have passed an inspection. Permitting requirements make bringing a motorboat from home impractical for most short-term visitors, and Jet Skis are banned. Electric-powered and all paddlecraft can get a **same-day inspection and free permit** to launch immediately. Inspections are available for **Lake McDonald** and lakes in **Many Glacier.** Check on the status of inspections at **Two Medicine,** as lack of staff precluded them in some years.

Due to vehicle length (21 ft/6.4 m) and height (10 ft/3.1 m) restrictions, towed boats and some rooftop-carried boats may not cross Going-to-the-Sun Road between Avalanche and Sun Point. McDonald Creek is closed to all boating due to nesting harlequin ducks.

LAKE MCDONALD
open for paddling mid-May-Oct.
With its monstrous shoreline, Lake McDonald is a treat for canoeing, kayaking, and paddleboarding, but watch for winds whipping up large whitecaps. When glassy waters prevail, nothing beats paddling at sunrise or sunset.

Apgar
Get inspections opposite the Apgar boat launch for **Lake McDonald** (7:30am-7pm daily mid-May-Oct., shorter hours May and late Sept.-Oct.). This is the only boat ramp for Lake McDonald, but hand-carried craft can launch from Sprague Creek Picnic Area or several pullouts along the lake after stopping in Apgar for

paddling Lake McDonald

inspection. When the lake is placid, it's prime paddling.

MANY GLACIER

Many Glacier has smaller lakes open for paddling late May-early September and surrounded by stunning scenery. Only nonmotorized boats are permitted: kayaks, rowboats, paddleboards, canoes, and small sailboats. First, get inspections and permits at the **Many Glacier Ranger Station** (7am-5pm daily late May-late Sept.; free); then, park on Many Glacier Road between the hotel turn-off and the picnic area to carry boats down a gravel path to the launch on Swiftcurrent Lake.

Swiftcurrent Lake

With less hefty winds than larger park lakes, paddlers can enjoy a lakeshore tour sometimes with sightings of moose or bears. Kayakers can cross Swiftcurrent Lake and paddle the connecting slow-moving **Cataract Creek** upstream to **Lake Josephine,** where a shoreline loop makes a scenic tour.

TWO MEDICINE

On calm days, kayaks, canoes, and paddleboards tour the shoreline of **Two Medicine Lake** (June-late Sept.). But it is one of the windiest lakes in the park, so keep an eye on waves; if whitecaps pop up, get off the water. Some paddlers prefer the tiny **Pray Lake** in the campground for its more protected water. Two Medicine Road terminates at the public boat ramp. Hand-propelled watercraft and nontrailered electric-powered boats are allowed, but Jet Skis and gas-engine motorboats are not. Check on the availability of inspections and permits before launching.

RENTALS

Glacier Park Boat Company operates watercraft rentals at Lake McDonald, Many Glacier, and Two Medicine boat docks. Rentals available include canoes, double kayaks, and small motorboats, and at Lake McDonald, paddleboards. Paddles and life jackets are included.

LAKE MCDONALD LODGE BOAT DOCK
406/888-5727 or 406/257-2426; https://glacierparkboats.com; $18-32/hour

MANY GLACIER HOTEL BOAT DOCK
406/257-2426; https:// glacierparkboats.com; daily mid-June-mid-Sept.; $20-26/hour; for use on Swiftcurrent Lake only

TWO MEDICINE BOAT DOCK
406/257-2426; https// glacierparkboats.com; $21-32/hour

WINTER SPORTS

Some roads and trails in the park become cross-country skiing and snowshoeing routes in winter. For route descriptions and maps, pick up *Skiing and Snowshoeing* in the visitor centers or online (www.nps.gov/glac). Skiers and snowshoers should be well equipped and versed in winter travel safety before venturing out.

GOING-TO-THE-SUN ROAD

Since winter buries Going-to-the-Sun

Road with snow from Lake McDonald Lodge to St. Mary, the road attracts cross-country skiers and snowshoers November-early April. Touring up the gated road's lower elevations goes through relatively avalanche-free zones. The gentle grade makes for good gliding suitable for beginners; however, the skier tracks can get icy. For snowshoers, etiquette requires blazing a separate snowshoe trail rather than flattening the parallel ski tracks.

In McDonald Valley, ski tours lead past McDonald Creek and Upper McDonald Creek Falls to **Avalanche Campground** (6 mi/9.7 km one-way). Some skiers head up to **Snyder Lakes** (8.4 mi/13.5 km round-trip), but be ready for the narrow trail descending through tight trees on the way back down.

Between Rising Sun and Avalanche Creek, Going-to-the-Sun Road sees significant avalanche activity and is best avoided.

AROUND APGAR

Winter converts the roads and trails around Apgar into easy cross-country ski and snowshoe paths late November-early April. Quiet and scenic, road skiing makes for easy route-finding with little avalanche danger at lower elevations. Roads are plowed into Apgar. Ski tours launch up **Camas Road** to go to **Fish Creek Campground** and **Rocky Point,** among other routes.

GUIDES

Dec.-Mar.; from $350 for 1 person, $180 pp for 2 or more

Two companies guide snowshoe and cross-country ski tours by reservation. Avalanche-certified guides tailor the best routes in certain snow conditions to your skills and supply lunches. Overnight snow-camping trips are also available.

cross-country skiing on Going-to-the-Sun Road

GLACIER ADVENTURE GUIDES
*406/892-2173 or 877/735-9514; www.
glacieradventureguides.com*

GLACIER TREKS
406/885-7882; www.tourglacier.com

PARK-RUN TOURS
Rangers guide free snowshoe tours from **Apgar Visitor Center**

(406/888-7800; www.nps.gov/
glac; weekends Jan.-mid-Mar.). The two-hour interpretive walks look for animal tracks and examine how flora and fauna adapt to harsh winters. Hikers should wear winter footwear, dress in layers, and bring water. Rent snowshoes from the park service.

FOOD

Glacier is a place for good home-style cooking, where tasty fresh-baked fruit pies are still the rage, rather than upscale or international fare. Seasonal restaurants cater to summer visitors; hours can shorten in spring or fall.

Many eateries and camp stores are operated by **Xanterra** (855/733-4522; www.glacier-nationalparklodges.com; daily mid-June-mid-Sept.). No reservations are accepted, so you may have to wait for a table in midsummer. Menus rely on local, fresh, and organic sourcing served with healthy, gluten-free, vegan, and child options, plus choices for toppings and portions. The restaurants serve craft cocktails, beer, and wine.

STANDOUTS
Russell's Fireside Dining Room
*288 Lake McDonald Lodge Loop;
855/733-4522; daily mid-May-late
Sept.*
At Lake McDonald Lodge, the headliner restaurant is Russell's Fireside Dining Room, decorated with painted Native American chandeliers and full of historical ambience. The north windows have a peekaboo lake view, but during dinner the blinds usually

need to be pulled down as the hot sun blazes in. Breakfast (6:30-10am; $9-18) is a choice of continental buffet, full buffet, or menu entrées. Lunch (11:30am-2pm; $10-18) serves small plates, burgers, sandwiches, salads, and pasta. Dinner (5-9:30pm; $17-30) can go casual with burgers, salads, and pasta or full-on dining with charcuterie, shared appetizers, and plated entrées of fish or meats.

Ptarmigan Dining Room
*Many Glacier Hotel, milepost
11.5, Many Glacier Rd.; front desk
406/732-4411; early June-mid-Sept.*
In Many Glacier Hotel, the Ptarmigan Dining Room underwent a renovation that unmasked the original railroad beams and restored its historical look. Massive windows look out on Swiftcurrent Lake, Grinnell Point, and Mount Wilbur. Unfortunately, the evening sun blares hot in the windows, so sometimes the blinds are closed. For breakfast (6:30-10am; $10-22), choose between a continental buffet or hot entrée buffet, or order off the menu. Lunch (11:30am-2:30pm; $14-23) serves small plates, sandwiches, and burgers. Dinner (5-9pm; $26-45) has prime rib, Wagyu steak, duck, fish, or bison. Grab small plates, sandwiches, salads, and

Ptarmigan Dining Room at Many Glacier Hotel

GLACIER NATIONAL PARK FOOD

NAME	LOCATION	TYPE
Eddie's Café & Mercantile	Apgar	sit-down restaurant
★ Russell's Fireside Dining Room	Lake McDonald Lodge	sit-down restaurant
Lucke's Lounge	Lake McDonald Lodge	sit-down bar
Lake McDonald Campstore	Lake McDonald Lodge	convenience store
Two Dog Flats Grill	Rising Sun	sit-down restaurant
Rising Sun Camp Store	Rising Sun Motor Inn	convenience store
★ Ptarmigan Dining Room	Many Glacier Hotel	sit-down restaurant
'Nell's	Swiftcurrent Motor Inn, Many Glacier	sit-down restaurant and takeout
Heidi's Snack Shop	Many Glacier Hotel	convenience store
Swiftcurrent Campstore	Swiftcurrent Motor Inn, Many Glacier	convenience store
Two Medicine Campstore	Two Medicine	convenience store

pasta in the adjacent **Swiss Room bar** (noon-3pm and 5-8pm; $13-22).

BEST PICNIC SPOTS

Except for Sun Point, fires are permitted in fire rings at the picnic areas below. Bring your own firewood, or purchase at camp stores, since gathering it is prohibited.

Lake McDonald
APGAR PICNIC AREA
Southwest corner of Lake McDonald, off Going-to-the-Sun Road
Apgar Picnic Area offers a beautiful uplake view to the Continental Divide. The picnic area has beach access, and there are picnic tables, flush toilets, and fire rings with grills.

FOOD	PRICE	HOURS
casual American	moderate	8am–10pm daily May–mid-Sept.
traditional American	moderate–splurge	6:30–10am, 11:30am–2pm, and 5–9:30pm daily mid-May–late Sept.
casual American and drinks	moderate	11:30am–2pm daily mid-May–late Sept.
groceries, camping and hiking supplies		7am–9pm daily mid-June–mid-Sept.
casual American	moderate	7–10am and 11:30am–9pm daily early June–early Sept.
snacks and light lunches		7am–9pm daily mid-June–mid-Sept.
traditional American	moderate–splurge	6:30–10am, 11:30am–2:30pm, 5–9pm daily mid-June–mid-Sept.
casual American	moderate	7–10am and 11am–9pm daily mid-June–mid-Sept.
groceries	budget	6:30am–9pm daily mid-June–mid-Sept.
groceries, camping and hiking supplies	budget	7am–9pm daily mid-June–mid-Sept.
snacks and light lunches	budget	8:30am–6pm daily summer

On weekends and holidays, plan to nab a table early.

Going-to-the-Sun Road
AVALANCHE CREEK PICNIC AREA
Across Going-to-the-Sun Road from Avalanche Creek Campground
Picnic sites at Avalanche Creek are under cedar shade adjacent to McDonald Creek, but due to bears, do not leave your picnic gear unattended. Trailheads for Trail of the Cedars and Avalanche Lake are across the street. The picnic area has vault-toilet restrooms. Fires in the fire rings with grills are permitted.

SUN POINT PICNIC AREA
Sun Point Picnic Area has great views

up St. Mary Valley to the Continental Divide, but watch the paper plates, as the wind can howl. Trails lead to Sun Point and Baring Falls. It has vault toilets. Fires are not permitted.

Many Glacier
MANY GLACIER PICNIC AREA
Many Glacier Rd. milepost 12.2
Many Glacier's small picnic area gets crammed with picnickers toting binoculars to scan for bears on Mount Altyn. This popular picnic site and trailhead crowds in midsummer. If you want to roast marshmallows in one of the firepits, buy firewood at the Swiftcurrent Campstore.

Two Medicine
TWO MEDICINE PICNIC AREA
Two Medicine picnic area is adjacent to the campground. With running water and flush toilets, it is in a scenic spot right on the shore of Two Medicine Lake amid cottonwoods. Most of the sites have some trees, which provide a good windbreak on days when the wind howls, but scant shade on hot days. Sites include a picnic table and a fire ring with a grill, but buy firewood from the camp store.

CAMPING

Reservations
Advance reservations (877/444-6777; www.recreation.gov) start six months in advance for Apgar, Fish Creek, Sprague Creek, Avalanche, St. Mary, Two Medicine, and Many Glacier campgrounds. A few campsites are available four days in advance at Apgar, Sprague Creek, Avalanche, Many Glacier, and Two Medicine campgrounds. Apgar and Two Medicine also hold a few campsites to reserve one day in advance. Reserve group campsites 12 months in advance for **St. Mary** and **Apgar.** Your campground reservation will gain you entry without a road reservation for the specific road that has your campground.

Tips
Rather than moving campgrounds frequently, you are better off staying in one campground and driving to other locations to experience the park. For reservations six months in advance, research your campgrounds up front and know which campsites would be appropriate for you. Then, be logged into your account online, ready to select your desired site right at 8am mountain time.

For **first-come, first-served campgrounds,** check for fill times in the days leading up to your stay via texts; sign up for alerts by texting the letters GNPCGS to 333-111. You'll need to make a **vehicle ticket reservation** for roads with first-come, first-served campgrounds.

STANDOUTS
Rising Sun Campground
6 mi (9.7 km) west of St. Mary; late May-mid-Sept.; $20
Located only 12 mi (19.3 km) east of Logan Pass and 6 mi (9.7 km) west of St. Mary, Rising Sun Campground tucks on the lower hillside of Otokomi Mountain by St. Mary Lake. The sun drops down early behind

Goat Mountain, creating a long twilight. Remnants of the 2015 Reynolds Creek Fire linger on the hillside above the upper campsites. The first-come, first-served 83-site campground is a few minutes' walk to a restaurant, a camp store, and hot showers. Beach access is across Going-to-the-Sun Road, with a picnic area, boat ramp, and boat tours. The Otokomi Lake trailhead is behind the adjacent inn. RVs can only be 25 ft (7.6 m). Campers without Going-to-the-Sun Road vehicle reservation tickets can reach this campground from St. Mary. The campground fills in early morning; plan to be there by 7am to look for a site as soon as one opens.

Many Glacier Campground

end of Many Glacier Rd.; late May-mid-Sept.; $23

Many Glacier Campground packs 109 treed sites at the base of Grinnell Point. As the most coveted campground in the park, **reservations** for half of the campsites go fast for peak season (June-mid-Sept.; $23); most are released six months in advance, while a few are reserveable four days in advance. The other half are saved for first-come, first-served campers, and you must be in line before 7am to wait to get one when it opens up. June-July, camping may be restricted to hard-sided vehicles only (no tents) due to bear activity. A few sites can fit RVs up to 35 ft (11 m), but most fit RVs only up to 21 ft (6.4 m). Nearby trails depart for Iceberg Lake as well as Ptarmigan Tunnel and Swiftcurrent Pass. From the picnic area, a five-minute walk down the road, trails depart to Lake Josephine and Grinnell Lake, Grinnell Glacier, and Piegan Pass. Across the parking lot, Swiftcurrent Motor Inn has a restaurant, laundry, hot showers, and a camp store. In fall (mid-Sept.-Oct.), after the campground water is turned off for the season, first-come, first-served **primitive camping** ($10) is allowed, with vault toilets as the only service.

Two Medicine Campground on Pray Lake

GLACIER NATIONAL PARK CAMPGROUNDS

NAME	LOCATION	SEASON
Apgar Campground	Apgar	year-round (no water early Oct.-late Apr.)
Fish Creek Campground	Lake McDonald	June-early Sept.
Sprague Creek Campground	Lake McDonald	mid-May-mid-Sept
Avalanche Campground	Going-to-the-Sun Road	mid-July-early Sept.
★ Rising Sun Campground	St. Mary Lake	early June-early Sept.
St. Mary Campground	St. Mary	year-round
★ Many Glacier Campground	Many Glacier	June-mid-Sept.
★ Two Medicine Campground	Two Medicine	June-mid-Sept.

SITES AND AMENITIES	RV LIMIT	PRICE	RESERVATIONS
25 tent and RV sites, 169 tent-only sites, drinking water, flush toilets, dump station	25 sites for RVs up to 40 ft (12.2 m)	$23 Apr.-early Oct., $10 Apr. and most of Oct., free Nov.-Mar.	yes
80 tent and RV sites, 98 tent-only sites, drinking water, flush toilets, showers, dump station	18 sites for RVs up to 35 ft (11 m), 62 sites for RVs up to 27 ft (8 m)	$23	yes
25 tent and RV sites, drinking water, flush toilets	RVs up to 21 ft (6.4 m)	$23	yes late May-mid-Sept.
87 tent and RV sites, drinking water, flush toilets	RVs up to 26 ft (7.9 m)	$23	yes
83 tent and RV sites, drinking water, flush toilets, showers, dump station	RVs up to 25 ft (7.6 m)	$20	no
183 tent and RV sites, drinking water, flush toilets, showers, dump station	RVs up to 35 ft (11 m)	$20-23	yes late May-mid-Aug.
109 tent and RV sites, drinking water, flush toilets, dump station	some sites for RVs up to 35 ft (11 m), most sites RVs up to 21 ft (6.4 m)	$23	yes June-mid-Sept.
99 tent and RV sites, drinking water, flush toilets, dump station	13 sites for RVs up to 32 ft (9.7 m)	$23	yes June-mid-Sept.

GLACIER NATIONAL PARK CAMPGROUNDS (CONT.)

NAME	LOCATION	SEASON
Kintla Lake Campground	North Fork	June-mid-Sept.
Bowman Lake Campground	North Fork	mid May-early Sept.
Quartz Creek Campground	North Fork	July-early Sept.
Logging Creek Campground	North Fork	late June-late Sept.
Cut Bank Campground	Cut Bank	late May-mid-Sept.

Two Medicine Campground

406/888-7800; late May-late Sept.; $20

Two Medicine Campground yields views of bears foraging on Rising Wolf Mountain, especially from the A and C loops. Riverfront sites are 95, 99, and 100. In early summer, ruby-crowned kinglets call out "teacher, teacher" from the trees. The 99-site campground surrounds the calmer waters of small Pray Lake, a good place for paddling, fishing, or chilly swimming. Tenters should choose sheltered sites in A and B loops due to abrupt high winds that can flatten poles. Flush toilets, water, and a dump station are provided, and the outdoor amphitheater hosts ranger and Native America Speaks programs. A seven-minute walk or a few-minute drive connects with the boat tour and rental dock. Only 13 sites can handle RVs up to 32 ft (9.7 m). Reservations (www. recreation.gov) are required June to mid-September; most are available six months in advance, with a few released four days in advance and one day in advance. First-come, first-served primitive camping (late Sept.-Oct.; $10) has vault toilets and no water.

SITES AND AMENITIES	RV LIMIT	PRICE	RESERVATIONS
13 tent and small RV sites, drinking water, pit toilet; dump station	21 ft (6.4 m) maximum vehicle length, no trailers	$15	no
48 tent and small RV sites, drinking water, vault toilets, dump station	21 ft (6.4 m) maximum vehicle length, no trailers	$15	no
7 tent and small RV sites, pit toilets	21 ft (6.4 m) maximum vehicle length, no trailers	$10	no
7 tent and small RV sites, pit toilets	21 ft (6.4 m) maximum vehicle length, no trailers	$10	no
14 tent or small RV sites, vault toilets	21 ft (6.4 m) maximum vehicle length, no trailers	$10	no

LODGING

Accommodations have en suite bathrooms, unless otherwise indicated. Lodges generally do not have TVs, elevators, or air-conditioning. At the large, drive-up hotels, Wi-Fi is usually available in the lobby.

Reservations

Advance reservations for all in-park lodgings are **imperative,** especially for July and August. Contact **Xanterra** (855/733-4522; www.glaciernationalparklodges.com) 13 months in advance for Many Glacier Hotel, Lake McDonald Lodge, Rising Sun Motor Inn, Swiftcurrent Motor Inn, and Apgar Village Inn. Make reservations 13-16 months ahead with **Pursuit Glacier Park Collection** (844/868-7474; www.glacierparkcollection.com) for Apgar Village Lodge and Motel Lake McDonald. For Granite Park Chalet and Sperry Chalet, make reservations in early January through **Belton Chalets** (406/387-5654 or 888/345-2649; www.graniteparkchalet.com or www.sperrychalet.com).

GLACIER NATIONAL PARK LODGING

NAME	LOCATION
Apgar Village Inn	Apgar
Apgar Village Lodge and Cabins	Apgar
★ Lake McDonald Lodge	Lake McDonald
Motel Lake McDonald	Lake McDonald
Rising Sun Motor Inn	Going-to-the-Sun Road
★ Granite Park Chalet	Going-to-the-Sun Road
★ Sperry Chalet	Going-to-the-Sun Road
★ Many Glacier Hotel	Many Glacier
Swiftcurrent Motor Inn	Many Glacier

Tips

For your best chance at getting a reservation, book the **first day of the month** when reservations open, as inside-park lodgings often fill fast. Flexibility in dates can also help secure a reservation. Sometimes, you can pick up a last-minute reservation from a cancellation. Call to check on these rather than looking online.

SEASON	OPTIONS	PRICE
late May-late-Sept.	guest rooms, some with kitchenettes; family units that sleep up to six	rooms starting at $225
mid-May-Sept.	20 motel rooms; 28 rustic cabins, some with kitchens	rooms starting at $150
mid-May-late Sept.	main lodge rooms; cabin rooms; Cobb House two-room suites; Snyder Hall with shared bathrooms	rooms starting at $135
mid-June-mid-Sept.	motel rooms	rooms starting at $180
mid-June-mid-Sept.	motel rooms	rooms starting at $182
early July-early Sept.	hike-in camper chalet (no road access) with 12 rooms that sleep 2-6 people each; shared vault toilets; no running water; linen service available ($25)	$135 first person in room, $95 per added person
early July-early Sept.	hike-in camper lodge (no road access) with private rooms that sleep 2-6 people each (bedding included); shared vault toilets; running cold water; basic meals included	$275 for first person in room, $185 per additional person in room
early June-mid-Sept.	guest rooms and suites	rooms starting at $250
mid-June-mid-Sept.	cabins, with private or shared bathrooms; motel rooms	rooms starting at $140

STANDOUTS
Lake McDonald Lodge
288 Lake McDonald Lodge Loop; reservations 855/733-4522, front desk 406/888-5431; www. *glaciernationalparklodges.com; mid-May-late Sept.; $135-595*

A National Historic Landmark, Lake McDonald Lodge graces the southeast lakeshore. It centers around a massive stone fireplace and hunting

Lake McDonald Lodge

suites with televisions. Wi-Fi is available in the lobby and reading room.

Granite Park Chalet

Hike-in from Logan Pass or The Loop on Going-to-the-Sun Road; 406/387-5654 or 888/345-2649; www.graniteparkchalet.com; $135 first person in room, $95 per added person

Granite Park Chalet sits atop a knoll with a 360-degree view and bear-watching. This rustic chalet, which has 12 guest rooms sleeping 2-6 people each and outdoor vault toilets, functions like a hostel: Bring your own sleeping bag, eating utensils, and food to cook in the kitchen. Meals are not supplied. With **no running water,** you must haul water for cooking and washing from 0.2 mi (0.3 km) away. As an option, purchase linen service ($40 for sheets, a pillow, and blankets), preorder freeze-dried food ($2-15/item), and buy environmentally friendly disposable plates and utensils. No alcohol is sold or allowed in the dining hall, but you can pack along beverages for sipping in guest rooms and haul the containers out with you along with all of your garbage. Reach the chalet from Logan Pass (7.4 mi/11.9 km), The Loop (4 mi/6.4 km), or Swiftcurrent (7.6 mi/12.2 km). Book in early January.

Sperry Chalet

Hike-in from Lake McDonald Lodge or Jackson Glacier Overlook on Going-to-the-Sun Road; 406/387-5654 or 888/345-2649; www.sperrychalet.com; $275 first person in room, $185 per added person

Sperry Chalet offers hikers and horseback riders three meals and a warm bed, which means hauling only a day pack with some extra clothing. Set in a timbered cirque, the chalet has a dining hall, lodge, and several

lodge-themed lobby full of trophy specimens hung by John Lewis, the original owner. The complex has four types of accommodations: main lodge rooms, cabin rooms, Cobb House suites, and Snyder Hall. A $3 million renovation in 2016-2017 revamped some cabins and lodge rooms. Dial back your expectations to the mid-1900s with telephones as the only in-room amenities, and you'll be delighted with the location and historical ambience. Some lakeside rooms have views. Most rooms are small with bathrooms converted from original closets. Upstairs rooms lack elevator access. Snyder Hall has shared bathrooms and the lowest rates. Cobb House has two-room

park service buildings. Private lodge rooms sleep 2-6 people each in bunks or beds with bedding included. Bring a headlamp to reach the vault toilets at night. Faucets put out cold water only. Country roasts rotate for nightly dinners. Trail lunches packed for you are plain, with a meat sandwich (no lettuce or tomato), candy bars, and fruit leather. However, outstanding bakery goods use traditional decades-old recipes for cookies, freshly baked breads, and pies. To reach Sperry, hike 6.2 mi (10 km) up from Lake McDonald or 14 mi (22.5 km) over two passes from Jackson Glacier Overlook.

Many Glacier Hotel
milepost 11.5, Many Glacier Rd.; reservations 855/733-4522 or front desk 406/732-4411; www. glaciernationalparklodges.com; early June-mid-Sept.; $250-650
A National Historic Landmark, Many Glacier Hotel is the largest of the park's lodges and the most popular due to its stunning location. Set on Swiftcurrent Lake, the immense hotel cowers below surrounding peaks. The lodge centers around its massive four-story lobby with a huge fireplace. Some guest rooms and suites (some with decks) face the lake, while east-side guest rooms get the sunrise, with a unique morning wake-up call as the horses jangle to the corral. A Swiss theme pervades the hotel, with bellhops dressed in lederhosen and gingerbread cutout deck railings. An extensive rehabilitation was completed 2017, but the baths are still small (many were created from the original closets). No elevators access the upper floors. Rooms have phones, and the lobby has slow Wi-Fi. A restaurant, lounge, convenience store, and gift shop are on-site.

Many Glacier Hotel

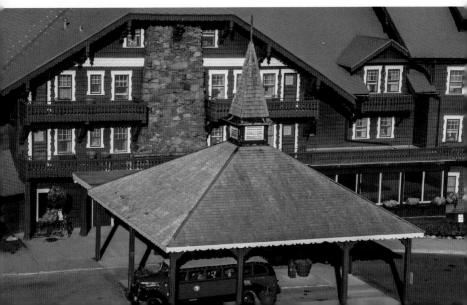

wildflowers in Many Glacier

INFORMATION AND SERVICES

For services, **Apgar,** near the West Glacier Entrance, is the biggest in-park hub, with a restaurant, camp store, two inns, a boat ramp, swimming beaches, visitor center, campground, picnic area and more. Most of Apgar is open May-September only.

St. Mary is the eastern portal to Going-to-the-Sun Road and a second park hub. At the junction of the Sun Road and US 89, the town clusters outside the park boundary along the highway. Only the visitor center and St. Mary Campground are within the park; lodging, restaurants, and grocery stores are on the Blackfeet Reservation outside the park.

Entrance Stations

Glacier has four main entrance stations. Despite staffing only during daylight hours in the summer, the entrances are open 24 hours per day. If they are not staffed, you can buy a park entrance pass at the self-serve kiosk just past the station. Seven-day passes cost $35 per vehicle, $30 per motorcycle, and $20 per biker, hiker, or pedestrian in summer; winter rates drop to $25, $20, and $15, respectively; **no cash is accepted.** All entrance stations hand out park maps and the park's newspaper. Those headed to the remote North Fork area of the park use the **Polebridge Entrance Station** and return via the **Camas Entrance** near Apgar.

Four roads require **vehicle ticket reservations** (www.recreation.gov; $2/vehicle) during peak season daily 6am-3pm. West-side accesses (Polebridge Entrance of the North Fork and West Glacier or Camas Entrance for Going-to-the-Sun Road) require tickets late May through mid-September. East-side accesses (Many Glacier, Two Medicine, and Rising Sun on Going-to-the-Sun Road from St. Mary) require tickets July-mid-September. Tickets are released online in one-month blocks four months in advance, and additional tickets are released one day in advance; they are not sold in the park. **Going-to-the-Sun Road** tickets are valid for three days; all other vehicle tickets are valid for one day. Check in advance online (www.nps.gov/glac) for potential adjustments.

West Glacier Entrance
Year-round
Crossing the West Glacier Bridge over the Middle Fork of the Flathead River officially is the entry to Glacier National Park. After the bridge, a parking pullout allows for photo-documenting your travel with the park sign. With 60 percent of Glacier's visitors entering here, be prepared for long lines on weekends and in summer. The West Glacier entrance station, which is usually staffed during daylight hours in summer and on weekends off-season, serves as the west entrance to Going-to-the-Sun Road. A self-pay kiosk is just beyond the entrance station.

St. Mary Entrance
Year-round
The eastern gateway for Going-to-the-Sun Road is St. Mary. This entrance station is staffed during daylight hours daily in summer and on weekends only fall-spring. You can go through the entrance and reach St. Mary Visitor Center, St. Mary Campground, and Sun Road shuttles without a road reservation for peak season. A self-pay kiosk is just past the entrance station.

Many Glacier Entrance
May-Oct.
On the Many Glacier Road, the Many Glacier Entrance is usually staffed daytime May-October. When unstaffed, use the self-pay kiosk just beyond the entrance station.

Two Medicine Entrance
Mid-May-Oct.
On Two Medicine Road, the Two Medicine Entrance is staffed during daylight hours daily in the summer. During shoulder

seasons, staffing is reduced to weekends only or not at all, but you can use the self-pay cash-only kiosk.

Visitor Centers

All three of Glacier's visitor centers are small. But you can get maps, ranger program information, *Junior Ranger Activity Guides,* boating and fishing regulations, trail conditions, and current road conditions especially on Going-to-the-Sun Road. They each have Glacier National Park Conservancy **bookstores** (406/892-3250; http://glacier.org), which also sell books online. Shuttles service all three visitor centers, too.

Apgar Visitor Center
Going-to-the-Sun Rd.; 406/888-7800; 8am-6pm daily mid-June-Aug., shorter hours mid-May-mid-June, Sept.-early Oct., weekends only in winter

Tucked in the woods at the four-way intersection two minutes north of Glacier's West Glacier Entrance, the small Apgar Visitor Center is the place to find ranger program schedules for guided walks on the west side of Glacier, plus astronomy programs nearby (daytime solar viewing and nighttime stargazing), and evening amphitheater presentations at campgrounds (Apgar, Fish Creek, and Avalanche). The parking lot accommodates big RVs, and you can leave your car all day to hop shuttles or meet up for concession-operated tours. The **Apgar Backcountry Permit Office** (406/888-7859 May-Oct., 406/888-7800 Nov.-Apr.; 7:30am-5pm daily June-Sept., 8am-4pm daily May and Oct.) is opposite the old red schoolhouse in Apgar. This is the main office for acquiring permits for overnight backpacking or paddling trips. Rush hour is the first 3 hours of each morning in July and August; lines begin forming before 6am. All permits must be picked up by 4:30pm.

Logan Pass Visitor Center
406/888-7800; 9am-7pm daily mid-June-Aug., shorter hours Labor Day-mid-Sept.

The one place everyone wants to go is Logan Pass, but its visitor center is a small, seasonal outpost with an information desk, a few displays, and a bookstore. You may have difficulty finding a parking spot 7am-3pm. Flush toilets are available downstairs and vault toilets at the parking lot. The center has a water bottle refill station, but no food or beverage sales. Due to the elevation, expect snow on the ground through June and harsher weather including wind, rain, or snow even in August. Don't be surprised if you left the lowlands in sunny summer only to arrive at Logan Pass in winter.

St. Mary Visitor Center
406/888-7800; 8am-5pm daily mid-June-early Oct., 8:30am-5pm late May-mid-June

Located at the St. Mary entrance to Glacier National Park, the St. Mary Visitor Center is the largest visitor center in the park. It houses a bookstore and displays on Indigenous cultural history. Inside the center, find **backcountry permits** (7:30am-5pm daily late May-late Sept.). The theater hosts slide presentations, evening naturalist programs, and the popular Two Medicine Lake Singers and Dancers (tickets required). Astronomy programs that celebrate this International Dark Sky Park take place outdoors, where you can see night sky features from the **Dusty Star Observatory** telescope on two high-resolution screens.

Cell Service and Internet

Glacier has very limited cell service reception and public Wi-Fi. Plan to download the apps, maps, podcasts, and PDFs you will need before you arrive. Limited cell reception is in Apgar on the southwest end of Lake McDonald (but no reception around Lake McDonald Lodge) and St. Mary; cell service is not available on most of Going-to-the-Sun Road and Logan Pass. Many Glacier, Two Medicine, and the North Fork also have no cell reception. Limited public Wi-Fi is available at Apgar and St. Mary Visitor Centers. Guests staying in lodges have access to limited Wi-Fi in lobbies.

TRANSPORTATION
Getting There
From Banff National Park

There are two routes from Banff National Park to Glacier National Park. For the **eastern route,** head east on the Trans-Canada Highway from the town of Banff to Calgary (80 mi/129 km; 90 minutes). From Calgary, head south for 113 mi (182 km) on AB 2 toward Fort Macleod. Continue from Fort Macleod south through Cardston to the Carway-Piegan border crossing (7am-11pm daily year-round). From Calgary to the border takes about 3 hours (165 mi/265 km). After crossing the Canadian-U.S. border onto US 89, drive 25 minutes (19 mi/31 km) to St. Mary for Going-to-the-Sun Road's east entrance. To enter the park at Many Glacier, after crossing the border, drive US 89 to Babb and turn right onto the Many Glacier Road to reach Many Glacier Hotel or Swiftcurrent in 40 minutes (22 mi/35 km). Total drive time from Calgary to Many Glacier or St. Mary is about 4 hours.

For the **western route,** travel south on BC 93 through Kootenay National Park and British Columbia toward Cranbrook. At 3.7 mi (6 km) before Cranbrook, merge with CA 3 heading 36 mi (58 km) east toward Elko. Take BC 93 south at Elko for 24 mi (39 km) toward Roosville on the Canadian-U.S. border (open 24 hours daily year-round). After crossing, continue south 63 mi (101 km) on US 93 through Eureka to Whitefish. Drive with caution: Deer frequent the road between Eureka and Whitefish, earning it the nickname "Deer Alley." In downtown Whitefish, US 93 turns south again at the third stoplight. Drive 2 mi (3.2 km) to the junction with MT 40 with signs for Glacier. Turn left onto MT 40, which joins US 2 just before Columbia Falls, and reaches West Glacier. Expect 6.5 hours driving time from Banff.

Vehicle Ticket Reservations

www.recreation.gov; $2/vehicle
Four roads require vehicle ticket reservations during peak season daily 6am-3pm. **West-side** accesses (Polebridge Entrance of the North Fork and West Glacier or Camas Entrance for Going-to-the-Sun Road) require tickets late May through mid-September. **East-side** accesses (Many Glacier, Two Medicine, and Rising Sun on Going-to-the-Sun Road from St. Mary) require tickets July-mid-September. Tickets are released online in one-month blocks four months in advance, and additional tickets are released one day in advance; they are not sold in the park. Going-to-the-Sun Road tickets are valid for three days; all other vehicle tickets are valid for one day. Check in advance online (www.nps.gov/glac) for potential adjustments.

Gas and Charging Stations
Inside the Park

There are **no gas stations** inside the park. Apgar Visitor Center parking lot has one **charging station.**

Outside the Park

In West Glacier, gas is available year-round with a credit card at **Glacier Highland** across from the train depot. Two gas stations are in **St. Mary** on US 89, one on either side of the junction with Going-to-the-Sun Road. Babb has a gas station across from Thronson's General Store. **East Glacier,** outside the park southeast of Two Medicine, also has gas stations.

The Glacier area has few charging stations. Electric vehicle drivers should use the map for public EV stations through Travel Montana (www.visitmt.com/plan-your-trip/getting-around) to plan routes carefully to access charging stations.

Parking

Apgar and St. Mary Visitor Centers

In Apgar, three small parking lots are in the village, and you can also park at the picnic area and boat dock. The largest parking lot, where RVs will find room, is at Apgar Visitor Center; a paved path connects to the village. You can park all day for free to hop the shuttle from the visitor center up Going-to-the-Sun Road.

The St. Mary Visitor Center has a large parking lot and is also a shuttle stop: To avoid parking hassles at Logan Pass, park your car here all day for free and catch the free shuttle up Going-to-the-Sun Road.

Logan Pass

In midsummer, the Logan Pass parking lot fills 7am-3pm. If the parking lot is full, forgo Logan Pass for the time being and return later in the day. While pullouts are 0.5 mi (0.8 km) east and west of the pass, the shoulderless road does not afford safe walking to the pass, and tromping across the fragile meadows is taboo.

Trailheads

Popular trailheads can pack out with parking by 8am in summer. These include the trailheads at Avalanche, The Loop, Logan Pass, and St. Mary Falls on Going-to-the-Sun Road.

Roads and Closures

Two-lane highways and roads dominate the park. Most roads are paved, although dirt and gravel byways are in the North Fork region.

Snow buries the Going-to-the-Sun Road in winter. The usual vehicle closure runs from Lake McDonald Lodge to St. Mary late October-spring. The Sun Road may also close temporarily in summer for weather or accidents.

Some of Glacier's roads can close before or after the peak season (when road reservations are required) for several hours 10am-3pm due to traffic congestion. These include Many Glacier Road, Two Medicine Road, and the Inside North Fork Road.

Find the status of roads in Glacier online (www.nps.gov/glac) or on the NPS app. The St. Mary and Apgar Visitor Centers have updates on road closures for weather, construction, or congestion. You can also receive text alerts about roads; send 333-111 the message "GNPROADS" to get alerts on closures, openings, and temporary restrictions.

Shuttles

Going-to-the-Sun Road

406/888-7800; www.nps.gov/glac
Going-to-the-Sun Road shuttles enable point-to-point hiking on some of Glacier's most spectacular trails and you won't be disappointed by full parking lots. Due to their popularity, waiting lines of an hour or more often form to board. Shuttles are just transportation (no interpretative guides), and most have bike racks and are wheelchair-accessible. Shuttle frequency decreases after Labor Day. For Logan Pass, be sure to take a day pack

with water, snacks, and extra clothing for fast-changing weather.

Shuttles stop at designated locations: trailheads, campgrounds, picnic areas, lodges, and Logan Pass. Get on or off at any of the stops denoted by interpretive signs. Three required stops have transfers to other shuttles: Avalanche, Logan Pass, and Sun Point. To cross the entire Sun Road from Apgar to St. Mary takes 3-4 shuttles.

West-side shuttles (7am-7pm daily July-Labor Day, 9am-5pm daily early-mid-Sept.) depart every 15-30 minutes. Heading east, the 28-passenger buses take about 45 minutes to reach Avalanche, the transfer stop to Logan Pass. From Avalanche to Logan Pass, shuttles depart every 15 minutes on Sprinters that carry 12-15 passengers for the 50-minute ride. For Logan Pass hikers, several morning **express shuttles** (15 passengers, until Labor Day) depart 7-8:30am to go nonstop from Apgar Visitor Center to Logan Pass. They leave every 15-30 minutes for the 90-minute drive.

East-side shuttles (8am-7pm daily July-Labor Day, 9am-5pm daily early-mid-Sept.) run between St. Mary Visitor Center and Logan Pass in two stages. Large shuttles (28 passengers) depart St. Mary every 30-40 minutes for the 20-minute ride to Sun Point. Debark here to catch one of the smaller shuttles (12-15 passengers) that go every 10-20 minutes for the 30-minute drive to Logan Pass. For hikers at Logan Pass, **express shuttles** (15 passengers, until Labor Day) depart 8-8:45am from St. Mary Visitor Center for the nonstop 50-minute ride to Logan Pass.

Xanterra Hiker Shuttle

855/733-4522; www.glaciernationalparklodges.com; July-mid-Sept.; one-way, adult $14, child $7
This hiker shuttle runs between St. Mary Visitor Center and Many Glacier with stops at Many Glacier Hotel and Swiftcurrent Motor Inn. The ride (45-50 minutes) is first-come, first-served, with limited seating, and departs several times daily in morning and late afternoon. Check the current schedule online and at Many Glacier Hotel or Swiftcurrent Motor Inn. Point-to-point hikers on the Highline-Swiftcurrent Pass Trails and Piegan Pass Trail use this shuttle to reach the Going-to-the-Sun Road shuttle at St. Mary.

East-Side Shuttle

844/868-7474; www.glacierparkcollection.com; daily June-Sept.; $20-40 one-way
For traveling between St. Mary, Two Medicine, and East Glacier, the East-Side Shuttle runs once each way per day. These shuttles allow for connecting with Sun Road or Many Glacier shuttles. A shuttle also goes six times per day from East Glacier to Two Medicine. Seats are first-come, first-served; pay the driver in cash when you board. Both shuttles originate at Glacier Park Lodge in East Glacier.

Fairmont Chateau Lake Louise

BANFF AND LAKE LOUISE

Banff National Park encompasses some of the world's most magnificent scenery. The snowcapped peaks of the Rocky Mountains form a spectacular backdrop for glacial lakes, fast-flowing rivers, and endless forests.

Deer, moose, elk, mountain goats, bighorn sheep, black and grizzly bears, wolves, and cougars inhabit the park's vast wilderness, while the human species is concentrated in the picture-postcard towns of Banff and Lake Louise. The town of Banff is near the park's southeast gate, 129 km (80 mi) west of Calgary. The village of Lake Louise, northwest of Banff along the Trans-Canada Highway, sits close to its namesake lake, which is regarded as one of the seven natural wonders of the world. The lake is rivaled for sheer beauty only by Moraine Lake, down the road.

One of the greatest draws of this 6,641-sq-km (2,564-square-mi) park is the accessibility of its natural wonders. Most highlights are close to the road system, but adventurous visitors can follow an excellent network of hiking trails to alpine lakes, along glacial valleys, and to spectacular viewpoints where crowds are scarce and human impact has been minimal.

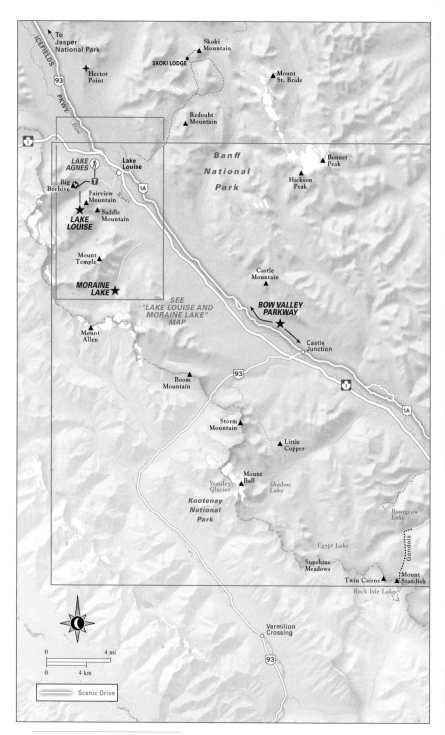

To Jasper
National Park

ICEFIELDS PKWY

93

Hector
Point

Skoki
Mountain

SKOKI LODGE

Mount
St. Bride

Bow

1

LAKE
AGNES

Lake
Louise

Redoubt
Mountain

Banff

National

Park

Bonnet
Peak

Big
Beehive

1A

Hickson
Peak

Fairview
Mountain

Saddle
Mountain

LAKE
LOUISE

River

Mount
Temple

Castle
Mountain

BOW VALLEY
PARKWAY

MORAINE
LAKE

SEE
"LAKE LOUISE AND
MORAINE LAKE"
MAP

Castle
Junction

Mount
Allen

1

1A

Boom
Mountain

93

Storm
Mountain

Little
Copper

Stanley
Glacier

Mount
Ball

Shadow
Lake

Kootenay
National
Park

Bourgeau
Lake

Egypt Lake

Gondola

Sunshine
Meadows

Mount
Standish

Twin Cairns

Rock Isle Lake

Vermilion
Crossing

93

0   4 mi

0   4 km

Scenic Drive

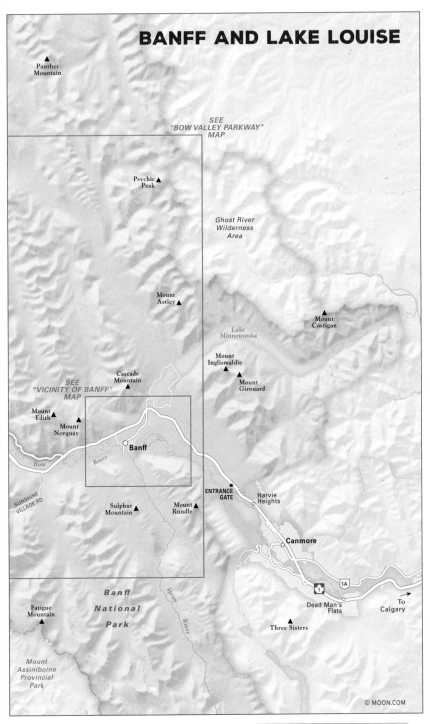

BANFF AND LAKE LOUISE

Panther
Mountain

SEE
"BOW VALLEY PARKWAY"
MAP

Psychic
Peak

Ghost River
Wilderness
Area

Mount
Astley

Lake
Minnewanka

Mount
Costigan

Mount
Inglismaldie

SEE
"VICINITY OF BANFF"
MAP

Cascade
Mountain

Mount
Girouard

Mount
Edith

Mount
Norquay

Bow

River

Banff

Mount
Rundle

ENTRANCE
GATE

Harvie
Heights

SUNSHINE
VILLAGE RD

Sulphur
Mountain

Canmore

Banff

National

Park

Spray

River

Fatigue
Mountain

Dead Man's
Flats

To
Calgary

Three Sisters

Mount
Assiniboine
Provincial
Park

© MOON.COM

2

TOP 3

⭐ **1. BOW VALLEY PARKWAY:** This scenic drive between Banff and Lake Louise provides views of abundant wildlife and many worthwhile stops (page 134).

⭐ **2. LAKE LOUISE:** Famous Lake Louise has hypnotized visitors with its beauty for more than 120 years (page 135).

⭐ **3. MORAINE LAKE:** This body of water qualifies as a double must-see, with the deep blue of the lake itself and the glaciated peaks surrounding it (page 144).

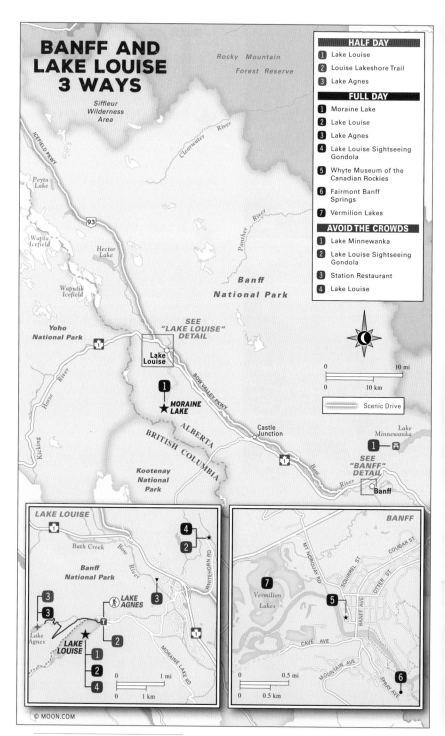

BANFF AND LAKE LOUISE 3 WAYS

Rocky Mountain Forest Reserve

Siffleur Wilderness Area

HALF DAY
1. Lake Louise
2. Louise Lakeshore Trail
3. Lake Agnes

FULL DAY
1. Moraine Lake
2. Lake Louise
3. Lake Agnes
4. Lake Louise Sightseeing Gondola
5. Whyte Museum of the Canadian Rockies
6. Fairmont Banff Springs
7. Vermilion Lakes

AVOID THE CROWDS
1. Lake Minnewanka
2. Lake Louise Sightseeing Gondola
3. Station Restaurant
4. Lake Louise

ICEFIELD PKWY

Peyto Lake

Clearwater River

Panther River

Wapta Icefield

93

Hector Lake

Waputik Icefield

Banff National Park

Yoho National Park

Horse River

Kicking

SEE "LAKE LOUISE" DETAIL

Lake Louise

BOW VALLEY PKWY

1 **MORAINE LAKE**

ALBERTA

BRITISH COLUMBIA

Castle Junction

Bow River

Lake Minnewanka

1

SEE "BANFF" DETAIL

Banff

Kootenay National Park

0 — 10 mi
0 — 10 km

Scenic Drive

LAKE LOUISE

Bath Creek

Bow River

Banff National Park

4
2

WHITEHORN RD

3
3

LAKE AGNES

3

Lake Agnes

T

LAKE LOUISE

2

1
2
4

MORAINE LAKE RD

0 — 1 mi
0 — 1 km

BANFF

MT NORQUAY RD

COUGAR ST

SQUIRREL ST

OTTER ST

7

Vermilion Lakes

5

BANFF AVE

CAVE AVE

MOUNTAIN AVE

SPRAY AVE

6

0 — 0.5 mi
0 — 0.5 km

© MOON.COM

BANFF AND LAKE LOUISE 3 WAYS

HALF DAY

Banff National Park encompasses a large area, so if you only have a half day, concentrate your time on the Lake Louise area, which is under an hour's drive from the town of Banff.

1 The parking lot at **Lake Louise** is often full well before dawn, but early risers are rewarded with the first rays of the sun hitting one of the world's most beautiful lakes (or book a shuttle from Banff to be assured of lake access).

2 The **Louise Lakeshore Trail** offers the best views, or take to the turquoise waters in a canoe.

3 Afterward, hike to **Lake Agnes** and enjoy tea and muffins at the historic backcountry teahouse.

FULL DAY

If your time is limited, the best way to ensure you don't miss the best that Banff National Park has to offer is to make shuttle bus reservations for Lake Louise and Moraine Lake.

1 Catch the shuttle from Banff to **Moraine Lake,** where the water is at its calmest early in the morning. Scramble up the Rockpile for the best views.

2 Catch the connector shuttle between Moraine Lake and **Lake Louise** (no reservations needed).

3 Lace up for a three-hour round-trip hike to **Lake Agnes,** where there is a delightful teahouse.

4 Ride the **Lake Louise Sightseeing Gondola** up Whitehorn Mountain for sweeping views of the entire Lake Louise area.

5 Return to Banff and wander along bustling Banff Avenue. Explore local history at the **Whyte Museum of the Canadian Rockies.**

6 Enjoy dinner at the iconic **Fairmont Banff Springs** hotel. Dine at the Rundle Patio for wonderful valley views, or splurge at 1888 Chop House.

7 After dinner, take advantage of the long days of summer to enjoy a late evening stroll or drive along **Vermilion Lakes.**

AVOID THE CROWDS

Millions of visitors who descend on Banff National Park every year gravitate to downtown Banff and famous lakes such as Louise and Moraine. In fact, Moraine Lake is so popular that the only access is by shuttle or tour bus (no public vehicles). An alternative is the itinerary below. Make reservations ahead of time for dinner at Station Restaurant in Lake Louise.

1 Walk along the shore of **Lake Minnewanka,** the largest lake in Banff National Park. The crowds thin as you walk farther.

2 Arrive in Lake Louise by midafternoon and you'll have missed most of the crowds riding the **Sightseeing Gondola.**

3 Head to dinner at Lake Louise's **Station Restaurant** to enjoy fine Canadian dining in an elegant setting.

4 End your day with an evening stroll along the shoreline of **Lake Louise.**

More Ways to Avoid the Crowds

- Experienced backpackers can hike out into the backcountry of the **Egypt Lake** region.
- Head out early to **Yoho National Park,** north and west of Banff and Lake Louise, and explore its highlights.

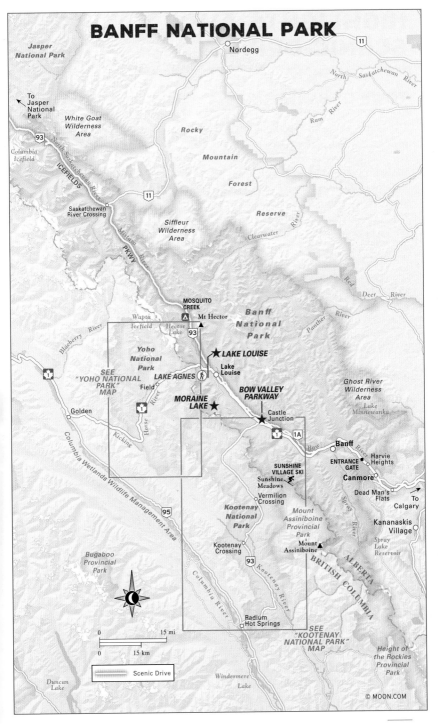

BANFF NATIONAL PARK

Jasper
National Park

Nordegg

11

To
Jasper
National
Park

93

White Goat
Wilderness
Area

Columbia
Icefield

ICEFIELDS

Saskatchewan
River Crossing

11

Rocky

Mountain

Forest

Reserve

North Saskatchewan River

Ram River

Clearwater River

Red Deer River

Panther River

Ghost River
Wilderness
Area

PKWY

Mistaya River

Siffleur
Wilderness
Area

MOSQUITO
CREEK

Mt Hector

93

Banff
National
Park

Wapta
Icefield

Hector
Lake

★ LAKE LOUISE

Blueberry River

Yoho
National
Park

LAKE AGNES

Field

Lake
Louise

BOW VALLEY
PARKWAY

MORAINE
LAKE ★

Castle
Junction

1

1A

SEE
"YOHO NATIONAL
PARK"
MAP

Golden

Kicking Horse River

Columbia Wetlands Wildlife Management Area

Bow River

Banff

Harvie
Heights

ENTRANCE
GATE

Canmore

Lake
Minnewanka

SUNSHINE
VILLAGE SKI

Sunshine
Meadows

Vermilion
Crossing

Dead Man's
Flats

To
Calgary

95

Kootenay
National
Park

Mount
Assiniboine
Provincial
Park

Spray River

Kananaskis
Village

Spray
Lake
Reservoir

Kootenay
Crossing

Mount
Assiniboine

93

Kootenay River

Bugaboo
Provincial
Park

BRITISH COLUMBIA

ALBERTA

Radium
Hot Springs

Columbia River

SEE
"KOOTENAY
NATIONAL
PARK"
MAP

Height
of the
Rockies
Provincial
Park

0   15 mi

0   15 km

Scenic Drive

Duncan
Lake

Windermere
Lake

© MOON.COM

HIGHLIGHTS AND SCENIC DRIVES

TOWN OF BANFF

Many visitors planning a trip to the national park don't realize that the town of Banff is a bustling commercial center. The town's location is magnificent. It is spread out along the **Bow River,** extending to the lower slopes of Sulphur Mountain to the south and Tunnel Mountain to the east. In one direction is the towering face of Mount Rundle, and in the other, framed by the buildings along Banff Avenue, is Cascade Mountain. Hotels and motels line the north end of Banff Avenue, while a profusion of shops, boutiques, cafés, and restaurants hugs the south end. Also at the south end, just over the Bow River, is the Park Administration Building. Here the road forks—to the right is the historic Cave and Basin Hot Springs, to the left the Fairmont Banff Springs and Banff Gondola. Some people are happy walking along the crowded streets or shopping in a unique setting; those more interested in some peace and quiet can easily slip into pristine wilderness just a five-minute walk from town.

Whyte Museum of the Canadian Rockies
111 Bear St.; 403/762-2291; www. whyte.org; 10am-5pm daily; adult C$10, senior C$9, child C$5

The Whyte Foundation was established in the mid-1950s by local artists Peter and Catharine Whyte to help preserve artistic and historical material relating to the Canadian Rockies. Their Whyte Museum of the Canadian Rockies opened in 1968 and has grown ever since. It now houses the world's largest collection

Banff Avenue

of Canadian Rockies literature and art. Included in the archives are more than 4,000 volumes, oral tapes of early pioneers and outfitters, antique postcards, old cameras, manuscripts, and a large photography collection. The highlight is the photography of Byron Harmon, whose black-and-white studies of mountain geography have shown people around the world the beauty of the Canadian Rockies. The downstairs gallery features changing art exhibitions. The museum also houses the library and archives of the Alpine Club of Canada. On the grounds are several heritage homes and cabins formerly occupied by local pioneers.

Buffalo Nations Luxton Museum

1 Birch Ave.; 403/762-2388; www. buffalonationsmuseum.com; 11am-5pm daily; adult C$9, senior C$8, child C$4

Looking like a stockade, the Buffalo Nations Luxton Museum overlooks the Bow River across from Central Park. It is dedicated to the heritage of the First Nations who once inhabited the Canadian Rockies and adjacent prairies. The museum was developed by prominent local resident Norman Luxton in the early 1900s. At that time it was within the Banff Trading Post, an adjacent gift shop that still stands. The museum contains memorabilia from Luxton's lifelong relationship with the Stoney people, including an elaborately decorated tepee, hunting equipment, arrowheads dating back 4,000 years, stuffed animals, original artwork, ceremonial pipes, and traditional clothing. Various aspects of First Nations culture—such as ceremonial gatherings, living in a tepee, and weaving—are also displayed. The Indian Trading

Post is one of Banff's more distinctive gift shops and is definitely worth a browse.

Cave and Basin National Historic Site

403/762-1566; 9:30am-5pm daily summer, 11am-5pm Wed.-Sun. rest of year; adult C$8.50, senior C$7, under 18 free

At the end of Cave Avenue, the Cave and Basin National Historic Site is the birthplace of Banff National Park and of the Canadian National Parks system. Here, in 1883, three men employed by the Canadian Pacific Railway (CPR) stumbled upon the hot springs and were soon lounging in the hot water—a real luxury in the Wild West. Bathhouses were installed in 1887, and bathers paid C$0.10 for a swim. Ironically, the soothing minerals in the water that had attracted millions of people to bathe here eventually caused the pools' demise. The minerals, combined with chlorine, produced sediments that ate away at the concrete structure until the pools were deemed unsuitable for swimming in 1993. Although the pools are now closed to swimming, the site is still one of Banff's most popular attractions. A narrow tunnel winds into the dimly lit cave, and short trails lead to the cave entrance and through a unique environment created by the hot water from the springs.

Banff Upper Hot Springs

Mountain Ave.; 403/762-1515; 10am-10pm daily; C$16.50 adults, C$14.25 seniors and children

The Banff Upper Hot Springs were first developed in 1901. The present building was completed in 1935, with extensive renovations made in 1996. Water flows out of the bedrock at 47°C (116.6°F) and is cooled to 40°C

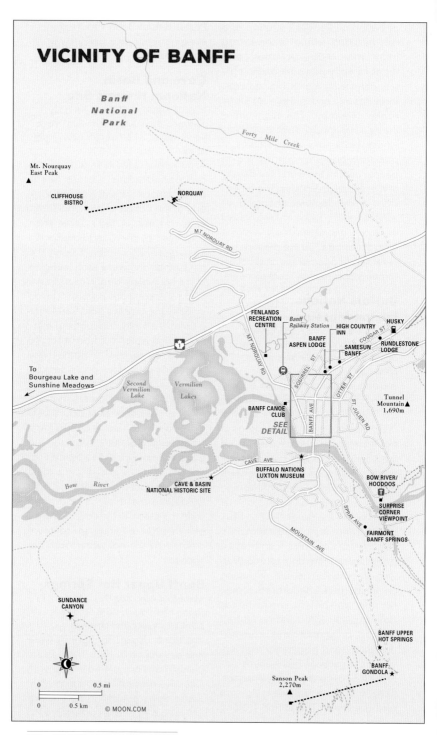

VICINITY OF BANFF

Banff National Park

Forty Mile Creek

Mt. Nourquay East Peak

CLIFFHOUSE BISTRO

NORQUAY

MT. NORQUAY RD

FENLANDS RECREATION CENTRE

Banff Railway Station

HIGH COUNTRY INN

HUSKY

BANFF ASPEN LODGE

SAMESUN BANFF

RUNDLESTONE LODGE

COUGAR ST

SQUIRREL ST

OTTER ST

ST. JULIEN RD

To Bourgeau Lake and Sunshine Meadows

Second Vermilion Lake

Vermilion Lakes

Tunnel Mountain 1,690m

BANFF CANOE CLUB

BANFF AVE

SEE DETAIL

CAVE AVE

Bow River

CAVE & BASIN NATIONAL HISTORIC SITE

BUFFALO NATIONS LUXTON MUSEUM

BOW RIVER/ HOODOOS

SURPRISE CORNER VIEWPOINT

SPRAY AVE

MOUNTAIN AVE

FAIRMONT BANFF SPRINGS

SUNDANCE CANYON

BANFF UPPER HOT SPRINGS

BANFF GONDOLA

Sanson Peak 2,270m

0   0.5 mi
0   0.5 km

© MOON.COM

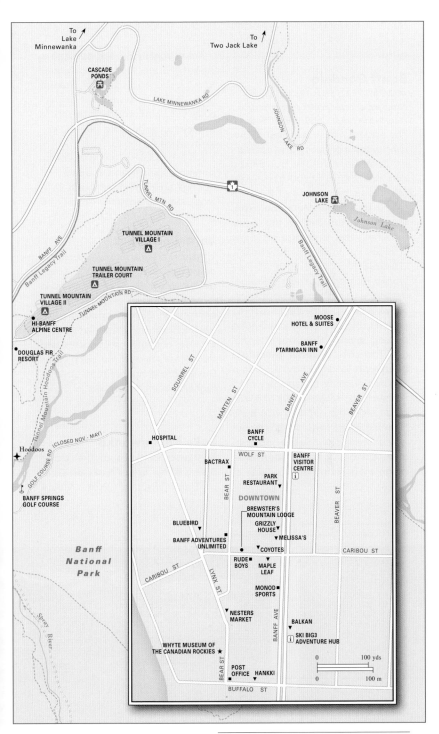

To Lake Minnewanka

To Two Jack Lake

CASCADE PONDS

LAKE MINNEWANKA RD

JOHNSON LAKE RD

TUNNEL MTN RD

JOHNSON LAKE

Johnson Lake

Banff Legacy Trail

TUNNEL MOUNTAIN VILLAGE I

TUNNEL MOUNTAIN TRAILER COURT

BANFF AVE

Banff Legacy Trail

TUNNEL MOUNTAIN VILLAGE II

TUNNEL MOUNTAIN RD

HI-BANFF ALPINE CENTRE

DOUGLAS FIR RESORT

Tunnel Mountain Hoodoos Trail

GOLF COURSE RD (CLOSED NOV - MAY)

Hoodoos

BANFF SPRINGS GOLF COURSE

Banff National Park

Spray River

MOOSE HOTEL & SUITES

BANFF PTARMIGAN INN

SQUIRREL ST

MARTEN ST

BANFF AVE

BEAVER ST

HOSPITAL

BANFF CYCLE

WOLF ST

BANFF VISITOR CENTRE

BACTRAX

BEAR ST

PARK RESTAURANT

BEAVER ST

DOWNTOWN

BREWSTER'S MOUNTAIN LODGE

BLUEBIRD

GRIZZLY HOUSE

BANFF ADVENTURES UNLIMITED

MELISSA'S

CARIBOU ST

COYOTES

CARIBOU ST

RUDE BOYS

MAPLE LEAF

LYNX ST

MONOD SPORTS

NESTERS MARKET

BANFF AVE

BALKAN

WHYTE MUSEUM OF THE CANADIAN ROCKIES

SKI BIG3 ADVENTURE HUB

0   100 yds

BEAR ST

POST OFFICE

HANKKI

0   100 m

BUFFALO ST

(104°F) in the main pool. Lockers and towel rental are a couple of dollars extra.

Banff Gondola

403/762-2523; 8am-10pm daily in summer, shorter hours rest of year; round-trip adult C$60, child C$40

The easiest way to get high above town without breaking a sweat is on the Banff Gondola. The four-person cars rise 700 m (2,300 ft) in eight minutes to the summit of 2,285-m (7,500-ft) **Sulphur Mountain.** From the observation deck at the upper terminal, the breathtaking view includes the town, the Bow Valley, Cascade Mountain, Lake Minnewanka, and the Fairholme Range. Inside the upper terminal are interactive displays, a theater, and three eateries. Bighorn sheep often hang around below the upper terminal. The short **Sulphur Mountain Boardwalk** leads along a ridge to a restored weather observatory atop Sanson Peak. Between 1903 and 1931, long before the gondola was built, Norman Sanson was the meteorological observer who collected data at the station. During this period he made more than 1,000 ascents of Sulphur Mountain, all in the line of duty.

From downtown, the gondola is 3.1 km (1.9 mi) south along Mountain Avenue. May-October, **Pursuit** (866/756-1904; www.banffjasper-collection.com) provides free shuttle service to the gondola from downtown hotels.

A 5.5-km (3.4-mi) hiking trail to the summit begins from the Upper Hot Springs parking lot. Although it's a long slog, you have the option of a gondola ride down (C$40 one-way).

Vermilion Lakes

This series of three shallow lakes forms an expansive montane wetland supporting a variety of mammals and more than 200 species of birds. The entire area is excellent for wildlife viewing, especially in winter when it provides habitat for elk, coyotes, and the occasional wolf. Vermilion Lakes Drive, paralleling the Trans-Canada Highway immediately west of Banff, provides the easiest access to the area.

Lake Minnewanka

Minnewanka (Lake of the Water Spirit) is the largest body of water in Banff National Park. Mount

---

Banff Upper Hot Springs (left); Lake Minnewanka (right)

Inglismaldie (2,964 m/9,720 ft) and the Fairholme Range form an imposing backdrop. The reservoir was first constructed in 1912, and additional dams were built in 1922 and 1941 to supply hydroelectric power to Banff. Even if you don't feel up to an energetic hike, it's worth parking at the facility area and going for a short walk along the lakeshore. You'll pass a concession selling snacks and drinks along the way, go past the tour boat dock, and reach an area with tables—the perfect place for a picnic. You should continue farther around the lake as well—with the added benefit of escaping the crowds. The lake is also great for fishing.

Banff Lake Cruise (866/474-4766; www.banffjaspercollection.com; 4-8 times daily mid-May-early Oct.; adult C$72, child C$36) is a 90-minute cruise to the far reaches of the lake, passing the Devil's Gap formation.

SUNSHINE MEADOWS

Sunshine Meadows, straddling the Continental Divide, is a unique and beautiful region of the Canadian Rockies. It's best known as home to **Sunshine Village,** a self-contained alpine resort accessible only by gondola from the valley floor. But for a few short months each summer, the area is clear of snow and becomes a wonderland for hiking. Large amounts of precipitation create a lush cover of vegetation—over 300 species of wildflowers alone have been recorded here.

From Sunshine Village, trails radiate across the alpine meadow, which is covered in a colorful carpet of fireweed, glacier lilies, mountain avens, white mountain heather, and forget-me-nots (the meadows are in full bloom mid-July-early Aug.). The

Rock Isle Lake in Sunshine Meadows

most popular destination is **Rock Isle Lake,** an easy 1.8-km (1.1-mi) jaunt from the upper village that crosses the Continental Divide while only gaining 100 m (330 ft) of elevation. Another option is to ride the **Standish Chairlift** (included with gondola ride) to a lofty viewing deck where on a clear day **Mount Assiniboine** (3,618 m/11,870 ft), known as the "Matterhorn of the Rockies," is easily distinguished to the south. From the viewing deck, after a short, steep descent, hiking options include a loop around **Grizzly and Larix Lakes** (page 146). If the weather is cooperating, it won't matter which direction you head (so long as it's along a formed trail); you'll experience the Canadian Rockies in all their glory.

It's possible to walk the 6-km (3.7-mi) restricted-access road up to the meadows, but a more practical alternative is to take the **Banff Sunshine Summer Gondola** (403/705-4000; www.banffsunshinemeadows.com; 8am-6pm daily late June-mid-Sept.; adult C$65, senior C$59, child C$32). To get to the base of the gondola from Banff, follow the Trans-Canada

Highway 9 km (5.6 mi) west to Sunshine Village Road, which continues a similar distance along Healy Creek to the Sunshine Village parking lot.

★ BOW VALLEY PARKWAY

Two roads link Banff to Lake Louise. The Trans-Canada Highway is the quicker route and more popular with through traffic. The other is the more scenic 52-km (32-mi) Bow Valley Parkway, which branches off the Trans-Canada Highway 5 km (3.1 mi) west of Banff. Cyclists will appreciate this paved road's two long, divided sections and low speed limit (60 kph/37 mph). Along this route are several impressive viewpoints, picnic areas, good hiking, lodges, campgrounds, and one of the park's best restaurants. Note: In May, June, and September, the southern end of the parkway (as far north as Johnston Canyon) is closed to vehicles,

allowing cyclists to enjoy the road at a leisurely pace. This closure has been extended in recent years throughout summer. For up-to-date information, visit https://parkscanada.ca/banffnow.

Scenic Drive

DRIVING DISTANCE: 52 km (32 mi) one-way
DRIVING TIME: 1 hour one-way
START: Banff
END: Lake Louise

As you enter the parkway, you pass a short side road to the creek-side **Fireside** day-use area. At **Backswamp Viewpoint,** you can look upstream to a swampy wetland filled with aquatic vegetation.

MULESHOE

Farther along the road, 5.5 km (3.4 mi) from the beginning of the route, is another wetland and day-use area at Muleshoe. Across the parkway is a 1-km (0.6-mi) trail that climbs to

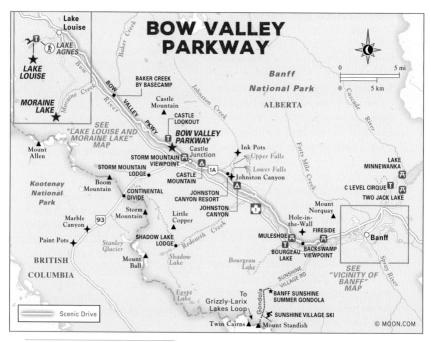

a viewpoint overlooking the valley. (The slope around this trail is infested with wood ticks during late spring and early summer, so be sure to check yourself carefully after hiking in this area.) To the east, **Hole-in-the-Wall** is visible. This large-mouthed cave was created by the Bow Glacier, which once filled the valley.

Beyond Muleshoe the road inexplicably divides for a few car lengths. The road then passes through particularly hilly terrain, part of a massive rockslide that occurred approximately 8,000 years ago.

JOHNSTON CANYON

Approximately 17.7 km (11 mi) along the parkway, Johnston Creek drops over a series of spectacular waterfalls, deep within the chasm it has carved into the limestone bedrock. The canyon is not nearly as deep as Maligne Canyon in Jasper National Park—30 m (100 ft) at its deepest, compared to 50 m (165 ft) at Maligne—but the catwalk that leads to the lower falls has been built through the depths of the canyon rather than along its lip, making it seem just as spectacular. The **lower falls** are 1 km (0.6 mi) from the Bow Valley Parkway, while the equally spectacular **upper falls** are a farther 1.6 km (1 mi) upstream by easy hiking trail. Beyond this point, the trail continues 3.1 km (1.9 mi) to the **Ink Pots,** shallow pools of spring-fed water. While in the canyon, look for fast-moving black swifts zipping through the air.

Past Johnston Canyon, at the west end of Moose Meadows, a small plaque marks the former site of the late 1800s boomtown **Silver City.**

CASTLE MOUNTAIN

Beyond Silver City, the aptly named Castle Mountain comes into view. It's one of the park's most recognizable peaks and most interesting geographical features. The road skirts the base of the mountain, passes **Castle Junction** (with gas, groceries, and accommodations) where Highway 93 jogs west to Kootenay National Park, and climbs a small hill to **Storm Mountain Viewpoint,** which provides more stunning views and a picnic area. The next commercial facility is **Baker Creek by Basecamp** (403/522-3761, www.basecampresorts.com), with cabins and light snacks from the deli.

MORANT'S CURVE VIEWPOINT

Then it's 7.1 km (4.4 mi) more to a viewpoint at **Morant's Curve,** from where rail line, river, and mountains combine for perfect symmetry. After passing another day-use area, the Bow Valley Parkway rejoins the Trans-Canada Highway at Lake Louise.

★ LAKE LOUISE

In summer, about 20,000 visitors per day make the journey from the Bow Valley floor up to Lake Louise, famous for its stunning turquoise coloring. To be assured access to the lake, make **reservations** on the frequent shuttles from Lake Louise Park & Ride at the gondola (https://reservation.pc.gc.ca). An alternative to the shuttle is one of two hiking **trails** that begin in the village (allow 1 hour each way) and end at the public parking lot, where a trail leads to the lake's eastern shore. From this vantage point the dramatic setting can be fully appreciated. The lake is 2.4 km (1.5 mi) long, 500 m (1,640 ft) wide, and up to 90 m (295 ft) deep. Its cold waters reach a maximum high temperature of 4°C (39°F) in August.

YOHO NATIONAL PARK

Yoho, a Cree word that translates to "amazement," is a fitting name for this park on the western slopes of the Canadian Rockies.

Its wild and rugged landscape holds spectacular waterfalls, extensive ice fields, a lake to rival those in Banff, and one of the world's most intriguing fossil beds. In addition, you'll find some of the finest hiking in all Canada on the park's 300-km (186-mi) trail system.

The Trans-Canada Highway (Highway 1) bisects the 131,300-ha (324,450-acre) park on its run between Lake Louise (Alberta) and Golden (British Columbia). Yoho borders Banff National Park, making it an easy add-on to a Glacier, Banff, and Jasper trip. Unless you're traveling straight through and not stopping or have a Discovery Pass for all of Canada's national parks, you'll need a National Parks Day Pass (adult C$10.50) to visit Yoho.

Within the park are lodges, road-accessible campgrounds, and the small town of Field, where you'll find basic services. Yoho is open year-round, although road conditions in winter can be treacherous and occasional closures occur on Kicking Horse Pass. The road out to Takakkaw Falls is closed through winter, and it often doesn't reopen until late June.

HIGHLIGHTS
Emerald Lake
One of the jewels of the Canadian Rockies, this beautiful lake is surrounded by a forest of Engelmann spruce, as well as many peaks more than 3,000 m (9,840 ft) high. It is covered in ice most of the year but comes alive with activity for a few short months in summer when hikers take advantage of the magnificent surroundings.

Takakkaw Falls
Takakkaw Falls is the most impressive waterfall in the Canadian Rockies. The falls are fed by the Daly and Des Poilus Glaciers of the Waputik Icefield, which straddles the Continental Divide. Meaning "wonderful" in the language of the Cree, Takakkaw tumbles 254 m (830 ft) over a sheer rock wall at the lip of the Yoho Valley, creating a spray bedecked by rainbows. It can be seen from the parking lot, but it's well worth the easy 10-minute stroll over the Yoho River to appreciate the sight in all its glory.

Lake O'Hara
Nestled in a high bowl of lush alpine meadows, Lake O'Hara, 10.9 km (6.8 mi) from the nearest public road, is surrounded by dozens of smaller alpine lakes and framed by spectacular peaks permanently mantled in snow. The entire area is webbed by a network of hiking trails radiating in all directions, making it the premier hiking region

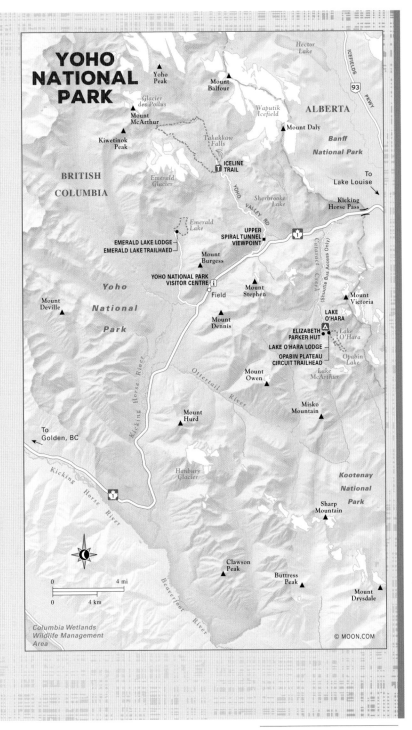

YOHO NATIONAL PARK

Yoho Peak

Mount Balfour

Hector Lake

ICEFIELDS PKWY

93

ALBERTA

Glacier des Poilus

Mount McArthur

Waputik Icefield

Mount Daly

Kiwetinok Peak

Takakkaw Falls

Banff National Park

BRITISH COLUMBIA

ICELINE TRAIL

Emerald Glacier

YOHO VALLEY RD

Sherbrooke Lake

To Lake Louise

Kicking Horse Pass

Emerald Lake

EMERALD LAKE LODGE
EMERALD LAKE TRAILHAED

UPPER SPIRAL TUNNEL VIEWPOINT

1

Mount Burgess

YOHO NATIONAL PARK VISITOR CENTRE

Field

Mount Stephen

Yoho

National

Park

Cataract Creek (Shuttle Bus Access Only)

Mount Victoria

Mount Deville

Mount Dennis

LAKE O'HARA

ELIZABETH PARKER HUT

Lake O'Hara

LAKE O'HARA LODGE

OPABIN PLATEAU CIRCUIT TRAILHEAD

Opabin Lake

Kicking Horse River

Ottertail River

Mount Owen

Lake McArthur

Misko Mountain

To Golden, BC

Mount Hurd

Kicking Horse River

Hanbury Glacier

Kootenay

National

Park

Sharp Mountain

0   4 mi
0   4 km

Clawson Peak

Buttress Peak

Mount Drysdale

Beaverfoot River

Columbia Wetlands Wildlife Management Area

© MOON.COM

in the park. What makes this destination all the more special is that a quota system limits the number of visitors. It's possible to walk to Lake O'Hara, but most visitors take the shuttle bus (https://reserva-tion.pc.gc.ca; mid-June-early Oct.) along a road closed to the pub-lic. Check the website for reservation details. Several overnight op-tions are available at the lake, including the **Elizabeth Parker Hut** (403/678-3200; www.alpineclubofcanada.ca), **Lake O'Hara Lodge** (250/343-6418; www.lakeohara.com), and a campground (www.reservation.pc.gc.ca), but each should be booked well in advance.

SCENIC DRIVE
As with all other parks of the Canadian Rockies, you don't need to travel deep into the backcountry to view Yoho's most spectacular fea-tures—many are visible from the roadside.

Yoho Valley Road
Fed by the Wapta Icefield in the far north of the park, the **Yoho River** flows through this spectacularly narrow valley, dropping more than 200 m (660 ft) in the last 1 km (0.6 mi) before its confluence with the Kicking Horse River. The road leading up the valley, which is usual-ly open and snow-free by late June, passes the park's main camp-ground, climbs a *very* tight series of switchbacks (watch for buses reversing through the middle section), and emerges at **Upper Spiral Tunnel Viewpoint,** which offers a different perspective on the afore-mentioned tunnel. A further 300 m (0.2 mi) along the road is a **pullout** for viewing the confluence of the Yoho and Kicking Horse Rivers—a particularly impressive sight, as the former is glacier-fed and there-fore silty, while the latter is lake-fed and clear. Yoho Valley Road ends 14 km (8.7 mi) from the main highway at **Takakkaw Falls.**

HIKES
Emerald Lake
DISTANCE: 5.1 km (3.2 mi) round-trip
DURATION: 1.5 hours round-trip
ELEVATION GAIN: minimal
RATING: easy
TRAILHEAD: Emerald Lake parking lot, 9 km (5.6 mi) from the Trans-Canada Highway

One of the easiest yet most enjoyable walks in Yoho is around the park's most famous lake. The trail encircles the lake and can be hiked in either direction. The best views are from the western shoreline, where a massive avalanche has cleared away the forest of Engel-mann spruce. Across the lake from this point, **Mount Burgess** can be seen rising an impressive 2,600 m (8,530 ft). Traveling in a clockwise direction, beyond the avalanche slope, the trail to Emerald Basin veers off to the left, crossing a small bridge at the 2.3-km (1.4-mi)

Emerald Lake, Yoho National Park

mark. Beyond the lake's inlet, the vegetation changes dramatically. A lush forest of towering western red cedar creates a canopy, protecting moss-covered fallen trees, thimbleberry, and bunchberry extending to the water's edge. Just over 1 km (0.6 mi) from the bridge, the trail divides: The left fork leads back to the parking lot via a small forest-encircled pond, or continue straight ahead through the grounds of Emerald Lake Lodge.

Iceline Trail

DISTANCE: 6.4 km (4 mi) one-way
DURATION: 2.5 hours one-way
ELEVATION GAIN: 690 m (2,260 ft)
RATING: moderate-strenuous
TRAILHEAD: HI-Yoho (Whiskey Jack Hostel); park in the Takakkaw Falls lot up the road from the hostel

The Iceline is one of the most spectacular day hikes in the Canadian Rockies. The length given is from HI-Yoho to the highest point along the trail (2,250 m/7,380 ft). From the hostel, the trail begins a steep and steady 1-km (0.6-mi) climb to a point where two options present themselves: The Iceline Trail is to the right, and Yoho Lake is to the left. After another 20 minutes of walking, the Iceline Trail option enters its highlight—a 4-km (2.5-mi) traverse of a moraine below Emerald Glacier. Views across the valley improve as the trail climbs to its crest and passes a string of small lakes filled with glacial meltwater. Many day hikers return from this point, although officially the trail continues into Little Yoho River Valley.

Opabin Plateau Circuit

DISTANCE: 6 km (3.7 mi) round-trip
DURATION: 2 hours round-trip
ELEVATION GAIN: 250 m (820 ft)
RATING: easy-moderate
TRAILHEAD: Lake O'Hara; access via reserved summer shuttle bus (https://reservation.pc.gc.ca)

This plateau high above the tree line and dotted with small lakes is one of the most picturesque destinations in the Canadian Rockies. Two trails lead up to the plateau, which itself is laced with trails. The most direct route is the Opabin Plateau West Circuit, which branches right from the Shoreline Trail 300 m (0.2 mi) beyond Lake O'Hara Lodge. It then passes Mary Lake, climbs steeply, and reaches the plateau in about 1.9 km (1.2 mi). Opabin Prospect is an excellent lookout along the edge of the plateau. From this point, take the right fork to continue to the head of the cirque and Opabin Lake. This section of trail passes through a lightly forested area of larch that comes alive with color the second week of September. From Opabin Lake, the East Circuit traverses the lower slopes of Yukness Mountain, passing Hungabee Lake, then descending steeply to Lake O'Hara and ending back along the Shoreline Trail 600 m (0.4 mi) east of Lake O'Hara Lodge.

FOOD AND LODGING

Truffle Pigs Bistro
100 Centre St.; 250/343-6303; 11am-9pm daily; C$24-44
In downtown Field, Truffle Pigs Bistro is one of those unexpected finds that make traveling such a joy. In the evening this place really shines, with dishes as creative as yam and brisket poutine to start and as simple as eggplant lasagna for a main.

Emerald Lake Lodge
Emerald Lake; 250/343-6321 or 800/663-6336; www.crmr.com; from C$600 s or d
Emerald Lake Lodge is a gracious, luxury-class accommodation along the southern shore of one of the Canadian Rockies' most magnificent lakes. The original lodge was built in 1902 in the same tradition as the Fairmont Chateau Lake Louise and Fairmont Banff Springs—as a playground for wealthy travelers. No original buildings remain (although the original framework is used in the main building); instead, guests lap up the luxury of richly decorated duplex-style units and freestanding cabins. Each spacious unit is outfitted in a heritage theme and has a wood-burning fireplace, private balcony, and luxurious bathroom. A restaurant, lounge, and lakefront café are on-site.

INFORMATION
The main source of information about the park is the **Yoho National Park Visitor Centre** (250/343-6783 or 250/343-6783; 9am-5pm daily May-mid-Oct., until 7pm daily in summer) on the Trans-Canada Highway at Field. For more information, check out the **Parks Canada** website (https://parks.canada.ca/yoho).

GETTING THERE
The Trans-Canada Highway passes through the heart of Yoho National Park; it's 84 km (52 mi) from the town of Banff to Field. Public transportation to and around the park is limited—you will need to have your own vehicle or a rental. For park road conditions, call 403/762-1450.

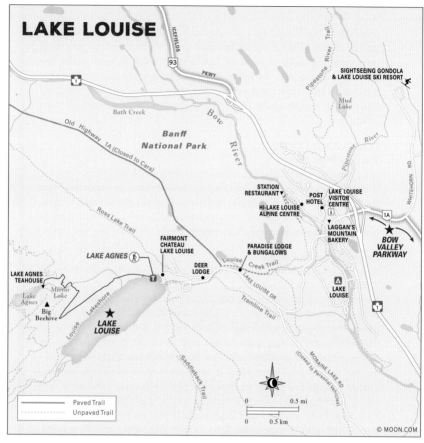

LAKE LOUISE

LAKE LOUISE

ICEFIELDS
93
PKWY

Bath Creek

Bow River

Banff
National Park

Old Highway 1A (Closed to Cars)

Ross Lake Trail

Pipestone River Trail

SIGHTSEEING GONDOLA
& LAKE LOUISE SKI RESORT

Mud
Lake

Pipestone River

WHITEHORN RD

STATION
RESTAURANT
POST
HOTEL
HI-LAKE LOUISE
ALPINE CENTRE
LAKE LOUISE
VISITOR
CENTRE
i
LAGGAN'S
MOUNTAIN
BAKERY
1A
BOW
VALLEY
PARKWAY

FAIRMONT
CHATEAU
LAKE LOUISE

LAKE AGNES

DEER
LODGE
PARADISE LODGE
& BUNGALOWS
Louise Creek Trail
LAKE LOUISE DR
LAKE
LOUISE

LAKE AGNES
TEAHOUSE
Lake
Agnes
Mirror
Lake
Big
Beehive
Lakeshore
Tramline Trail

Louise

LAKE
LOUISE

Saddleback Trail

MORAINE LAKE RD
(Closed to Personal Vehicles)

Paved Trail
Unpaved Trail

0   0.5 mi
0   0.5 km

© MOON.COM

Near the **Fairmont Chateau Lake Louise,** which is a tourist attraction in itself, you'll find some of the park's best hiking, canoeing, and horseback riding. The snow-covered peak at the back of the lake is **Mount Victoria** (3,459 m/11,350 ft), which sits on the Continental Divide. Mount Victoria, first climbed in 1897, remains one of the park's most popular peaks for mountaineers. Although the difficult northeast face (facing the lake) was first successfully ascended in 1922, the most popular and easiest route to the summit is along the southeast ridge, approached from Abbot Pass.

Sightseeing Gondola

9am-4pm daily late May-Sept., until 5pm in July-Aug.; adult C$60, senior $49, child C$25

During summer, the main ski lift at the **Lake Louise Ski Resort** (403/522-3555; www.skilouise.com) whisks visitors up the face of Mount Whitehorn in either open chairs or enclosed gondola cars. At an altitude of more than 1.9 km (1.2 mi) above sea level, the view from the top—across the Bow Valley, Lake Louise, and the Continental Divide—is among the most spectacular in the Canadian Rockies. Short trails lead through the forest and across open meadows. Visitors are free to walk these trails, but it

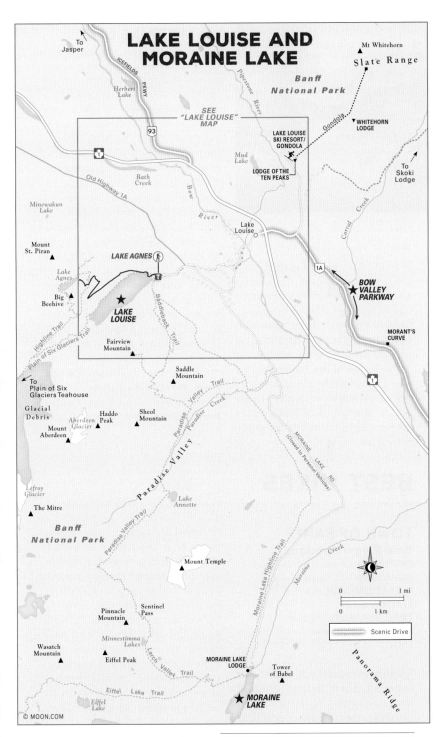

LAKE LOUISE AND MORAINE LAKE

To Jasper

Mt Whitehorn

Slate Range

ICEFIELDS PKWY

Herbert Lake

Banff National Park

Pipestone River

SEE "LAKE LOUISE" MAP

Gondola

93

LAKE LOUISE SKI RESORT/ GONDOLA

WHITEHORN LODGE

1

Old Highway 1A

Bath Creek

Mud Lake

LODGE OF THE TEN PEAKS

To Skoki Lodge

Minewakun Lake

Bow River

Lake Louise

Corral Creek

Mount St. Piran

LAKE AGNES

1A

Lake Agnes

Big Beehive

LAKE LOUISE

Saddleback Trail

BOW VALLEY PARKWAY

MORANT'S CURVE

Highline Trail

Fairview Mountain

Plain of Six Glaciers Trail

Saddle Mountain

1

To Plain of Six Glaciers Teahouse

Paradise Valley Trail

Paradise Creek

Glacial Debris

Haddo Peak

Sheol Mountain

MORAINE LAKE RD (Closed to Personal Vehicles)

Aberdeen Glacier

Mount Aberdeen

Paradise Valley

Lefroy Glacier

Lake Annette

The Mitre

Banff National Park

Paradise Valley Trail

Mount Temple

Moraine Creek

Moraine Lake Highline Trail

Pinnacle Mountain

Sentinel Pass

Wasatch Mountain

Minnestimma Lakes

Eiffel Peak

Larch Valley Trail

MORAINE LAKE LODGE

Tower of Babel

Panorama Ridge

Eiffel Lake Trail

Eiffel Lake

MORAINE LAKE

0   1 mi

0   1 km

Scenic Drive

© MOON.COM

Moraine Lake

★ MORAINE LAKE

Although less than half the size of Lake Louise, Moraine Lake is just as spectacular and worthy of just as much time. It is up a winding road 12.9 km (8 mi) off Lake Louise Drive. Its rugged setting, nestled in the Valley of the Ten Peaks among the towering mountains of the main ranges, has provided inspiration for millions of people around the world. Despite its name, the lake was not dammed by a glacial moraine; in fact, the large rock pile that blocks its waters was deposited by major rockfalls from the Tower of Babel to the south.

The lake often remains frozen until June, and the access road is closed all winter. When the road is open, usually mid-June to early October, there are no personal vehicles allowed on the road and the main access is by **shuttle bus from Banff** (www.roamtransit. com) or from the **Lake Louise Park & Ride** (https://reservation. pc.gc.ca).

pays to join a **guided walk** if you'd like to learn about the surrounding environment. After working up an appetite (and working off breakfast), head to the bistro in the **Whitehorn Lodge,** try the outdoor barbecue, or, back at the base area, enjoy lunch at the **Lodge of the Ten Peaks,** the resort's impressive post-and-beam day lodge. Ride-and-dine packages are an excellent deal. Free shuttles run from Lake Louise accommodations to the day lodge.

BEST HIKES

TOWN OF BANFF
Bow River/Hoodoos
DISTANCE: 4.8 km (3 mi) one-way
DURATION: 1-1.5 hours one-way
ELEVATION GAIN: minimal
EFFORT: easy
TRAIL SURFACE: unpaved
TRAILHEAD: Surprise Corner, Buffalo Street

From a viewpoint famous for its Fairmont Banff Springs outlook, the trail descends to the Bow River, passing under the sheer east face

of Tunnel Mountain. It then follows the river a short distance before climbing into a meadow where deer and elk often graze. From this perspective the north face of Mount Rundle is particularly imposing. As the trail climbs, you'll hear the traffic on Tunnel Mountain Road long before you see it. The trail ends at a viewpoint above the hoodoos, strange-looking limestone-and-gravel columns jutting mysteriously out of the forest. An alternative to returning the same way is to catch a Roam Transit bus (every 30 minutes; C$2) from Tunnel Mountain Campground.

C Level Cirque

DISTANCE: 4 km (2.5 mi) one-way
DURATION: 1.5 hours one-way
ELEVATION GAIN: 457 m (1,500 ft)
EFFORT: moderate
TRAIL SURFACE: unpaved
TRAILHEAD: Upper Bankhead Day Use Area, Lake Minnewanka Road, 3.5 km (2.2 mi) beyond the Trans-Canada Highway underpass

From a day-use area on the site of an abandoned mining town, the trail climbs steadily through a forest of lodgepole pine, aspen, and spruce to a pile of tailings and broken-down concrete walls. Soon after, there is a panoramic view of Lake Minnewanka, and then the trail reenters the forest before ending in a small cirque with views down the Bow Valley. The cirque is carved into the eastern face of Cascade Mountain, where snow often lingers until July. When the snow melts, the lush soil is covered in a carpet of colorful wildflowers.

Bourgeau Lake

DISTANCE: 7.6 km (4.7 mi) one-way
DURATION: 2.5 hours one-way
ELEVATION GAIN: 730 m (2,400 ft)
EFFORT: strenuous
TRAIL SURFACE: unpaved
TRAILHEAD: signposted parking lot, Trans-Canada Highway, 3.1 km (1.9 mi) west of Sunshine Village Road Junction

This trail follows Wolverine Creek to a small subalpine lake nestled at the base of an impressive limestone amphitheater. Although the trail is moderately steep, plenty of distractions along the way are worthy of a stop (and rest). Back across the Bow Valley, the Sawback Range is easy to distinguish. As the forest of lodgepole pine turns to spruce, the trail passes under the cliffs of Mount Bourgeau and crosses Wolverine Creek (below a spot where it tumbles photogenically over exposed bedrock). After strenuous switchbacks, the trail climbs into the cirque containing Bourgeau Lake. As you explore the lake's rocky shore, you'll hear noisy marmots and pikas, even if you don't see them.

Bourgeau Lake (left); view of Lake Louise from the Plain of Six Glaciers Trail (right)

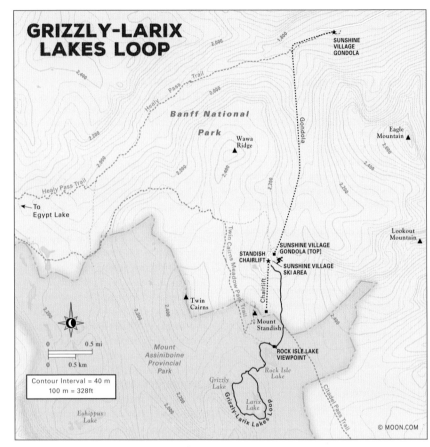

SUNSHINE MEADOWS
Grizzly-Larix Lakes Loop
DISTANCE: 8.5 km (5.3 mi) round-trip
DURATION: 3 hours round-trip
ELEVATION GAIN: 105 m (350 ft)
EFFORT: easy-moderate
TRAIL SURFACE: unpaved
TRAILHEAD: Sunshine Village, reached by gondola from the valley floor 17.7 km (11 mi) from the town of Banff

The trail that loops around Grizzly and Larix Lakes is the most popular outing in the Sunshine Meadows region. Following a broad gravel track from the center of Sunshine Village, you make a steady but brief climb to the Great Divide, passing through the last scattered stands of alpine fir into a treeless alpine landscape. On the 2,305-m (7,560-ft) summit, views stretch south across the vast Sunshine Meadows to the distant pyramid of Mount Assiniboine. West of the divide, you descend to **Rock Isle Lake Viewpoint,** one of the most photogenic scenes in the region. From this point, the trail climbs over a low, rocky hill to where the lake's outlet stream plunges down steep limestone slabs, and then drops through open forest and lush meadows filled with wildflowers.

Soon the trail splits to begin a 2.4-km (1.5-mi) loop around Grizzly and Larix Lakes. Keep right and descend to Grizzly Lake. From the lake's inlet bridge, the trail turns left and contours the lip of the basin to a fine viewpoint over the Simpson Valley. Larix, the larger of the two lakes, is just beyond the viewpoint.

BOW VALLEY PARKWAY
Castle Lookout
DISTANCE: 3.7 km (2.3 mi) one-way
DURATION: 90 minutes one-way
ELEVATION GAIN: 520 m (1,700 ft)
EFFORT: moderate
TRAIL SURFACE: unpaved
TRAILHEAD: Bow Valley Parkway, 5 km (3.1 mi) northwest of Castle Junction

However you travel through the Bow Valley, you can't help but be impressed by Castle Mountain rising proudly from the forest floor. This trail takes you above the tree line on the mountain's west face to the site of the Mount Eisenhower fire lookout, abandoned in the 1970s and burned in the 1980s. From the Bow Valley Parkway, the trail follows a wide pathway for 1.4 km (0.9 mi) to an abandoned cabin in a forest of lodgepole pine and spruce. It then becomes narrower and steeper, switchbacking through a meadow before climbing through a narrow band of rock and leveling off near the lookout site. Magnificent panoramas of the Bow Valley spread out before you in both directions. Storm Mountain can be seen directly across the valley.

LAKE LOUISE
Louise Lakeshore
DISTANCE: 1.9 km (1.2 mi) one-way
DURATION: 30 minutes one-way
ELEVATION GAIN: none
EFFORT: easy
TRAIL SURFACE: unpaved
TRAILHEAD: Lake Louise, 4 km (2.5 mi) from Trans-Canada Highway

Probably the busiest trail in all the Canadian Rockies, this one follows the north shore of Lake Louise from in front of the Fairmont Chateau Lake Louise to the west end of the lake. Here numerous braided glacial streams empty their silt-filled waters into Lake Louise. Along the trail's length are benches for sitting and pondering what English mountaineer James Outram once described as "a gem of composition and of coloring ... perhaps unrivalled anywhere."

Plain of Six Glaciers
DISTANCE: 5.3 km (3.3 mi) one-way
DURATION: 1.5 hours one-way
ELEVATION GAIN: 370 m (1,215 ft)
EFFORT: moderate
TRAIL SURFACE: unpaved
TRAILHEAD: Lake Louise

Hikers along this trail are rewarded not only with panoramic views of the glaciated peaks of the main range but also with a rustic trail's-end teahouse serving homemade goodies baked on a wood-fired stove. For the first 1.9 km (1.2 mi), the trail follows the **Louise Lakeshore Trail** to the western end of the lake. From there it begins a steady climb through a forest of spruce and subalpine fir. It enters an open area where an avalanche has come tumbling down (a colorful carpet of wildflowers in midsummer), then passes through a forested area into a vast wasteland of moraines produced by

TOP HIKE
LAKE AGNES

DISTANCE: 3.5 km (2.2 mi) one-way
DURATION: 1.5 hours one-way
ELEVATION GAIN: 400 m (1,312 ft)
EFFORT: moderate
TRAIL SURFACE: unpaved
TRAILHEAD: Lake Louise

This moderately strenuous hike is one of the park's most popular. It begins in front of the château, branching right near the beginning of the Louise

Lakeshore Trail. For the first 2.6 km (1.6 mi), the trail climbs steeply, switch-backing through a forest of subalpine fir and Engelmann spruce, crossing a horse trail, and leveling out at tiny **Mirror Lake.** Here the old, traditional trail veers right (use it if the ground is wet or snowy), while a more direct route veers left. The final elevation gain along both trails is made easier by a flight of steps beside **Bridal Veil Falls.** The trail ends at its namesake subalpine lake, which is nestled in a hanging valley. It's also where you'll find the rustic **Lake Agnes Teahouse** (8am-5pm daily early June-mid-Oct.; cash only), which offers homemade soups, healthy sandwiches, and a wide assortment of teas.

From the teahouse, a 1-km (0.6-mi) trail leads to **Little Beehive** and impressive views of the Bow Valley. Another trail leads around the northern shore of Lake Agnes, climbing 1. 6 km (0.9 mi) to **Big Beehive.**

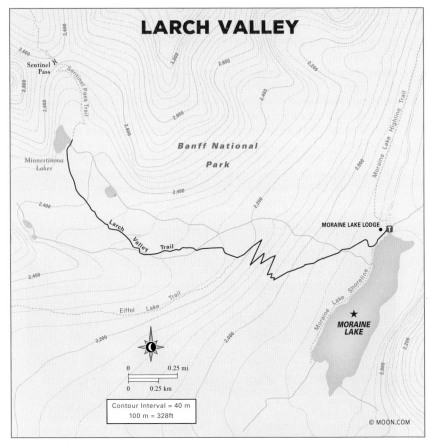

LARCH VALLEY

Banff National Park

Sentinel Pass

Minnestimma Lakes

Moraine Lake Lodge

Larch Valley Trail

Eiffel Lake Trail

★ MORAINE LAKE

Moraine Lake Shoreline

Moraine Lake Highline Trail

Sentinel Pass Trail

0   0.25 mi

0   0.25 km

Contour Interval = 40 m
100 m = 328ft

© MOON.COM

the advance and retreat of Victoria Glacier. Views of surrounding peaks continue to improve until the trail enters a stunted forest. Eventually the trail arrives at the **Plain of Six Glaciers Teahouse** (9am-5pm daily mid-June-early Oct.; cash only). It operates the same way now as it did back when it was built by the CPR at the turn of the 20th century: Supplies are packed in by horse, and all cooking is done in a rustic kitchen.

After resting, continue 1 km (0.6 mi) on the narrow top of a lateral moraine. From here the trail's namesakes are visible. From left to right, the glaciers are Aberdeen, Upper Lefroy, Lower Lefroy, Upper Victoria, Lower Victoria, and Pope's. Between Mount Lefroy (3,441 m/11,290 ft) and Mount Victoria (3,459 m/11,350 ft) is Abbot Pass, named for Philip Abbot, who died attempting to climb Mount Lefroy in 1896.

Big Beehive

DISTANCE: 5 km (3.1 mi) one-way
DURATION: 2 hours one-way
ELEVATION GAIN: 520 m (1,710 ft)
EFFORT: moderate
TRAIL SURFACE: unpaved
TRAILHEAD: Lake Louise

The lookout atop the larger of the two "beehives" is one of the best places to admire the Bow Valley, which lies over 500 m (1,640 ft) directly below.

The various trails to the summit have one thing in common: All are steep. But the rewards are worth every drop of sweat along the way. The most popular route follows the Lake Agnes Trail for the first 3.5 km (2.2 mi) to Lake Agnes. From the teahouse, a trail leads to the western end of the lake, then switchbacks steeply up an exposed north-facing ridge. At the crest of the ridge, the trail forks. To the right it descends to the Plain of Six Glaciers Trail; to the left it continues 300 m (0.2 mi) to a log gazebo. Across Lake Louise is Fairview Mountain (2,745 m/9,000 ft), and behind this peak is the distinctive shape of Mount Temple (3,549 m/11,645 ft). Views also extend up the lake to Mount Lefroy and northeast to the Lake Louise Ski Resort. Views from the edge of the cliff are spectacular, but be very careful—it's a long, long way down. By returning down the Lake Louise side of the Big Beehive via the Highline Trail, the loop is 11.5 km (7.1 mi).

MORAINE LAKE
Larch Valley
DISTANCE: 2.9 km (1.8 mi) one-way
DURATION: 1 hour one-way
ELEVATION GAIN: 400 m (1,310 ft)
EFFORT: moderate
TRAIL SURFACE: unpaved
TRAILHEAD: Moraine Lake, 12.9 km (8 mi) from Lake Louise Drive

In mid- to late September, when the larch trees have turned a magnificent gold and the sun is shining, few

Larch Valley

spots can match the beauty of this valley, but don't expect to find much solitude. Although the most popular time for visiting the valley is fall, it is a worthy destination all summer, when the open meadows are filled with colorful wildflowers. The trail begins just past Moraine Lake Lodge and climbs fairly steeply, with occasional glimpses of Moraine Lake below. After reaching the junction of the Eiffel Lake Trail, keep right, passing through an open forest of larch and into the meadow beyond. The range of larch is restricted within the park, and this is one of the few areas where they are prolific. Mount Fay (3,235 m/10,615 ft) is the dominant peak on the skyline, rising above the other mountains that make up the Valley of the Ten Peaks. Continue up a further 1 km (0.6 mi) to the two Minnestimma Lakes, where views back to the Ten Peaks are unforgettable.

looking across Minnestimma Lakes to Larch Valley

BACKPACKING

For those with relevant experience, heading into the backcountry of Banff National Park is a great way to escape the crowds encountered on day hikes. One of the most popular regions for a backcountry trip is **Egypt Lake,** a 12.1-km (7.5-mi) walk from the nearest road. Here you'll find a campground and hut that sleeps 12, from where trails lead to alpine lakes and passes high above the tree line. If you are not equipped for backcountry travel, lodges at Shadow Lake and in the Skoki Valley provide an alternate way to visit these regions.

If you are planning an overnight camping trip into the backcountry, you *must* make reservations well in advance through the **Parks Canada Reservation Service** (877/737-3783; https://reservation.pc.gc.ca).

SHADOW LAKE

LENGTH: 14 km (8.7 mi) one-way
TRAILHEAD: Redearth Creek Parking Area, Trans-Canada Highway, 10.9 km (6.8 mi) west of Sunshine Village Junction

Shadow is one of the many impressive subalpine lakes along the Continental Divide and, for those staying at **Shadow Lake Lodge** (403/678-3200; www.shadowlakelodge.com; mid-June-early Sept.; starting at C$800 s or d) or the backcountry campground, a popular base for day trips to Ball Pass, Gibbon Pass, and Haiduk Lake. The trail follows an abandoned road for 10.9 km (6.8 mi) before forking right and climbing into the forest. The campground is 1.9 km (1.2 mi) beyond this junction, and just 300 m (0.2 mi) farther is Shadow Lake Lodge. The lake is nearly 1.9 km (1.2 mi) long and is best viewed from the bridge over its outlet stream.

SKOKI VALLEY

LENGTH: 14.3 km (8.9 mi) one-way
TRAILHEAD: end of Fish Creek Road, off Whitehorn Road 1.8 km (1.1 mi) north of Lake Louise interchange

The trail into historic **Skoki Lodge** (403/256-8473 or 800/258-7669; www.skoki.com; late June-early Oct.; C$250-550 pp) accesses endless hiking opportunities tucked behind

looking over Skoki Lakes (left); paddleboarding on Vermilion Lakes (right)

the Lake Louise Ski Resort. The first 3.4 km (2.1 mi) of the trail are along a gravel access road. Guests of Skoki Lodge ride a shuttle for this first stretch, lessening the hiking distance to 10.9 km (6.8 mi). From the end of the road, the trail climbs to Boulder Pass, passing Halfway Hut (a rustic shelter; no camping) and a short side trail to Hidden Lake. The pass harbors a large population of pikas and marmots. The trail then follows the north shore of Ptarmigan Lake before climbing again to Deception Pass, named for its false summit. It then descends into Skoki Valley, passing a side trail to the Skoki Lakes and eventually reaching Skoki Lodge. Just over 1 km (less than 1 mi) beyond the lodge is a campground, an excellent base for exploring the region for those with reservations.

BIKING

Whether you have your own bike or you rent one from the many bicycle shops in Banff or Lake Louise, cycling in the park is for everyone. Popular paved routes for road biking include the road to **Lake Minnewanka** (16 km/10 mi), along the **Bow Valley Parkway** (52 km/32 mi), and the **Banff Legacy Trail** to Canmore (26.8 km/16.6 mi).

Several unpaved trails radiating from Banff and passing through the backcountry have been designated as bicycle trails. These include a network of trails on the east side of Tunnel Mountain, the Rundle Riverside to Canmore, and the Spray River Loop.

Before heading into the backcountry, download the *Mountain Biking and Cycling Guide* from the Brochures page of the Parks Canada website (https://parks.canada.ca/banff). Backcountry riders are particularly susceptible to sudden bear encounters. Be alert and make loud noises when passing through heavy vegetation.

SUNDANCE CANYON

Sundance Canyon is a rewarding destination across the Bow River from downtown. Starting at Cave and Basin National Historic Site, this easy ride is 5.3 km (3.3 mi) one-way and is paved. Occasional glimpses of the Sawback Range are afforded by breaks in the forest. At the end of the paved section is a bike rack, from where you can continue on foot along a 2.1-km (1.3-mi) hiking trail that loops through an overhanging canyon formed by Sundance Creek's powerful waters.

SPRAY RIVER LOOP

This popular mountain biking route (11.9 km/7.4 mi round-trip) starts at the Fairmont Banff Springs hotel and heads uphill, following the Spray River closely, for 6 km (3.7 mi). After crossing the river, it's downhill all the way to the Fairmont Banff Springs Golf Course. A worthwhile stop on the inbound leg is at a cliff face where Rundlestone used for the famous hotel's facade was quarried.

RENTALS

Road bikes and road/mountain hybrid bikes rent for about C$70 per day, and e-bikes for about C$120 per day. Renting front- and full-suspension mountain bikes runs approximately C$25-30 per hour and C$80-100 per day.

KOOTENAY NATIONAL PARK

If you're driving up to Banff through the Columbia Valley from the west side of Glacier National Park, you will pass through Kootenay National Park (National Parks Day Pass adult C$10.50). You could just admire the mountain vistas from the road, but if you want to take a break from driving, here are a few options for where to stop.

RADIUM HOT SPRINGS
250/347-9485; 10:30am-10pm daily in summer, 11:30am-9pm daily the rest of the year; adult C$16.50, senior and child C$14.25
Located just 3.1 km (1.9 mi) from the point where Highway 93 crosses into the park from the south, this hot spring pool gushes with mineral waters. A soak here makes a great antidote for drive-stiffened muscles.

SCENIC VIEWPOINTS
For a quick stretch in some beautiful scenery, stop at one or all of the following viewpoints along Highway 93:

- **Olive Lake,** just east of Sinclair Pass

- **Hector Gorge,** north of Kootenay Crossing

- **Numa Falls,** where the Vermilion River tumbles over exposed bedrock

MARBLE CANYON AND THE PAINT POTS
Get a close-up look at two different natural features—Marble Canyon, an ice-carved, marble-streaked canyon, and

Numa Falls

the Paint Pots, circular ponds stained red, orange, and yellow by oxide-bearing springs—by following short trails that can both be completed in an hour or less.

STANLEY GLACIER
If you have a bit more time, hike up to Stanley Glacier (4.2 km/2.6 mi one-way), which will take around three hours round-trip. The stunning views are worth every step.

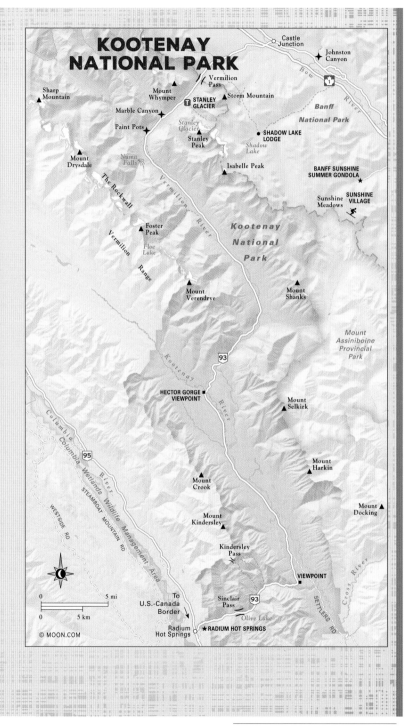

KOOTENAY NATIONAL PARK

Castle Junction

Johnston Canyon

Sharp Mountain

Mount Whymper

Vermilion Pass

Storm Mountain

Marble Canyon

STANLEY GLACIER

Banff National Park

Paint Pots

Stanley Glacier

Bow River

Stanley Peak

SHADOW LAKE LODGE

Shadow Lake

Mount Drysdale

Numa Falls

Isabelle Peak

BANFF SUNSHINE SUMMER GONDOLA

The Rockwall

Vermilion River

Kootenay National Park

Sunshine Meadows

SUNSHINE VILLAGE

Foster Peak

Floe Lake

Vermilion Range

Mount Verendrye

Mount Shanks

Mount Assiniboine Provincial Park

Kootenay River

93

HECTOR GORGE VIEWPOINT

Mount Selkirk

Columbia River

Columbia Wetlands Wildlife Management Area

95

Mount Harkin

STEAMBOAT MOUNTAIN RD.

WESTSIDE RD.

Mount Crook

Mount Docking

Mount Kindersley

Kindersley Pass

VIEWPOINT

Cross River

SETTLERS RD.

0   5 mi

0   5 km

To U.S.-Canada Border

Sinclair Pass

93

Olive Lake

© MOON.COM

Radium Hot Springs

★ RADIUM HOT SPRINGS

BANFF CYCLE
Cascade Shops, 317 Banff Ave., Banff; 403/985-4848; www.banffcycle.com; summer only

BANFF ADVENTURES UNLIMITED
211 Bear St., Banff; 403/762-4554; www. banffadventures.com

BACTRAX
225 Bear St., Banff; 403/762-8177; https://snowtips-bactrax.com

PADDLING

BOW RIVER
On a quiet stretch of the Bow River at the north end of Wolf Street, **Banff Canoe Club** (403/762-5005; www. banffcanoeclub.com; 9am-9pm daily mid-June-Sept.; C$55 one hour, C$30 each additional hour) rents canoes and paddleboards. From here you can paddle upstream, or along Echo Creek to First Vermilion Lake. It's an extremely peaceful way to leave the bustle of Banff behind, especially the Echo Creek option, where beavers are often spotted at dusk.

WINTER SPORTS

From November to May, the entire park transforms itself into a winter playground covered in a blanket of snow. Three world-class winter resorts are in Banff National Park.

DOWNHILL SKIING
Apart from an abundance of snow, the resorts in Banff National Park have something else in common—spectacular views, which alone are worth the price of a lift ticket. Although the resorts operate independently, the **Ski Big3 Adventure Hub** (114 Banff Ave.; 403/762-4754; www.skibig3.com; 8am-9pm daily) represents all three and is the place to get information on multiday ticketing and transportation.

Norquay
403/762-4421; www.banffnorquay. com; mid-Nov.-mid-Apr.; lift tickets adult C$115, youth and senior C$87, child C$45
Norquay is a small but steep hill overlooking the town of Banff. There are some great cruising runs and a well-respected ski school, but also the experts-only North American Chair (the one you can see from town), which opens up the famous double-black-diamond Lone Pine run. A magnificent post-and-beam day lodge nestled below the main runs is flanked on one side by a wide deck that catches the afternoon sun, while holding a cafeteria, restaurant, and bar inside. A shuttle bus makes pickups from Banff hotels for the short 6-km (3.7-mi) ride up to the resort.

Sunshine Village
403/762-6500 or 877/542-2633; www.skibanff.com; late Nov.-late

May; day passes adult C$156, senior and youth C$120, child C$60

Perched high in the mountains on the Continental Divide, Sunshine Village has lots going for it—more than 6 m (20 ft) of snow annually, wide-open bowls, a season stretching for nearly 200 days, North America's only heated chairlift, and the only slope-side accommodations in the park. Aside from the infamous experts-only Delirium Dive, the area is best known for its excellent beginner and intermediate terrain. The total vertical rise is 1,070 m (3,510 ft), and the longest run (down to the lower parking lot) is 8 km (5 mi).

Lake Louise Ski Resort
403/522-3555 or 877/253-6888; www.skilouise.com; Nov.-early May; lift tickets adult C$154, senior and youth C$119, child C$60

The Lake Louise Resort, Canada's second-largest ski resort, comprises 1,700 ha (4,200 acres) of gentle trails, mogul fields, long cruising runs, steep chutes, and vast bowls filled with famous Rocky Mountain powder.

The resort, which has more than 100 named runs, spreads over four distinct mountain faces. The front side has a vertical drop of 1,000 m (3,280 ft) and is served by eight lifts, including four high-speed quads and western Canada's only six-passenger chairlift.

Free shuttle buses run regularly from Banff and Lake Louise accommodations to the hill.

Rentals and Sales
Each resort has ski and snowboard rental and sales facilities, but getting your gear down in town is often easier. Basic rental packages—skis, poles, and boots—are C$50-60 per day, while high-performance packages range C$70-100. Snowboards and boots rent for C$50-70 per day.

MONOD SPORTS
129 Banff Ave., Banff; 403/762-4571; www.monodsports.com

RUDE BOYS
Snowboards only; 205 Caribou St., Banff; 403/762-8211; www.rudeboys.com

ICE-SKATING
Of all the ice-skating rinks in Canada, the one on frozen **Lake Louise,** in front of the château, is surely the most spectacular. Spotlights allow skating after dark. The rink is generally open mid-December-mid-April.

BANFF NATIONAL PARK FOOD

NAME	ADDRESS	TYPE
TOWN OF BANFF		
Nesters Market	122 Bear St., Banff	grocery
Whitebark	Banff Aspen Lodge, 401 Banff Ave., Banff	café
Melissa's	201 Banff Ave., Banff	restaurant/bar
★ **Park**	219 Banff Ave., Banff	sit-down restaurant
Maple Leaf	137 Banff Ave., Banff	sit-down restaurant
Balkan	120 Banff Ave., Banff	sit-down restaurant
Grizzly House	207 Banff Ave., Banff	sit-down restaurant
Hankki	208 Buffalo St., Banff	sit-down restaurant
★ **Rundle Patio**	Fairmont Banff Springs	sit-down restaurant
Bluebird	218 Lynx St., Banff	sit-down restaurant
Coyotes	206 Caribou St.	sit-down restaurant
★ **Cliffhouse Bistro**	Mt. Norquay Rd.	sit-down restaurant
BOW VALLEY PARKWAY		
★ **Storm Mountain Lodge**	Hwy 93, off Bow Valley Parkway	sit-down restaurant
LAKE LOUISE		
★ **Laggan's Mountain Bakery**	Samson Mall, Lake Louise	café
Bill Peyto's Café	HI-Lake Louise Alpine Centre, 203 Village Rd., Lake Louise	sit-down restaurant
Post Hotel	200 Pipestone Dr., Lake Louise	sit-down restaurant
The Station Restaurant	200 Sentinel Rd., Lake Louise	sit-down restaurant
Fairview Bar and Restaurant	Fairmont Chateau Lake Louise	sit-down restaurant

FOOD	PRICE	HOURS
groceries	budget	8am-11pm daily in summer, shorter hours the rest of the year
coffee and baked goods	budget	6:30am-6pm daily
classic North American	moderate	8am-2am daily
classic Canadian	moderate	11:30am-10pm daily
contemporary Canadian	splurge	10am-10pm daily
European	moderate	11:30am-9pm Sun.-Thurs., 11:30am-10pm Fri.-Sat.
fondue	splurge	11:30am-10pm daily
Korean	budget	11:30am-9pm daily
Canadian	moderate	11:30am-sunset daily
steakhouse	splurge	5-9pm daily
Southwestern	moderate	8am-9pm daily
contemporary Canadian	moderate	mid-June-early Oct. 11am-6pm daily
classic Canadian	moderate	5-8:30pm daily May-mid-Oct., 5-8:30pm Fri.-Sun. early Dec.-Apr.
coffee and baked goods	budget	7am-7pm daily, until 5pm outside summer
casual	moderate	7:30am-9:30pm daily
European	splurge	6:30-10pm daily
Canadian	splurge	11:30am-2pm and 5-9pm daily
Canadian	splurge	5:30-10pm daily

FOOD

Whether you're in search of an inexpensive snack for the family or silver service, you can find it in the town of Banff, which has more than 80 restaurants (more per capita than any other town or city across Canada). The quality of food and service varies greatly. Some restaurants revolve solely around the tourist trade, while others have reputations that attract diners from Calgary who have been known to stay overnight just to eat at their favorite haunt.

Around Lake Louise, there are good dining options serving all budgets.

STANDOUTS

Park
219 Banff Ave., Banff; 403/762-5114; www.parkdistillery.com; 11:30am-10pm daily; C$24-69
Park does a wonderful job of combining classic campfire cooking with modern dining trends—all within a massive space in the heart of downtown that perfectly reflects the food and the history of the park, with a massive stone fireplace and seating choices that include a balcony overlooking Banff Avenue and communal tables beside the open kitchen. Many of the dishes are cooked over a wood-fired grill or on a rotisserie, creating deliciously smoky campfire-like flavors: You could start with rotisserie chicken chowder or corn bread smothered in maple-rum butter, and then choose from mains such as pork-and-beans or AAA T-bone. Craft beers and house-distilled spirits round out this excellent choice.

Rundle Patio
Fairmont Banff Springs, 405 Spray Ave., Banff; 403/762-6860; www.fairmont.com/banff-springs; 11am-sunset daily summer; C$22-35
The Rundle Patio is an outdoor dining space that features magnificent views down the Bow Valley. The menu is filled with dishes that are perfect to share, but you can also simply kick back with a drink from the extensive wine list.

Cliffhouse Bistro
Mount Norquay Rd., 6 km (3.7 mi) from downtown Banff; 403/762-4421; www.banffnorquay.com;

Cascade Ponds Day Use Area (left); Lake Minnewanka Day Use Area (right)

mid-June-early Oct. 11am-6pm daily; lunches C$18-30

For something unique, plan on riding the chairlift at Norquay to the Cliff-house Bistro. Access is by chairlift (adult C$45, child C$28) to a 1950s stone building that has been creatively revamped to bring back its vintage glory, complete with views across the Bow Valley and a log fireplace. You can enjoy the panorama over tea or coffee, or order lunches such as panini, salads, and nachos to share.

Storm Mountain Lodge
Hwy 93; 403/762-4155; https:// stormmountainlodge.com/cuisine; 5-8:30pm daily May-mid-Oct. and 5-8:30pm Fri.-Sun. early Dec.-Apr.; C$26-59

The food at Storm Mountain Lodge is excellent, but it's the ambience you'll remember—an intoxicating blend of historic appeal and rustic mountain charm. The chef uses mostly organic produce with seasonally available game and seafood—bison, venison, wild salmon, and the like—to create tasty and interesting dishes well suited to the I-must-be-in-the-Canadian-wilderness surroundings. Storm Mountain Lodge is a 25-minute drive northwest from Banff; take the Trans-Canada Highway toward Lake Louise and head west at the Castle Mountain interchange.

Laggan's Mountain Bakery
Samson Mall, 101 Village Rd., Lake Louise; 403/552-2017; www.laggans. com; 7am-7pm daily, until 4pm outside of summer; lunches C$8-12

If you don't feel like a cooked breakfast, start your day off at Laggan's Mountain Bakery, *the* place to hang out with a coffee and a freshly baked breakfast croissant, pastry, cake, or muffin. The chocolate brownie is delicious (order two slices to save having to line up twice). If the few tables are full, order takeout and enjoy your meal on the riverbank behind the mall.

BEST PICNIC SPOTS
Cascade Ponds Day Use Area
Lake Minnewanka Rd., 4 km (2.5 mi) north of downtown Banff

Picnic tables, many with firepits (wood supplied), ring the shoreline at Cascade Ponds, but as the closest day-use area to downtown Banff, it gets busy.

Two Jack Lake Day Use Area
Lake Minnewanka Rd., 8 km (5 mi) north of downtown Banff

This is another very popular day-use area close to town, and tables here are in high demand on summer weekends, but the views across the lake to Mount Rundle are stunning.

Lake Minnewanka Day Use Area
Lake Minnewanka Rd., 6.4 km (4 mi) north of downtown Banff

One of Banff's largest day-use areas is along the rocky shoreline of Lake Minnewanka, although the farthest tables are a 10-minute walk from the parking lot. Fire grills and wood are supplied.

Johnson Lake Day Use Area
Lake Minnewanka Rd., 9.7 km (6 mi) north of downtown Banff

If you hear locals talk about going to the "beach," they are probably referring to Johnson Lake, with relatively warm water for swimming. If the picnic tables are full, there's room to spread out a blanket on the grassy slope.

Storm Mountain Viewpoint Day Use Area

Bow Valley Parkway, 3.7 km (2.3 mi) north of Castle Junction

As the Bow Valley Parkway crests a ridge just north of Castle Junction, it passes a viewpoint that doubles as a day-use area, with a few picnic tables ideally located to catch sweeping views across the Bow Valley to Storm Mountain.

Fairview Day Use Area

Lake Louise Dr., between the village and lake

Most visitors to Lake Louise looking to enjoy a picnic do so along the lakeshore. The only official day-use area is nestled in a subalpine forest along the road leading up to the lake.

CAMPING

Within Banff National Park, 13 auto-accessible campgrounds (5 on Icefields Parkway) hold more than 2,400 sites. Although the town of Banff has five of these facilities with more than 1,500 sites in its immediate vicinity, you should make reservations well in advance. The three largest campgrounds are strung out over 1.4 km (0.9 mi) along Tunnel Mountain Road, with the nearest sites 2.6 km (1.6 mi) from town.

Open fires are permitted in designated areas throughout most campgrounds, but you must purchase a firewood permit (C$9.80 per site per night) to burn wood, which is provided at no cost.

Reservations

Sites at most campgrounds can be reserved through the **Parks Canada Reservation Service** (877/737-3783; https://reservation.pc.gc.ca) starting early in the year (check the website for reservation opening dates), and it's strongly recommended that you do reserve if you require electrical hookups or want to stay at one of the more popular campgrounds, such as Two Jack Lakeside (a campground notorious for having every site booked for the entire season within minutes of the reservation system opening).

Tips

If you missed out on reserving a site in the vicinity of Banff or Lake Louise, neighboring Kootenay and Yoho National Parks have campgrounds, although in most cases you will still need reservations.

Two Jack Lakeside Campground

STANDOUTS
Two Jack Lakeside Campground
late May-early Oct.; C$30

Along Lake Minnewanka Road northeast of town are two campgrounds offering fewer services than the others, but with sites that offer more privacy. The pick of the two is Two Jack Lakeside Campground, for which you will need advance reservations. It features 74 sites tucked into trees at the south end of Two Jack Lake, popular for canoeing, kayaking, and paddleboarding. Facilities include hot showers, kitchen shelters, drinking water, and flush toilets.

It's just over 6 km (3.7 mi) from the Trans-Canada Highway underpass.

Lake Louise Campground
serviced section year-round, unserviced section June-Sept.; C$35 serviced site, C$30 unserviced site

Exit the Trans-Canada Highway at the Lake Louise interchange, 56 km (35 mi) northwest of Banff, and take the first left beyond Samson Mall and under the railway bridge to reach Lake Louise Campground, within easy walking distance of the village. The campground is divided into two sections by the Bow River but is linked by the Bow River Loop hiking trail that leads into the village along either side of the river. Individual sites

BANFF NATIONAL PARK CAMPGROUNDS

NAME	LOCATION	SEASON
Tunnel Mountain Village I Campground	east of downtown Banff	mid–May–early Oct.
Tunnel Mountain Village II Campground	east of downtown Banff	year-round
Tunnel Mountain Trailer Court	east of downtown Banff	mid–May–early Oct.
★ Two Jack Lakeside Campground	Lake Minnewanka Road	late May–early-Oct.
Two Jack Main Campground	Lake Minnewanka Road	late June–mid-Sept.
Johnston Canyon Campground	Bow Valley Parkway	late June–mid-Sept.
Castle Mountain Campground	Bow Valley Parkway	mid–May–Aug.
★ Lake Louise Campground	Lake Louise	serviced section year-round, unserviced section June-Sept.

SITES AND AMENITIES	RV LIMIT	PRICE	RESERVATIONS
618 tent sites, drinking water, flush toilets, showers, dump station	n/a	C$30	yes
209 tent and RV sites, drinking water, flush toilets, showers, dump station, electrical hookups	no limit	C$35–40	yes
322 tent and RV sites, drinking water, flush toilets, showers, dump station, electrical hookups	no limit	C$40	yes
74 tent sites, drinking water, flush toilets, showers	n/a	C$30	yes
380 tent and RV sites, drinking water, flush toilets, showers, dump station	RVs up to 8 m (27 ft)	C$23	yes
132 tent and RV sites, drinking water, flush toilets, showers, dump station	RVs up to 8 m (27 ft)	C$29	yes
43 tent and RV sites, drinking water, flush toilets	RVs up to 7.3 m (24 ft)	C$23	no
395 tent and RV sites, drinking water, flush toilets, showers, dump station, electrical hookups (serviced section)	no limit	C$35 serviced sites, C$30 tents	yes

BANFF NATIONAL PARK LODGING

NAME	ADDRESS
TOWN OF BANFF	
★ Brewster's Mountain Lodge	208 Caribou St., Banff
Banff Ptarmigan Inn	337 Banff Ave., Banff
Moose Hotel & Suites	345 Banff Ave., Banff
Banff Aspen Lodge	401 Banff Ave., Banff
High Country Inn	419 Banff Ave,. Banff
Samesun Banff	433 Banff Ave., Banff
Rundlestone Lodge	537 Banff Ave., Banff
HI-Banff Alpine Centre	801 Hidden Ridge Way, Banff
Douglas Fir Resort	525 Tunnel Mountain Rd., Banff
★ Fairmont Banff Springs	405 Spray Ave., Banff
BOW VALLEY PARKWAY	
Johnston Canyon Resort	Bow Valley Parkway
Baker Creek by Basecamp	Bow Valley Parkway
★ Storm Mountain Lodge	Hwy 93, off Bow Valley Parkway
LAKE LOUISE	
HI-Lake Louise Alpine Centre	203 Village Rd., Lake Louise
★ Post Hotel	200 Pipestone Dr., Lake Louise
★ Paradise Lodge and Bungalows	105 Lake Louise Dr., Lake Louise
Deer Lodge	109 Lake Louise Dr., Lake Louise

SEASON	OPTIONS	PRICE
year-round	hotel rooms; loft suites	rooms starting at C$450
year-round	hotel rooms	rooms starting at C$480
year-round	one- and two-bedroom suites	suites starting at C$500
year-round	hotel rooms	rooms starting at C$380
year-round	hotel rooms	rooms starting at C$350
year-round	dormitory rooms (some women-only rooms)	dorm C$50-60, $240 s or d
year-round	hotel rooms	rooms starting at C$420
year-round	two-, four-, and six-bed dormitory rooms; four-bed cabins	nonmember dorm C$55-65, nonmember private room starting at C$220
year-round	condo-style units	units starting at C$400
year-round	hotel rooms	rooms starting at C$1,200
mid-May-early Oct.	cabins, some with kitchens	cabins starting at C$420
year-round	cabins with kitchens suites	cabins starting at C$700
year-round (closed Mon.-Wed. in fall)	cabins	cabins starting at C$370
year-round	dormitory rooms with 4-5 beds; private rooms	nonmember dorm C$62-75, nonmember private room from C$240
year-round	bungalow-style rooms, some with kitchens	rooms starting at C$600
mid-May-early Oct.	cabins, some with kitchens; suites	cabins starting at C$610
year-round	hotel rooms	rooms starting at C$390

NAME	ADDRESS
★ Fairmont Chateau Lake Louise	111 Lake Louise Dr., Lake Louise
MORAINE LAKE	
Moraine Lake Lodge	Moraine Lake Rd.

throughout are close together, but some privacy and shade are provided by towering lodgepole pines. Just under 200 serviced (powered) sites are grouped together at the end of the road; this section also has showers and flush toilets. Across the river are 216 unserviced sites, each with a fire ring and picnic table. Amenities include kitchen shelters and a modern bathroom complex with hot showers. A dump station is near the entrance to the campground (C$8 per use).

LODGING

Finding a room in Banff National Park in summer is nearly as hard as trying to justify its price. By late afternoon, just about every room in the park will be occupied, and basic hotel rooms start at almost C$500. It

Fairmont Banff Springs

SEASON	OPTIONS	PRICE
year-round	hotel rooms	rooms starting at C$1,200
June-Sept.	hotel rooms	rooms starting at C$1,400

is also worth noting that prices vary according to demand. The park's off-season is October-May, and hotels offer rate reductions during this period. Shop around, and you may find a bargain.

In summer, accommodations at Lake Louise are even harder to come by than in Banff, so it's essential to make reservations well in advance.

All rates quoted are for a standard room in the high season (June-Sept.). Rooms have en suite bathrooms, unless otherwise indicated.

Reservations
In July and August and during the Christmas holidays, you should make reservations as far in advance as possible. Contact hotels directly for the best rates.

Tips
Hotel rooms in **Canmore,** a 20-minute drive east of Banff, are significantly less expensive than within the park.

STANDOUTS
Town of Banff
BREWSTER'S MOUNTAIN LODGE
208 Caribou St., Banff; 403/762-2900 or 888/762-2900; www.brewstermountainlodge.com; C$450-600 s or d
More than 100 years since Jim and Bill Brewster guided their first guests through the park, their descendants are still actively involved in the tourist industry, operating the central and very stylish Brewster's Mountain Lodge. The building features an eye-catching log exterior with an equally impressive lobby. The Western theme is continued in the 77 upstairs rooms. Standard rooms feature two queen-size beds, deluxe rooms offer a jetted tub and sitting area, and loft suites are designed for families. Packages provide good value here, while off-season rates are slashed up to 60 percent.

FAIRMONT BANFF SPRINGS
405 Spray Ave., Banff; 403/762-2211; www.fairmont.com; starting at C$1,200 s or d
The 739-room Fairmont Banff Springs is Banff's best-known accommodation. Earlier this century, the hotel came under the ownership of Fairmont Hotels and Resorts, losing its century-old tag as a Canadian Pacific hotel and in the process its ties to the historic railway company that constructed the original hotel back in 1888. Even though the rooms have been modernized, many date to the 1920s, and as is common in older establishments, these accommodations are small. But room size is only a minor

Post Hotel

with a log bed, covered deck, a wood-burning fireplace, and bathroom with claw-foot tub. They don't have phones, internet, or TVs, so there's little to distract you from the past. Look for fall and spring deals that include a breakfast and dinner for around the room-only price in summer. Outside, the wilderness beckons, with Storm Mountain as a backdrop. The lodge is at Vermilion Pass, a 25-minute drive from Banff or Lake Louise (head west from the Castle Mountain interchange).

Lake Louise
POST HOTEL
200 Pipestone Dr., Lake Louise Village; 403/522-3989 or 800/661-1586; www.posthotel.com; C$600-1,200 s or d
Originally called Lake Louise Ski Lodge, the Post Hotel is one of only a handful of Canadian accommodations that have been accepted into the prestigious Relais & Châteaux organization. Bordered to the east and south by the Pipestone River, it may lack views of Lake Louise, but it is as elegant—in a modern, woodsy way—as the château. Each bungalow-style room is furnished with Canadian pine and has a balcony. Many rooms have whirlpools and fireplaces, while some have kitchens. Other facilities include the upscale Temple Mountain Spa, an indoor pool, a steam room, and a library. The hotel has 17 different room types, with 26 different rates depending on the view. Between the main lodge and the Pipestone River are four sought-after cabins, each with a wood-burning fireplace.

PARADISE LODGE AND BUNGALOWS
105 Lake Louise Dr., Lake Louise; 403/522-3595; www.paradiselodge.

consideration when staying in this historic gem. With 12 eateries, four lounges, a luxurious spa facility, an indoor pool, elegant public spaces, a 27-hole golf course, tennis courts, horseback riding, and enough twisting, turning hallways, towers, and shops to warrant a detailed map, you'll not want to spend much time in your room. (Unless, of course, you are in the top floor Crown Suite.) During summer, rack rates for a regular room are C$1,200, discounted to around C$700 or less the rest of the year. Many summer visitors stay as part of a package—the place to find these is on the website www.fairmont.com. Packages may simply include breakfast, while others will have you golfing, horseback riding, or relaxing in the spa.

Bow Valley Parkway
STORM MOUNTAIN LODGE
Hwy. 93; 403/762-4155; https://stormmountainlodge.com; daily, Thurs.-Mon. in fall; C$370-500 s or d
Constructed by the Canadian Pacific Railway in 1922, Storm Mountain Lodge features 14 historic cabins restored to their former rustic glory. Each has its original log walls, along

com; mid-May-early Oct.; starting at C$610 s or d

This family-operated lodge provides outstanding value in a wonderfully tranquil setting. Spread out around well-manicured gardens are 21 attractive cabins in four configurations. Each has a rustic yet warm and inviting interior, with comfortable beds, a separate sitting area, and an en suite bathroom. Each cabin has a small fridge, microwave, and coffeemaker, while the larger ones have full kitchens and separate bedrooms. Instead of television, children are kept happy with a playground that includes a sandbox and jungle gym. The least-expensive cabins, complete with a classic cast-iron stove/fireplace combo, are C$610 s or d, or pay C$720 for a cabin with a big deck and sweeping valley views. Twenty-four luxury suites, each with a fireplace, TV, one or two bedrooms, and fabulous mountain views, start at C$620, or C$700 with a kitchen. To get there from the valley floor, follow Lake Louise Drive toward the Fairmont Chateau Lake Louise for 3.1 km (1.9 mi); the lake itself is just 1 km (0.6 mi) farther up the hill.

FAIRMONT CHATEAU LAKE LOUISE

111 Lake Louise Dr., Lake Louise; 403/522-3511 or 866/540-4413; www. fairmont.com; starting at C$1,200

The famously fabulous Fairmont Chateau Lake Louise, a historic 539-room hotel on the shore of Lake Louise, has views equal to any mountain resort in the world. But all this historic charm and mountain scenery come at a price. Official rates drop as low as C$600 s or d outside of summer, with accommodation and ski pass packages sometimes advertised for around C$700 d. Children younger than 18 sharing with parents are free, but if you bring a pet, it'll be an extra C$60.

Fairmont Chateau Lake Louise

INFORMATION AND SERVICES

Service Hubs

Banff

The town of Banff is a bustling commercial center within the boundaries of Banff National Park, where travelers can find services and supplies.

Lake Louise

The community of Lake Louise is another hub for services within the park.

Entrance Gate

The main fee station is located on the eastern approach to the park. Heading to Banff from Calgary, the Trans-Canada Highway passes through the town of Canmore, then enters the park, where tollbooths are open 24 hours daily year-round.

Visitor Centers

Banff Visitor Centre

224 Banff Ave.; 8am-8pm daily June-Aug., 9am-5pm daily Sept.-May
Many sources of information are available in the park and its commercial facilities. Once you've arrived, the best place to make your first stop is the Banff Visitor Centre. This central complex houses information desks for Parks Canada (403/762-1550) and Banff Lake Louise Tourism (403/762-0270), as well as a retail outlet that stocks guidebooks, maps, and bear spray.

Lake Louise Visitor Centre

403/522-3833; 9am-7pm daily early June-Aug., 9am-5pm daily rest of year
Lake Louise Visitor Centre is beside Samson Mall on Village Road in the heart of Lake Louise Village. This excellent Parks Canada facility has interpretive exhibits, slide and video displays, and staff on hand

to answer questions, recommend hikes suited to your ability, and help you out with transit and parking queries.

TRANSPORTATION

Getting There

Air

Calgary International Airport (YYC), 129 km (80 mi) east, is the closest airport to Banff National Park. To get to the town of Banff, drive west on the Trans-Canada Highway; allow 90 minutes for the trip.

Another option is **Vancouver International Airport** (YVR), which is larger, but farther away. From Vancouver, the drive to Lake Louise is approximately 779 km (484 mi) east along the Trans-Canada Highway and takes about 10 hours.

From Glacier National Park

If you find yourself at **West Glacier,** on the park's west side, the quickest way to get to Banff is to head north on Highway 93 to the U.S.-Canada border; from there it's 430 km (267 mi) to Banff along Highway 93/95 via Cranbrook and Kootenay National Park. From West Glacier, allow six hours.

From **St. Mary,** on the east side of Glacier National Park, the most direct route to Banff National Park is to take Highway 2 north to Calgary (3 hours) and then to head west on the Trans-Canada Highway. The total distance between St. Mary and Banff is 420 km (260 mi); allow 4.5 hours.

From Jasper National Park

From Jasper in the north, the Icefields Parkway leads 230 km (143 mi) south to Lake Louise; allow around 3.5 hours for the drive. To get from Jasper to the town of Banff, the drive is 286 km (178 mi) total and takes at least four hours. Driving times can vary given the speed restrictions and often heavy traffic on this route.

Between Banff and Lake Louise

The community of Lake Louise is beside the Trans-Canada Highway 56 km (35 mi) northwest of Banff. The drive takes about 50 minutes.

Gas and Charging Stations

Gas stations are scattered through the town of Banff, including **Husky** (601 Banff Ave.; 24 hours daily) a little northeast of downtown. Charging stations are at some hotels and beside the Banff Visitor Centre. Lake Louise also has two gas stations and charging stations at the Lake Louise Ski Resort.

Parking

The downtown core of Banff is busy year-round, but especially so between late June and early September after 10am. If you're staying in a hotel along Banff Avenue or on Tunnel Mountain, don't drive into town—**walk** or catch a **Banff Transit bus** (check www.roamtransit.com for a schedule).

If you do drive into downtown, don't let not finding a parking spot on Banff Avenue ruin your holiday. Head to the **Fenlands Banff Recreation Centre** on Mount Norquay Road, the large parking lot on the east side of the Banff Railway Station, or the **parking garage** at the corner of Bear and Lynx Streets. Paid parking is in effect year-round throughout downtown.

For travelers with **RVs** or **trailers,** finding a downtown parking spot can be a challenge. If you must bring your rig into town, try the RV-only parking spots on Railway Avenue opposite the railway station and at the corner of Lynx and Wolf Streets.

The website **www.banffparking. ca** is an excellent resource that includes real-time updates of various parking areas, including the number of empty stalls at parking lots through town.

Lake Louise is very busy year-round; paid parking is in effect throughout summer, but a much easier option than trying to find parking is to catch a shuttle (see below). Moraine Lake Road is closed to personal vehicles year-round. The only access is via the shuttles discussed below, by commercial tour bus, or for guests staying at Moraine Lake Lodge.

Buses and Shuttles

Parks Canada Shuttles

In summer and fall, Parks Canada operates buses from the **Park & Ride** at the Lake Louise Ski Resort, across the valley from the lake. Buses leave from here for Lake Louise itself and Moraine Lake, with a connector bus linking the two lakes. Shuttles operate continuously between 8am and 6pm, with earlier departures at the busiest times of year. The round-trip fare to either destination is adult C$10, senior or child C$5. For reservations go to https://reservation.pc.gc.ca; for more information, visit www.https://parks.canada.ca/banffnow.

Roam Transit

403/762-0606; https://roamtransit.com; C$2-10 per sector

Roam Transit operates bus service along two routes through the town of Banff: one from the Banff Gondola north along Banff Avenue, the other from the Fairmont Banff Springs to the Tunnel Mountain campgrounds. Roam buses also run out to Lake Minnewanka, Canmore, and Lake Louise and Moraine Lake (summer only). Reservations are required for routes to Lake Louise and Moraine Lake, and you should make these well in advance in summer and fall.

Icefields Parkway

ICEFIELDS PARKWAY

The 230-km (143-mi) Icefields Parkway between Lake Louise and Jasper is one of the most scenic, exciting, and inspiring mountain roads ever built. From Lake Louise this paved route parallels the Continental Divide, following in the shadow of the highest, most rugged mountains in the Canadian Rockies. The first 122 km (76 mi) to Sunwapta Pass—the boundary between Banff and Jasper National Parks—can be driven in two hours, and the entire parkway in under four hours. But it's likely you'll want to spend at least a day, probably more, stopping at each of the 13 viewpoints, hiking the trails, watching the abundant wildlife, and just generally enjoying one of the world's most magnificent landscapes.

The parkway remains open year-round, although winter brings with it some special considerations. The road is often closed for short periods for avalanche control. Check road conditions before setting out. And be sure to fill up with gas; no services are available between November and April.

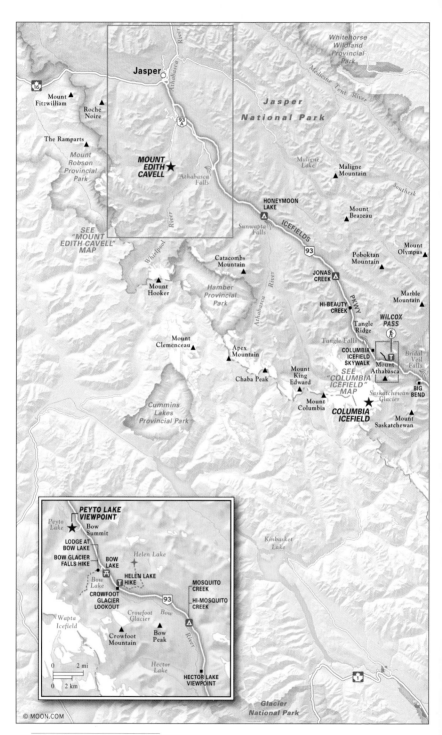

Jasper

Jasper
National Park

Whitehorse
Wildland
Provincial
Park

Mount
Fitzwilliam

Roche
Noire

The Ramparts

Mount
Robson
Provincial
Park

MOUNT
EDITH
CAVELL

Athabasca
Falls

SEE
"MOUNT
EDITH
CAVELL"
MAP

Maligne
Lake

Maligne
Mountain

Mount
Brazeau

HONEYMOON
LAKE

ICEFIELDS

Sunwapta
Falls

Catacombs
Mountain

Hamber
Provincial
Park

Athabasca

River

Poboktan
Mountain

Mount
Olympus

JONAS
CREEK

Mount
Hooker

Whirlpool

River

HI-BEAUTY
CREEK

PKWY

Tangle
Ridge

Marble
Mountain

WILCOX
PASS

Tangle Falls

Mount
Clemenceau

Apex
Mountain

COLUMBIA
ICEFIELD
SKYWALK

Bridal
Veil
Falls

SEE
"COLUMBIA
ICEFIELD"
MAP

Mount
Athabasca

Chaba Peak

Mount
King
Edward

Cummins
Lakes
Provincial
Park

BIG
BEND

Saskatchewan
Glacier

Mount
Columbia

COLUMBIA
ICEFIELD

Mount
Saskatchewan

Kimbasket
Lake

PEYTO LAKE
VIEWPOINT

Peyto
Lake

Bow
Summit

LODGE AT
BOW LAKE

Helen Lake

BOW GLACIER
FALLS HIKE

BOW
LAKE

Bow
Lake

HELEN LAKE
HIKE

MOSQUITO
CREEK

CROWFOOT
GLACIER
LOOKOUT

HI-MOSQUITO
CREEK

Wapta
Icefield

Crowfoot
Glacier

Bow

Crowfoot
Mountain

Bow
Peak

River

Hector Lake

0   2 mi

0   2 km

HECTOR LAKE
VIEWPOINT

Glacier
National Park

© MOON.COM

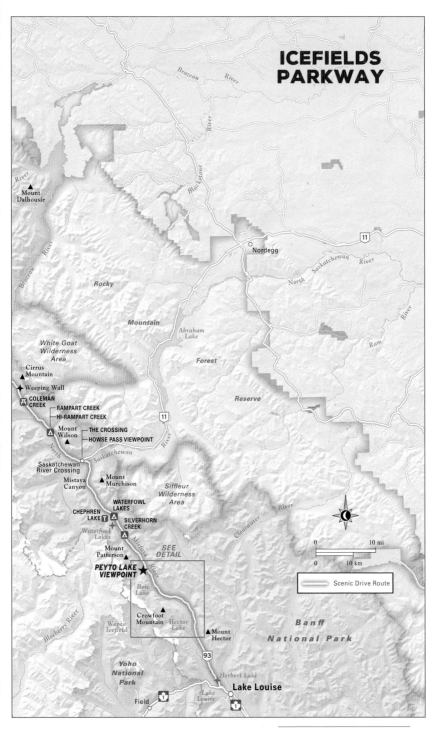

ICEFIELDS PARKWAY

Brazeau River

River

Blackstone River

11

Nordegg

North Saskatchewan River

Ram River

Rocky

Mountain

Abraham Lake

Forest

Reserve

River

White Goat Wilderness Area

Cirrus Mountain

Weeping Wall

COLEMAN CREEK

RAMPART CREEK
HI-RAMPART CREEK

Mount Wilson

THE CROSSING
HOWSE PASS VIEWPOINT

11

River

North Saskatchewan

Saskatchewan River Crossing

Mistaya Canyon

Mount Murchison

Siffleur Wilderness Area

WATERFOWL LAKES

CHEPHREN LAKE

SILVERHORN CREEK

Waterfowl Lakes

Clearwater River

Mount Patterson

SEE DETAIL

PEYTO LAKE VIEWPOINT

Mistaya River

Bow Lake

Banff

Blaeberry River

Wapta Icefield

Crowfoot Mountain

Hector Lake

Mount Hector

National Park

93

Yoho National Park

Herbert Lake

Field

1

Lake Louise

Lake Louise

0   10 mi
0   10 km

Scenic Drive Route

3

TOP 3

⭐ **1. PEYTO LAKE VIEWPOINT:** Hidden from the parkway, a short trail from Bow Summit leads to a wooden viewing deck overlooking this magnificent turquoise lake (page 192).

⭐ **2. COLUMBIA ICEFIELD:** Don't miss this glacial area at the southern end of Jasper National Park. Take the Ice Explorer tour to get a close-up view of this natural wonder (page 195).

⭐ **3. MOUNT EDITH CAVELL:** Although this peak is visible from various points, no vista is as memorable as that from its base, reachable by road from Highway 93A. For a neck-straining view, take the Cavell Meadows Trail (page 202).

2

ICEFIELDS PARKWAY 3 WAYS

HALF DAY

The Icefields Parkway is chock-full of highlights that can be seen from your vehicle, so it is possible to drive the route in a half-day, but I'd recommend longer if time allows. If your schedule does limit you to a half-day, leave early in the morning if possible to minimize the time spent crawling along in a long line of midday traffic. The following itinerary is from south to north.

1 **Bow Lake,** 35 km (22 mi) north of the Trans-Canada Highway, is a good first stop, and it only takes a few minutes to drink in the lake's stunning beauty.

2 Just up the road at Bow Summit, it's a 10-minute walk to a **viewing platform** high above **Peyto Lake.**

3 At the **Columbia Icefield,** 127 km (79 mi) north of the Trans-Canada Highway, the best way to soak up the ice-field-and-mountain panorama is from the outside viewing area at the Icefield Centre, which overlooks the Athabasca Glacier.

4 From the ice field, it's 105 km (65 mi) to Jasper. Even with a stop at roadside **Athabasca Falls,** the stretch takes a little under 90 minutes.

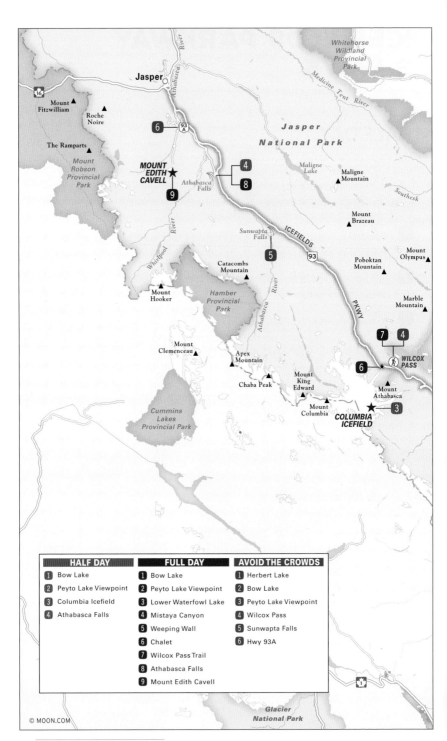

HALF DAY	**FULL DAY**	**AVOID THE CROWDS**
1 Bow Lake	1 Bow Lake	1 Herbert Lake
2 Peyto Lake Viewpoint	2 Peyto Lake Viewpoint	2 Bow Lake
3 Columbia Icefield	3 Lower Waterfowl Lake	3 Peyto Lake Viewpoint
4 Athabasca Falls	4 Mistaya Canyon	4 Wilcox Pass
	5 Weeping Wall	5 Sunwapta Falls
	6 Chalet	6 Hwy 93A
	7 Wilcox Pass Trail	
	8 Athabasca Falls	
	9 Mount Edith Cavell	

© MOON.COM

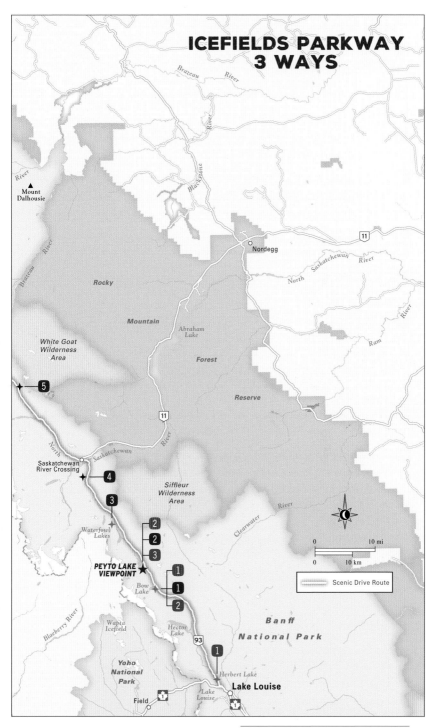

ICEFIELDS PARKWAY
3 WAYS

Mount
Dalhousie

11

Nordegg

Rocky

Mountain

Abraham
Lake

White Goat
Wilderness
Area

Forest

Reserve

5

11

Saskatchewan
River Crossing

4

Siffleur
Wilderness
Area

3

2

2

3

Waterfowl
Lakes

PEYTO LAKE
VIEWPOINT ★

1

1

2

Bow
Lake

Banff

National Park

Wapta
Icefield

Hector
Lake

93

1

Yoho
National
Park

Herbert Lake

Lake Louise

Field

Lake
Louise

1

0   10 mi

0   10 km

▨▨▨▨ Scenic Drive Route

FULL DAY

1 At **Bow Lake,** 35 km (22 mi) north of Lake Louise, park at the lake's north end and wander along the rocky shoreline to soak up the scene.

2 Your next stop should be **Peyto Lake Viewpoint,** a short drive beyond Bow Lake.

3 From there, stop at the roadside lookout beside **Lower Waterfowl Lake** to see its turquoise waters.

4 If you started out early, you'll have time for more stops before reaching the Columbia Icefield. **Mistaya Canyon,** where the Mistaya River squeezes between narrow walls, should be one of them.

5 The **Weeping Wall**—so called for its multiple waterfalls—is another top stop.

6 At the Columbia Icefield, have an early lunch at **Chalet,** dining outside if the weather is good.

7 The Columbia Icefield can be overwhelming, both for its size and the number of ways to spend your time. If you are a keen hiker, strike out on the **Wilcox Pass Trail.** Otherwise, if you'd like to get up close to a glacier, take an Ice Explorer tour out onto the Athabasca Glacier. Both these options take around three hours.

8 Stop at **Athabasca Falls** to appreciate the power of nature as water is forced over a narrow ledge and into a deep canyon.

9 From Athabasca Falls, it's an easy 32-km (20-mi) run to the end of the route at the town of Jasper, but it's worth the detour along Cavell Road to the base of **Mount Edith Cavell.** Allow 30 minutes to walk along the interpretive trail directly below this imposing peak.

AVOID THE CROWDS

Avoiding the crowds along the Icefields Parkway is more about when you travel the route rather than where you stop along the way. With the long days of summer, an early start from Banff or Lake Louise allows you to see the highlights along the parkway's south end, but after a few stops and a hike, the crowds will have caught up to you. You may not avoid the crowds completely, but you can at least minimize them by following this itinerary.

1 Depart Banff or Lake Louise at dawn and make your first stop **Herbert Lake,** which is often perfectly calm in the morning.

2 Continue north to **Bow Lake,** which is larger and has a more spectacular backdrop.

3 At Bow Summit, take the short trail to the **Peyto Lake Viewpoint.**

4 At the Columbia Icefield, hike to **Wilcox Pass** and take the side trail to Wilcox Ridge for panoramic views of the ice field. By the time you finish the three-hour hike, crowds will have descended on the Icefield Centre, but there are a few picnic tables scattered around the north end of the parking lot that are the perfect place for lunch.

5 Of the two major waterfalls you pass en route to Jasper, **Sunwapta Falls** is less crowded than Athabasca, but equally impressive.

6 For the final stretch to Jasper, the original Icefields Parkway (now known as **Hwy 93A**) is a quiet route on the west side of the Athabasca River.

HIGHLIGHTS AND BEST HIKES

LAKE LOUISE TO CROWFOOT GLACIER

The Icefields Parkway forks right from the Trans-Canada Highway just north of Lake Louise. The impressive scenery begins immediately.

Herbert Lake

Just 3.1 km (1.9 mi) from the junction is Herbert Lake, formed during the last ice age when retreating glaciers deposited a pile of rubble known as a *moraine* across a shallow valley and water filled in behind it. The lake is a perfect place for early-morning or early-evening photography, when the Waputik Range and distinctively shaped **Mount Temple** are reflected in its waters.

Mount Hector

Traveling north, you'll notice numerous depressions in the steep, shaded slopes of the Waputik Range across the Bow Valley. The cooler climate on these north-facing slopes makes them prone to glaciation. Cirques were cut by small local glaciers. On the opposite side of the road, Mount Hector (3,394 m/11,130 ft), easily recognized by its layered peak, soon comes into view.

Hector Lake Viewpoint

Hector Lake Viewpoint is 16.1 km (10 mi) from the junction. Although the lake itself is a long way from the highway, the emerald-green waters nestled below a massive wall of limestone form a breathtaking scene. **Bow Peak,** seen when looking northward along the highway, is only 2,868 m (9,410 ft) high but is completely detached from the Waputik Range, making it a popular destination for climbers.

CROWFOOT GLACIER AND BOW LAKE
Crowfoot Glacier Lookout

The aptly named Crowfoot Glacier can best be appreciated from a lookout 17 km (10.6 mi) north of Hector Lake Viewpoint. The glacier sits on a wide ledge near the top of Crowfoot Mountain, from where its glacial claws cling to the mountain's steep slopes. The retreat of this glacier has been dramatic. In the 1960s, two of the claws extended to the base of the lower cliff. Today they are a shadow of their former selves, barely reaching over the cliff edge.

Helen Lake Hike

DISTANCE: 6 km (3.7 mi) one-way
DURATION: 2.5 hours one-way
ELEVATION GAIN: 457 m (1,500 ft)
EFFORT: moderate
TRAIL SURFACE: unpaved
TRAILHEAD: across the Icefields Parkway from Crowfoot Glacier Lookout, 32 km (20 mi) northwest of the junction with the Trans-Canada Highway

The trail to Helen Lake is one of the easiest ways to access a true alpine environment from any highway within Banff National Park. The trail climbs steadily through a forest of Engelmann spruce and subalpine fir for the first 2.6 km (1.6 mi) to an avalanche slope, reaching the tree line and the first good viewpoint after 3.1 km (1.9 mi). The view across the valley is spectacular, with Crowfoot Glacier visible to the southwest. As the trail reaches a ridge, it turns sharply and passes through extensive meadows of wildflowers that are at their peak in late July and early August. The trail then crosses a stream and climbs to the glacial cirque where Helen Lake lies. Listen and look for hoary marmots along the last section of trail and around the lakeshore.

For those with the time and energy, it's possible to continue an additional 3.1 km (1.9 mi) to Dolomite Pass; the trail switchbacks steeply up 100 vertical m (330 vertical ft) in less than 1 km (0.6 mi), then descends an additional 1 km (0.6 mi) to Katherine Lake and beyond to the pass.

Bow Lake

The sparkling, translucent waters of Bow Lake, 1.9 km (1.2 mi) beyond Crowfoot Glacier Viewpoint, are among the most beautiful that can be seen from the Icefields Parkway. The lake was created when moraines deposited by retreating glaciers dammed subsequent meltwater. On still days, the water reflects the snowy peaks, their sheer cliffs, and the scree slopes that run into the lake. At the southeast end

Helen Lake Hike (top); Helen Lake (bottom)

WATERFALLS ALONG
THE ICEFIELDS PARKWAY

This route may be named for its ice fields and glaciers, but there are many easily reached waterfalls, including some that can be seen from the highway.

Tangle Falls

- **Bow Glacier Falls:** The view of this waterfall, from the north end of Bow Lake, 35.9 km (22.3 mi) along the parkway, puts the grandeur of the setting into perspective, as you can see its source, the Bow Glacier, high above.

- **Weeping Wall:** Water flow down an imposing cliff, 105.6 km (65.6 mi) north of the Trans-Canada Highway, stains the sheer limestone and gives this natural feature its interesting name.

- **Tangle Falls:** Famously photogenic, this waterfall plunges over slabs of 500-million-year-old limestone right beside the highway 8 km (5 mi) north of the Icefield Centre.

- **Sunwapta Falls:** Around 48 km (30 mi) north of the Icefield Centre, a short side road leads to Sunwapta Falls. Here, the Sunwapta River makes an abrupt turn and drops down a cliff, then flows through a narrow canyon.

- **Athabasca Falls:** Continuing north 22.5 km (14 mi) from Sunwapta, the Athabasca River thunders over a limestone ledge and funnels through a gorge. Viewpoints on both sides of the river add to the experience.

of the lake, a day-use area offers waterfront picnic tables and a trail to a swampy area at the lake's outlet. At the upper end of the lake, you'll find the historic **Lodge at Bow Lake** and the trailhead for a walk to **Bow Glacier Falls.**

BOW GLACIER FALLS HIKE
DISTANCE: 3.4 km (2.1 mi) one-way
DURATION: 1 hour one-way
ELEVATION GAIN: 130 m (430 ft)
EFFORT: easy
TRAIL SURFACE: unpaved
TRAILHEAD: Lodge at Bow Lake, 35.9 km (22.3 mi) northwest of the Trans-Canada Highway

This hike skirts one of the most beautiful lakes in the region before ending at a narrow but spectacular waterfall. From the public parking lot in front of the lodge, follow the shore through to a gravel outwash area at the northwest end of the lake. Across the lake are reflected views of Crowfoot Mountain. The trail then begins a short but steep climb up the rim of a canyon before leveling out at the edge of a vast moraine of gravel, scree, and boulders. Pick your way through the 800 m (0.5 mi) of rough ground that remains to reach the base of Bow Glacier Falls. (The namesake glacier can be seen above the falls from the trailhead, but not from the falls themselves.)

BOW SUMMIT

The road leaves Bow Lake and climbs to Bow Summit. As you look back toward the lake, its true turquoise color becomes apparent, and the Crowfoot Glacier reveals its unique shape. At an elevation of 2,069 m (6,790 ft), this pass is one of the highest points crossed by a public road in Canada. It is also the beginning of the **Bow River,** the one you may have camped beside at Lake Louise or photographed flowing through the town of Banff.

★ Peyto Lake Viewpoint

From the parking lot at Bow Summit, a paved trail leads 500 m (0.3 mi) to one of the most breathtaking views you could ever imagine. Far below the viewpoint is Peyto Lake, an impossibly intense green lake whose hues change according to season. Before heavy melting of nearby glaciers begins (in June or early July), the lake is dark blue. As summer progresses, meltwater flows across a delta and into the lake. This water is laden with finely ground particles of rock debris known as rock flour, which remains suspended in the water. It is not the mineral content of the rock flour that is responsible for the lake's unique color, but rather the particles reflecting the blue-green sector of the light spectrum. As the amount of suspended rock flour changes, so does the color of the lake.

The lake is one of many park landmarks named for early outfitter Bill Peyto. In 1898, Peyto was part of an expedition camped at Bow Lake. Seeking solitude (as he was wont to do), he slipped off during the night to sleep near this lake. Other members of the party coined the name Peyto's Lake, and it stuck.

BESIDE THE CONTINENTAL DIVIDE
Mount Patterson

From Bow Summit, the parkway descends to a **viewpoint** directly across the Mistaya River from Mount Patterson (3,197 m/10,490 ft). Snowbird Glacier clings precariously to the mountain's steep northeast face, and the mountain's lower, wooded slopes are heavily scarred where rock and ice slides have swept down the mountainside.

Upper Waterfowl Lake

A trail leads down to the shore of Upper Waterfowl Lake, providing one of the park's best opportunities to view moose, which feed on the abundant aquatic vegetation. Rock and other debris that have been carried down nearby valley systems have built up, forming a wide alluvial fan, nearly blocking the Mistaya River and creating Upper Waterfowl Lake.

Bow Glacier Falls

Lower Waterfowl Lake

Lower Waterfowl Lake, downstream and to the north of Upper Waterfowl Lake, gets all the attention for its beautiful turquoise hue. A small pullout along its shoreline is the best vantage point, although if you want to linger longer, the campground on the lake's southern shore is one of the best situated in Banff National Park.

Chephren Lake Hike

DISTANCE: 4 km (2.5 mi) one-way
DURATION: 60–90 minutes one-way
ELEVATION GAIN: 100 m (330 ft)
EFFORT: easy
TRAIL SURFACE: unpaved
TRAILHEAD: Waterfowl Lakes Campground, Icefields Parkway, 57 km (35 mi) northwest from the Trans-Canada Highway

This pale-green body of water (pronounced kef-ren) is hidden from the Icefields Parkway but easily reached. The official trailhead is a bridge across the Mistaya River at the back of Waterfowl Lakes Campground (behind site 86). If you're not registered at the campground, park at the end of the unpaved road running along the front of the campground and walk 300 m (0.2 mi) down the well-worn path to the river crossing. From across the river, the trail dives headlong into a subalpine forest, reaching a crudely signposted junction after 1.6 km (1 mi). Take the right fork. This leads 2.4 km (1.5 mi) to Chephren Lake, descending steeply at the end (this stretch of trail is often muddy). The lake is nestled under the buttresses of Mount Chephren. To the left, farther up the lake, is Howse Peak.

The trail to smaller **Cirque Lake** (4.5 km/2.8 mi from the trailhead) branches left 1.6 km (1 mi) along this trail. It is less heavily used, but this

lake is popular with anglers for its healthy population of rainbow trout.

Mount Murchison

Continuing north takes travelers to Mount Murchison (3,337 m/10,950 ft) on the east side of the parkway. Although not one of the park's highest mountains, this gray and yellow massif of Cambrian rock comprises 10 individual peaks, covering an area of 3,000 ha (7,400 acres).

Mistaya Canyon

From a parking lot 14.3 km (8.9 mi) northeast of Waterfowl Lakes Campground, a short trail descends into the montane forest to Mistaya Canyon. Here the effects of erosion can be appreciated as the Mistaya River leaves the floor of the Mistaya Valley, plunging through a narrow-walled canyon into the North Saskatchewan Valley. The area is scarred with potholes where boulders have been whirled around by the action of fast-flowing water, carving deep depressions into the softer limestone bedrock below.

Saskatchewan River Crossing

The North Saskatchewan River posed a major problem for early travelers and later for the builders of the Icefields Parkway. This swift-running river eventually drains into Hudson Bay in eastern Canada. At 1 km (0.6 mi) past the bridge, you'll come to **Howse Pass Viewpoint.** From here the Howse and Mistaya Rivers can be seen converging with the North Saskatchewan at a silt-laden delta. From this viewpoint, numerous peaks can be seen to the west. Two sharp peaks are distinctive: **Mount Outram** (3,254 m/10,680 ft) is the closer; the farther is **Mount Forbes** (3,630 m/11,975 ft), the highest peak in Banff National Park. The "crossing" is also a junction with Highway 11 (also known as David Thompson Highway), which heads east, following the North Saskatchewan River. On the north side of the junction, **The Crossing Resort** (mid-Apr. to mid-Oct.) has the only gas between Lake Louise and Jasper, a restaurant, a pub, a gift shop, and motel rooms.

TO SUNWAPTA PASS

On the north side of the North Saskatchewan River is the towering hulk of **Mount Wilson** (3,261 m/10,700 ft), named for Banff outfitter Tom Wilson. The Icefields Parkway passes this massif on its western flanks.

Pullout

A **pullout** just past Rampart Creek Campground offers good views of **Mount Amery** to the west and **Mounts Sarbach, Chephren,** and **Murchison** to the south.

Weeping Wall

Beyond here is the Weeping Wall, a long cliff of gray limestone where a series of waterfalls tumbles more than 100 m (330 ft) down the steep slopes of **Cirrus Mountain.** In winter this wall of water freezes, making it a sought-after destination for ice climbers.

Big Bend

After ascending quickly, the road drops again and rounds the Big Bend, a sweeping section of road that makes an almost 360-degree curve in preparation for a long climb to Sunwapta Pass. Halfway up the 360-vertical-m (1,180-vertical-ft) climb is a **viewpoint** well worth a stop (cyclists will definitely appreciate a rest). From here vistas extend down the valley to the slopes of **Mount Saskatchewan** and, on the other side of the parkway, Cirrus Mountain. **Bridal Veil Falls Viewpoint,** farther up the road, has the added attraction of its namesake falls across the valley.

Parker's Ridge Hike

DISTANCE: 2.4 km (1.5 mi) one-way
DURATION: 1 hour one-way
ELEVATION GAIN: 210 m (690 ft)
EFFORT: easy-moderate
TRAIL SURFACE: unpaved
TRAILHEAD: Icefields Parkway, 4 km (2.5 mi) south of Sunwapta Pass

From the trailhead on the west side of the highway, this wide path gains elevation quickly through open meadows and scattered stands of subalpine fir. This fragile environment is easily destroyed, so it's important that you stay on the trail. During the short alpine summer, these meadows are carpeted with red heather, white mountain avens, and blue alpine forget-me-nots. From the summit of the ridge, you look down on the 1.9-km-wide (1.2-mi) **Saskatchewan Glacier** spreading out below. Note that this trail is often closed until early July due to lingering snow.

Sunwapta Pass

A cairn at Sunwapta Pass (2,023 m/6,640 ft), 4 km (2.5 mi) north of the Parker's Ridge trailhead, marks the boundary between Banff and Jasper National Parks. It also marks the divide between the North Saskatchewan and Sunwapta Rivers, whose waters drain into the Atlantic and Arctic Oceans, respectively. Going north, you enter **Jasper National Park** here.

★ COLUMBIA ICEFIELD

The largest and most accessible of 17 glacial areas along the Icefields

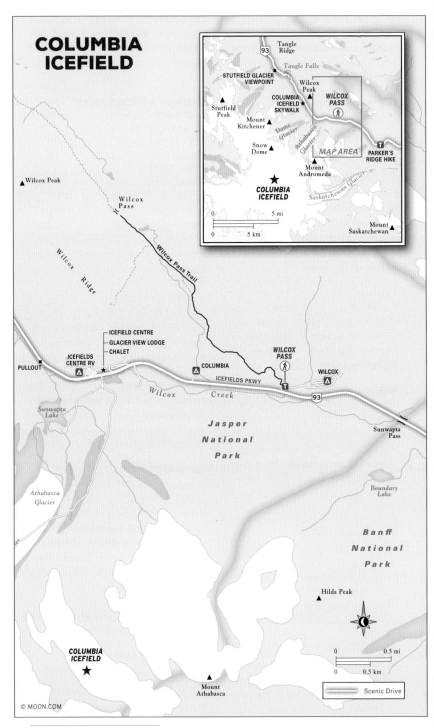

COLUMBIA ICEFIELD

Tangle Ridge

93

Tangle Falls

STUTFIELD GLACIER VIEWPOINT

Stutfield Peak

Wilcox Peak

COLUMBIA ICEFIELD SKYWALK

WILCOX PASS

Mount Kitchener

Dome Glacier

Athabasca Glacier

MAP AREA

Snow Dome

PARKER'S RIDGE HIKE

Mount Andromeda

Saskatchewan Glacier

COLUMBIA ICEFIELD

0   5 mi

0   5 km

Mount Saskatchewan

Wilcox Peak

Wilcox Pass

Wilcox Ridge

Wilcox Pass Trail

ICEFIELD CENTRE
GLACIER VIEW LODGE
CHALET

PULLOUT

ICEFIELDS CENTRE RV

WILCOX PASS

COLUMBIA

ICEFIELDS PKWY

Wilcox Creek

WILCOX

93

Sunwapta Lake

Jasper National Park

Sunwapta Pass

Athabasca Glacier

Boundary Lake

Banff National Park

Hilda Peak

COLUMBIA ICEFIELD

0   0.5 mi

0   0.5 km

Mount Athabasca

Scenic Drive

© MOON.COM

Parkway is the 325-sq-km (125-sq-mi) Columbia Icefield, beside the Icefields Parkway at the south end of Jasper National Park, 105 km (65 mi) south of Jasper and 127 km (79 mi) north of Lake Louise. It's a remnant of the last major glaciation that covered most of Canada 20,000 years ago, and it has survived because of its elevation at 1,900-2,800 m (6,230-9,190 ft) above sea level, cold temperatures, and heavy snowfalls. From the main body of the ice cap, which sits astride the Continental Divide, six glaciers creep down three main valleys. Of these, **Athabasca Glacier** is the most accessible and can be seen from the Icefields Parkway; it is one of the world's few glaciers that you can drive right up to.

The ice field is made more spectacular by the impressive peaks that surround it. **Mount Athabasca** (3,491 m/11,450 ft) dominates the skyline, and three glaciers cling to its flanks. **Dome Glacier** is also visible from the highway; although part of the Columbia Icefield, it is not actually connected. Instead, it is made of ice that breaks off the ice field 300 m (980 ft) above, supplemented by large quantities of snow each winter.

Icefield Centre

July-Aug. daily 9am-10pm, reduced hours May-June, Sept.-mid-Oct., closed mid-Oct.-Apr.

The Icefield Centre is nestled at the base of Mount Wilcox, overlooking the Athabasca Glacier. The center is the staging point for Ice Explorer tours of the glacier, but before heading out onto the ice field, don't miss the **Glacier Gallery** on the lower floor. This large display area details all aspects of the frozen world, including the story of glacier formation and movement. The centerpiece is a scaled-down fiberglass model of the Athabasca Glacier, which is surrounded by hands-on displays and audiovisual presentations.

Also in the gallery is a **Parks Canada desk** (780/852-6288, 10am-5pm daily early May-late Sept.).

There are a few places to eat and drink at the Icefield Centre. On the main level is a **Starbucks** outlet, while upstairs is **Chalet,** a casual self-serve café. Across the hallway is **Altitude Restaurant**, serving breakfast and dinner.

Athabasca Glacier

Athabasca Glacier is an impressive 600 ha (1,480 acres) in area and up to 100 m (330 ft) deep. The speed at which glaciers advance and retreat varies with the long-term climate. Athabasca Glacier has retreated to its current position from across the highway, a distance of more than 1.6 km (1 mi) in a little more than 100 years. Currently it retreats up to 2 m (6 ft) per year. The rubble between the toe of Athabasca Glacier and the highway is a mixture of rock, sand, and gravel known as **till,** deposited by the glacier as it retreats.

From the Icefields Parkway, an

Athabasca Glacier

TOP HIKE
WILCOX PASS

DISTANCE: 4 km (2.5 mi) one-way
DURATION: 1.5 hours one-way
ELEVATION GAIN: 340 m (1,115 ft)
EFFORT: moderate
TRAIL SURFACE: unpaved
TRAILHEAD: Wilcox Creek Campground, 3.1 km (1.9 mi) south of the Icefield Centre

Views of the **Columbia Icefield** from the Icefields Parkway pale in com-

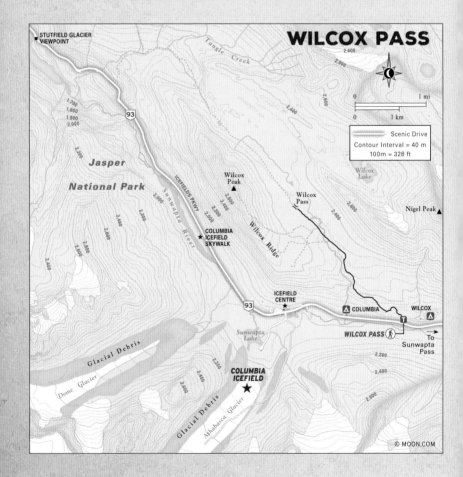

parison with those achieved along this trail, on the same side of the valley as the Icefield Centre. This trail was once used by northbound outfitters because, 120 years ago, the Athabasca Glacier covered the valley floor and had to be bypassed. Beginning from the Wilcox Creek Campground access road, the trail climbs through a stunted forest of Engelmann spruce and subalpine fir to a ridge with panoramic views of the valley, **Mount Athabasca,** and the **Athabasca Glacier.** Ascending gradually from there, the trail enters a fragile environment of alpine meadows.

unpaved road leads down through piles of till to a parking area beside Sunwapta Lake. An interesting alternative is to leave your vehicle beside the highway and take the 1.6-km (1-mi) hiking trail through the lunarlike landscape to the parking area. From this point, a short path leads up to a viewing area above the **toe of the glacier.** (Along the access road, look for the small markers showing how far the toe of the glacier reached in years past; the farthest marker is across the highway beside the stairs leading up to the Icefield Centre.)

The ice field can be dangerous for unprepared visitors. As with all glaciers, the broken surface of the Athabasca is especially hazardous because snow bridges can hide its deep crevasses. The crevasses are uncovered as the winter snows melt.

GLACIER TOUR
Pursuit; 403/762-6700 or 866/606-6700; www.banffjaspercollection.com; May-mid-Oct. daily 9am-6pm; adult C$125, child C$65; reserve online

Operated by Pursuit, Ice Explorers are specially developed vehicles with balloon tires that can travel over the crevassed surface and allow visitors to experience the glacier firsthand. The 90-minute tour of Athabasca Glacier, which begins with a bus ride from the Icefield Centre, includes time spent walking on the surface of the glacier. Try to reserve your tour for before 10am or after 3pm, after the tour buses have departed for the day. Early in the season, the glacier is still covered in a layer of snow and is therefore not as spectacular as during the summer. Full-day trips to the Columbia Icefield, which last nine hours and include the Ice Explorer excursion, are also available.

Sunwapta Lake
Sunwapta Lake, at the toe of the Athabasca Glacier, is the source of the Sunwapta River, which the Icefields Parkway follows for 48 km (30 mi) to Sunwapta Falls.

Pullout
Immediately north of the Icefield Centre, on the west side of the road, is an unheralded pullout where few travelers stop, but which allows for an excellent panorama of the area away from the crowds. Across the glacial-green Sunwapta River is a wasteland of till and a distinctive terminal moraine left behind by the retreating **Dome Glacier.** Between the Dome and Athabasca Glaciers is the 3,459-m (11,350-ft) **Snow Dome.**

ALONG THE SUNWAPTA RIVER
Columbia Icefield Skywalk
403/762-6700 or 866/606-6700; www.banffjaspercollection.com; 9am-6pm daily May-mid-Oct.; included with the Ice Explorer bus, or adult C$34, child C$17

The architecturally impressive Columbia Icefield Skywalk projects out into the Sunwapta Canyon 280 m (918 ft) above the valley floor around 6 km (3.7 mi) north of the Icefield Centre. Access is by shuttle bus from the Icefield Centre (no passenger vehicles are allowed to stop at the skywalk itself). A short interpretive trail leads along the canyon edge and then out onto the glass-floored skywalk. Looking upstream from the skywalk, you can see the massive, ice-draped slopes of **Mount Athabasca** (3,491 m/11,450 ft) framed by the walls of the valley—a truly inspiring view of this great mountain. Directly across the valley is the ice-capped east face of **Mount Kitchener.**

Tangle Falls

From the skywalk, northbound travelers lose 300 m (980 ft) of elevation over the next 4 km (2.5 mi), descending to the floor of the Sunwapta Valley. The first worthwhile stop is Tangle Falls; the waterfall is on the east side (on the right for northbound drivers) but parking is on the west side of the road, so be very careful when crossing over, both to park and when walking back across to view the falls. The waterfall is picturesque year-round, but extra special in winter when it is frozen solid.

Stutfield Glacier Viewpoint

Less than 1.9 km (1.2 mi) farther north, the road continues its descent to a viewpoint for Stutfield Glacier. Most of the glacier is hidden from view by a densely wooded ridge, but the valley floor below its toe is littered with till left by the glacier's retreat. The main body of the Columbia Icefield can be seen along the cliff top high above, and south of the glacier you can see Mount Kitchener.

About 6 km (3.7 mi) farther down the road is **Tangle Ridge,** a grayish-brown wall of limestone over which Beauty Creek cascades. At this point the Icefields Parkway runs alongside the Sunwapta River, following its braided course through the **Endless Range,** the eastern wall of a classic glacier-carved valley.

SUNWAPTA FALLS

A farther 40 km (25 mi) along the road, a 500-m (0.3-mi) spur at Sunwapta Falls Rocky Mountain Lodge leads to Sunwapta Falls. Here the Sunwapta River changes direction sharply and drops into a deep canyon. The best viewpoint is from the bridge across the river, but it's also worth following the path on the parking lot side of the river downstream along the rim of the canyon. About 1.9 km (1.2 mi) downstream, the river flows into the much wider Athabasca Valley at **Lower Sunwapta Falls.**

Columbia Icefield Skywalk (top); Goats and Glaciers Lookout (bottom)

GOATS AND GLACIERS LOOKOUT

After following the Athabasca River for 17.7 km (11 mi), the road ascends to a lookout with picnic tables offering panoramic river views. Below the lookout is a steep bank of exposed, glacially ground material containing natural deposits of salt. The local mountain goats spend most of their time on the steep slopes of **Mount Kerkeslin,** to the northeast, but occasionally cross the road and can be seen searching for the salt licks along the roadside or riverbank, trying to replenish lost nutrients.

ATHABASCA FALLS

Approximately 9 km (5.6 mi) beyond Goats and Glaciers Lookout and 32 km (20 mi) south of Jasper, the Athabasca River is forced through a narrow gorge and over a cliff into a cauldron of roaring water below. As the river slowly erodes the center of the riverbed, the falls will move upstream. Trails lead from a day-use area to various viewpoints above and below the falls. The trail branching under Highway 93A follows an abandoned river channel before emerging at the bottom of the canyon. Facilities at Athabasca Falls include picnic tables and restrooms.

DETOUR: WABASSO ROAD (HWY 93A)

At Athabasca Falls, an old stretch of the original Icefields Parkway (Wabasso Rd./Highway 93A) crosses the Athabasca River and continues along its west side for 25 km (15.5 mi) before rejoining the new parkway 6.9 km (4.3 mi) south of the town of Jasper. Along the route are close-up views of the Athabasca River and day-use areas, but the main reason for taking the road is to visit the base area of Mount Edith Cavell.

Geraldine Lakes Hike

DISTANCE: 5 km (3.1 mi) one-way
DURATION: 2 hours one-way
ELEVATION GAIN: 410 m (1,350 ft)
EFFORT: moderate
TRAIL SURFACE: unpaved
TRAILHEAD: Geraldine Fire Road, off Wabasso Rd., 1 km (0.6 mi) from Athabasca Falls

The first of the four Geraldine Lakes is an easy 1.9-km (1.2-mi) hike from the end of the 5.5-km (3.4-mi) Geraldine Fire Road. The forest-encircled lake reflects the north face of Mount Fryatt (3,361 m/11,030 ft). The trail continues along the northwest shore, climbs steeply past a scenic 100-m-high (330-ft) waterfall, and traverses some rough terrain where the trail becomes indistinct; follow the cairns. At the end of the valley is another waterfall. The trail climbs east of the waterfall to a ridge above the second of the lakes, 5 km (3.1 mi) from the trailhead. Although the trail officially ends here, it does continue to a campground at the south end of the lake. Two other lakes, accessible only by bushwhacking, are farther up the valley.

★ Mount Edith Cavell

This 3,363-m (11,033-ft) peak is the most distinctive and impressive in Jasper National Park. Known to Indigenous people as the "White Ghost" for its snowcapped summit, the mountain was given its official name in honor of a British nurse who was executed for helping prisoners of war escape German-occupied Belgium during World War I. The peak was first climbed that same year; today the most popular route to the summit is up the east ridge (to

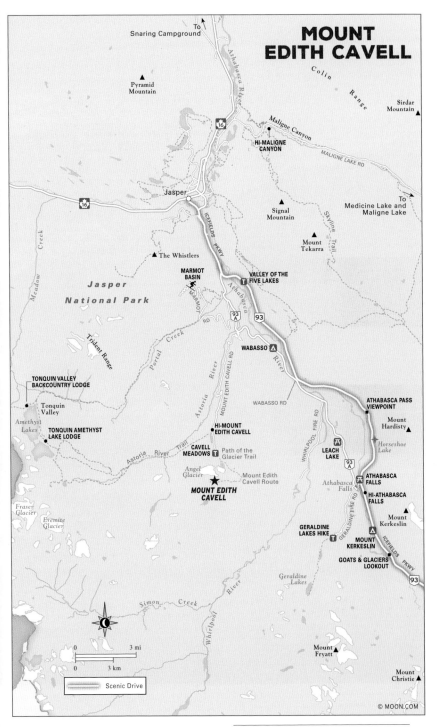

MOUNT EDITH CAVELL

To Snaring Campground

Colin Range

Pyramid Mountain

Sirdar Mountain

Athabasca River

16

Maligne Canyon

HI-MALIGNE CANYON

MALIGNE LAKE RD

Jasper

16

To Medicine Lake and Maligne Lake

Signal Mountain

Mount Tekarra

Skyline Trail

The Whistlers

MARMOT BASIN

ICEFIELDS PKWY

VALLEY OF THE FIVE LAKES

Jasper National Park

MARMOT RD

Athabasca River

93A

93

Meadow Creek

Trident Range

Portal Creek

WABASSO

TONQUIN VALLEY BACKCOUNTRY LODGE

Tonquin Valley

Astoria River

MOUNT EDITH CAVELL RD

WABASSO RD

Athabasca River

WHIRLPOOL FIRE RD

ATHABASCA PASS VIEWPOINT

Mount Hardisty

Amethyst Lakes

TONQUIN AMETHYST LAKE LODGE

Astoria River Trail

HI-MOUNT EDITH CAVELL

CAVELL MEADOWS

Path of the Glacier Trail

LEACH LAKE

Horseshoe Lake

93A

Angel Glacier

Mount Edith Cavell Route

ATHABASCA FALLS

★ MOUNT EDITH CAVELL

Athabasca Falls

HI-ATHABASCA FALLS

GERALDINE FIRE RD

Mount Kerkeslin

Fraser Glacier

Eremite Glacier

GERALDINE LAKES HIKE

MOUNT KERKESLIN

GOATS & GLACIERS LOOKOUT

ICEFIELDS PKWY

93

Geraldine Lakes

Whirlpool River

Simon Creek

0   3 mi

0   3 km

Scenic Drive

Mount Fryatt

Mount Christie

© MOON.COM

Mount Edith Cavell

the left of the summit). The imposing north face (facing the parking lot) has been climbed but is rated as an extremely difficult route.

The most impressive place to marvel at the mountain is from directly below the north face, at the end of Cavell Road. Located off Wabasso Road (Highway 93A), 12.9 km (8 mi) south from the town of Jasper and 19.3 km (12 mi) north of Athabasca Falls, Cavell Road ascends 300 m (980 ft) in 14.5 km (9 mi). Due to the many switchbacks, trailers must be left in the designated area at the bottom. Cavell Road is only open between mid-June and early October; it is closed the rest of the year. From the parking lot at the end of Cavell Road, you must strain your neck to take in the magnificent sight of the mountain's 1,500-m (4,920-ft) north face and **Angel Glacier,** which lies in a saddle on the mountain's lower slopes. On warm days, those who are patient may be lucky enough to witness an avalanche tumbling from the glacier, creating a roar that echoes across the valley. From the parking area, a short interpretive trail, **Path of the Glacier Trail** (1.2 km/0.75 mi; 1 hour round-trip), traverses barren moraines deposited by the receding Angel Glacier and leads to some great viewpoints.

Cavell Meadows Hike
DISTANCE: 6.1 km (3.8 mi) round-trip
DURATION: 2 hours round-trip
ELEVATION GAIN: 380 m (1,250 ft)
EFFORT: moderate
TRAIL SURFACE: unpaved
TRAILHEAD: parking lot at the end of Cavell Road, 27 km (17 mi) south of town

This trail, beginning from the parking lot beneath Mount Edith Cavell, provides access to an alpine meadow and panoramic views of Angel Glacier. The trail follows the paved Path of the Glacier Trail, then branches left, climbing steadily along a rocky ridge and then through a subalpine forest of Engelmann spruce, followed by stunted subalpine fir, to emerge facing the northeast face of Mount Edith Cavell and Angel Glacier. The view of the glacier from this point is nothing less than awesome, as the ice spills out of a cirque, clinging to a 300-m-high (984-ft) cliff face. The trail continues to higher viewpoints and an alpine meadow that, by mid-July, is filled with wildflowers.

ICEFIELDS PARKWAY TO JASPER
If you don't take Wabasso Road (Highway 93A) beyond Athabasca Falls to reach Mount Edith Cavell, continue north along the Icefields Parkway to access the following sights.

Horseshoe Lake
The first worthwhile stop along this route is Horseshoe Lake, reached along a 300-m (0.2-mi) trail from a parking lot 3.1 km (1.9 mi) north of Athabasca Falls. The southern end of this delightful little body of water is ringed by a band of cliffs popular with locals in summer as a cliff-diving spot but worth visiting for its scenery alone.

Athabasca Pass Viewpoint
About 1.9 km (1.2 mi) north of the Horseshoe Lake parking lot are a couple of lookouts with sweeping views across the Athabasca River to Athabasca Pass, used by David Thompson on his historic expedition across the continent. To the north of the pass lies Mount Edith Cavell.

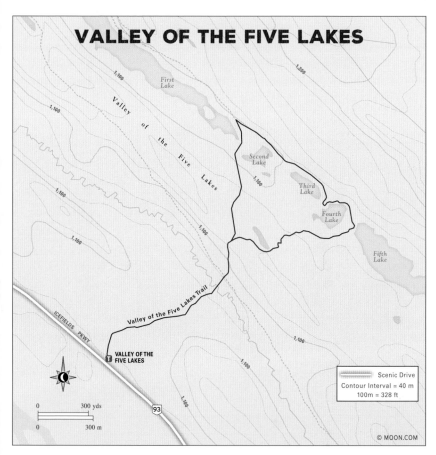

VALLEY OF THE FIVE LAKES

First Lake

Valley of the Five Lakes

Second Lake

Third Lake

Fourth Lake

Fifth Lake

Valley of the Five Lakes Trail

ICEFIELDS PKWY

VALLEY OF THE FIVE LAKES

1,100

1,100

1,100

1,100

1,100

1,100

1,100

1,100

1,200

1,300

93

| | Scenic Drive |
| Contour Interval = 40 m |
| 100m = 328 ft |

0 — 300 yds
0 — 300 m

© MOON.COM

From this lookout, it is 26 km (16 mi) to the town of Jasper.

Valley of the Five Lakes Hike

DISTANCE: 4.7 km (2.9 mi) round-trip
DURATION: 1.5 hours round-trip
ELEVATION GAIN: minimal
EFFORT: easy
TRAIL SURFACE: unpaved
TRAILHEAD: 10 km (6.2 mi) south along the Icefields Parkway of the town of Jasper

These shallow, turquoise lakes nestled in an open valley are small but make a worthwhile destination. From the trailhead and large parking lot, the trail passes through a forest of lodgepole pine, crosses a stream, and climbs a low ridge offering visitors a panoramic view of surrounding peaks. As the trail descends to the lakes, turn right at the first intersection to loop past the southernmost lake, then veer north to loop around the remaining lakes.

Valley of the Five Lakes

BACKPACKING

Before setting off on any hikes, whatever the length, go to the **Jasper Visitor Centre** in downtown Jasper or the Parks Canada desk in the **Icefield Centre** along the Icefields Parkway for waterproof Gem Trek hiking maps, trail conditions, and trail closures, or to purchase a copy of the *Canadian Rockies Trail Guide* by Brian Patton and Bart Robinson.

TONQUIN VALLEY
19 km (11.8 mi) one-way

For experienced backpackers only, this overnight trail starts opposite the hostel on Cavell Road and descends through a forest on the north side of Mount Edith Cavell for 5 km (3.1 mi), then crosses the Astoria River and begins a long ascent into the spectacular Tonquin Valley. Amethyst Lakes and the 1,000-m (3,280-ft) cliffs of the Ramparts first come into view after 12.9 km (8 mi). At the 16.9-km (10.5-mi) mark, the trail divides. To the left it climbs into Eremite Valley, where there is a campground. The right fork continues, following the Astoria River to the Tonquin Valley, Amethyst Lakes, and a choice of four campgrounds.

BIKING

Although the Icefields Parkway is steep and winding in places, it has a wide shoulder, making it ideal for an extended bike trip. Allow **four to seven days** to pedal north from Banff to Jasper, staying at hostels or camping along the route. This is the preferable direction to travel by bike because the elevation at the town of Jasper is more than 500 m (1,640 ft) lower than either Banff or Lake Louise. This is a trip for experienced riders only, as it features lots of elevation gain, long sections without services, and a great deal of vehicle traffic in midsummer.

FOOD

Dining choices along the Icefields Parkway are limited. Each of the three lodgings has a restaurant, The Crossing also has a store with groceries designed for campers, and the Icefield Centre has a range of dining outlets. Between mid-October and April, there are no services along the parkway. If you are planning a day trip, pick up lunch at Laggans in Lake Louise.

STANDOUTS
Chalet
Icefield Centre, Jasper National Park, 105 km (65 mi) south of Jasper

This casual self-serve café offers hot drinks, sandwiches, and other light meals. Seating is inside or out, with the outside tables offering unparalleled glacier views.

ICEFIELDS PARKWAY FOOD

NAME	LOCATION	TYPE
Lodge at Bow Lake	Banff National Park, 40 km (25 mi) north of Lake Louise on Icefields Parkway	sit-down restaurant
The Crossing	Banff National Park, 87 km (54 mi) north of Lake Louise on Icefields Parkway	sit-down restaurant
★ Chalet	Icefield Centre, Jasper National Park, 105 km (65 mi) south of Jasper	sit-down/takeout
Altitude Restaurant	Icefield Centre, Jasper National Park, 105 km (65 mi) south of Jasper	sit-down/takeout
Sunwapta Falls Rocky Mountain Lodge	Jasper National Park, 55 km (34 mi) south of Jasper	sit-down restaurant

BEST PICNIC SPOTS
Bow Lake Day Use Area
Banff National Park, 35 km (22 mi) north of Lake Louise
This small day-use area has easy access to one of Banff's most beautiful lakes. Spreading out a picnic on the pebbly shoreline is also an option.

Coleman Creek Day Use Area
Banff National Park, 100 km (62 mi) north of Lake Louise
Riverside Coleman Creek is one of the few day-use areas on the Banff side of the Icefields Parkway—but you'll need to plan ahead for a picnic, as it's a long way from the nearest town.

Athabasca Falls Day Use Area
Jasper National Park, 31 km (19 mi) south of the town of Jasper
Most visitors stop at Athabasca Falls to view the waterfall, but tables spread through the forest are the perfect place for a picnic.

Leach Lake Day Use Area
Wabasso Rd. (Highway 93A), Jasper National Park, 22.5 km (14 mi) south of the town of Jasper
There are only a couple of picnic tables at Leach Lake, but it's a quiet spot with mountain views and a dock.

FOOD	PRICE	HOURS
Canadian	splurge	6:30-9pm daily mid-June-Sept.
casual	moderate	7am-9pm daily early May-mid-Oct.
casual	budget	11am-6pm daily May-mid-Oct.
Canadian	splurge	7-9am, 6-9pm daily May-mid-Oct.
Canadian	splurge	8am-9pm daily May-early Oct.

CAMPING

Along the Icefields Parkway are 10 campgrounds. Most are rustic facilities with services limited to pit toilets, running water, firepits, and firewood. Many have limited sites for RVs or trailers, but this is clearly marked at the entry point. Within close proximity to the Columbia Icefield are three campgrounds—one designed only for tents, one for RVs and trailers, and the third a combo of both.

Reservations

Silverhorn and Rampart Creek Campgrounds in Banff National Park and Wabasso Campground in Jasper National Park are the only campgrounds in this chapter that can be reserved. Make reservations through **Parks Canada Reservation Service** (877/737-3783, https://reservation. pc.gc.ca) for C$12; check the website early in the year for the date that the reservation system opens as sites fill quickly.

Tips

The Icefields Parkway is one of the few regions of the Canadian Rockies national parks where most sites are first-come, first-served, but most campgrounds along the route have a limited number of sites, so plan on setting up camp as early in the afternoon as possible to have the best chance of getting a site.

ICEFIELDS PARKWAY CAMPGROUNDS

NAME	LOCATION	SEASON
Mosquito Creek Campground	Banff National Park, 24 km (15 mi) north of Lake Louise	June-early Oct.
Silverhorn Creek Campground	Banff National Park, 52 km (32 mi) north of Lake Louise	June-early Oct.
★ Waterfowl Lakes Campground	Banff National Park, 60 km (37 mi) north of Lake Louise	late June-early Sept.
Rampart Creek Campground	Banff National Park, 89 km (55 mi) north of Lake Louise	June-late Sept.
Wilcox Campground	Jasper National Park, 108 km (67 mi) south of Jasper	mid-June-mid-Sept.
Icefield Campground	Jasper National Park, 106 km (66 mi) south of Jasper	mid-June-early Oct.
Icefields Centre RV	Jasper National Park, 105 km (65 mi) south of Jasper	mid-May-early Oct.
Jonas Creek Campground	Jasper National Park, 76 km (47 mi) south of Jasper	mid-June-mid-Sept.
Honeymoon Lake Campground	Jasper National Park, 52 km (32 mi) south of Jasper	mid-May-mid-Sept.
Kerkeslin Campground	Jasper National Park, 35 km (22 mi) south of Jasper	June-early Sept.
★ Wabasso Campground	Jasper National Park, 16.1 km (10 mi) south of Jasper on Wabasso Rd. (Hwy 93A)	mid-May-mid-Sept.

SITES AND AMENITIES	RV LIMIT	PRICE	RESERVATIONS
38 tent and RV sites, drinking water, vault toilets	RVs up to 7 m (24 ft)	C$19	no
45 tent and RV sites, vault toilets	RVs up to 20 m (70 ft)	C$17	yes
116 tent and RV sites, drinking water, flush and vault toilets, dump station	RVs up to 7 m (24 ft)	C$23	no
51 tent and RV sites, drinking water, vault toilets	RVs up to 10 m (35 ft)	C$19	yes
46 tent and RV sites, pit toilets, dump station	RVs up to 8 m (27 ft)	C$26	no
33 tent-only sites, pit toilets	n/a	C$26	no
100 RV and trailer sites. No water or firepits	no limit	C$24	no
25 tent and RV sites, drinking water, pit toilets	RVs up to 7.6 m (25 ft)	C$26	no
35 tent and RV sites, drinking water, pit toilets	RVs up to 7.6 m (25 ft)	C$26	no
42 tent and RV sites, drinking water, pit toilets	RVs up to 7.6 m (25 ft)	C$26	no
231 tent and RV sites, drinking water, flush toilets, dump station, electrical hookups	RVs up to 10 m (35 ft)	C$32.50-39	yes

picnic table at Bow Lake (left); Wabasso Campground (right)

STANDOUTS
Waterfowl Lakes Campground
late June-early Sept.; C$23

Waterfowl Lakes Campground is 60 km (37 mi) north of Lake Louise along the Icefields Parkway. It features 116 sites between Upper and Lower Waterfowl Lakes, with a few sites in view of the lower lake. Facilities include drinking water, flush toilets, and kitchen shelters with wood-burning stoves. Rise early to watch the first rays of sun hit Mount Chephren from the shoreline of the lower lake, then plan on hiking the 4-km (2.5-mi) trail to **Chephren Lake**—you'll be among the first on the trail and back in time for a late breakfast.

Wabasso Campground
mid-May-mid-Sept.; C$32.50-39

Sites, some powered, at Wabasso Campground, along Wabasso Road approximately 16.1 km (10 mi) south of Jasper, are set among stands of spruce and aspen, with easy access to the Athabasca River. Facilities include heated bathrooms with flush toilets and hot and cold water.

LODGING

Waking up surrounded by wilderness is very special, and each of the lodging options along the Icefields Parkway offers this opportunity.

Along the route are four accommodations open between May and early October. The Lodge at Bow Lake is a historic log building overlooking a beautiful lake, The Crossing Resort is a complex of motel-style units, Glacier View Lodge overlooks the Columbia Icefield, and Sunwapta Falls Rocky Mountain Lodge has rooms and cabins to suit all budgets. Each of the four has a restaurant open to both guests and nonguests.

The four hostels are rustic affairs, with basic bunk beds and a common building for cooking and socializing.

Reservations
As there are fewer than 100 guest rooms along the entire length of the Icefields Parkway, you should make reservations well in advance.

Tips
If you are staying at any of the Icefields Parkway hostels, make sure you are self-sufficient and have packed food, as services along the route are limited.

STANDOUTS
Lodge at Bow Lake
403/522-0148; https://lodgeatbowlake.com; late May-early Oct.; C$850 s or d

Pioneer guide and outfitter Jimmy Simpson built the Lodge at Bow Lake (formerly known as Num-ti-jah Lodge) on the north shore of Bow Lake, 40 km (25 mi) north of Lake Louise, as a base for his outfitting operation in 1920. The desire to build a large structure when only short timbers were available led to the unusual octagonal shape of the main lodge. With a rustic mountain ambience that has changed little since Simpson's day, the lodge provides a memorable overnight stay. Under the distinctively red, steep-pitched roof of the main lodge are 16 rooms and a top-floor suite, and there's not a TV or phone in sight. Downstairs, guests soak up the warmth of a roaring log fire while mingling in a comfortable library filled with historical mountain literature. A modern-rustic dining room is open for breakfast and dinner daily.

Sunwapta Falls Rocky Mountain Lodge
780/852-4852 or 888/922-9222; www.sunwapta.com; May-mid-Oct.; C$330-500 s or d

Historic Sunwapta Falls Rocky Mountain Lodge is 55 km (34 mi) south of the town of Jasper and within walking distance of the picturesque waterfall for which it is named. It features 52 comfortable motel-like units, with either two queen beds or one queen bed and a fireplace; some have balconies. In the main lodge is a lunchtime self-serve restaurant popular with passing travelers. In the evening this same room is transformed into a restaurant featuring simply prepared Canadian game and seafood in the C$25-43 range.

Sunwapta Falls Rocky Mountain Lodge

ICEFIELDS PARKWAY LODGING

NAME	LOCATION
HI-Mosquito Creek	Banff National Park, 24 km (15 mi) north of Lake Louise
★ Lodge at Bow Lake	Banff National Park, 40 km (25 mi) north of Lake Louise
The Crossing	Banff National Park, 87 km (54 mi) north of Lake Louise
HI-Rampart Creek	Banff National Park, 89 km (55 mi) north of Lake Louise
Glacier View Lodge	Jasper National Park, 105 km (65 mi) south of Jasper
HI-Beauty Creek	Jasper National Park, 145 km (90 mi) north of Lake Louise
★ Sunwapta Falls Rocky Mountain Lodge	Jasper National Park, 55 km (34 mi) south of Jasper
HI-Athabasca Falls	Jasper National Park, 32 km (20 mi) south of Jasper
HI-Mount Edith Cavell	Jasper National Park, Cavell Road, 12.9 km (8 mi) off Hwy 93A

Lodge at Bow Lake

SEASON	OPTIONS	PRICE
May–Sept.	cabins with 4–6 beds	nonmembers C$42
late May–early Oct.	lodge rooms	C$850
mid–Apr.–mid–Oct.	hotel rooms	rooms starting at C$320
May–Sept.	cabins with 4–6 beds	nonmembers C$42
May–mid–Oct.	hotel rooms	rooms starting at C$520
May–Sept.	cabins with 12 beds	nonmembers C$42
May–mid–Oct.	motel rooms	rooms starting at C$330
May–Oct.	dormitory rooms (no showers and only pit toilets)	nonmembers C$42
mid–June–Sept.	dormitory rooms (no showers and only pit toilets)	nonmembers C$42

Icefields Parkway

INFORMATION AND SERVICES

Service Hubs

The only services along the Icefields Parkway are at the **Crossing Resort,** 87 km (54 mi) north of Lake Louise, where you will find gas, groceries, a large gift shop with basic camping supplies, and a restaurant. The Crossing is open mid-April to mid-October; the rest of the year there are no services the length of the parkway, so be sure to gas up in Banff, Lake Louise, or Jasper.

Entrance Gate

At each end of the Icefields Parkway is an entrance gate. By the time you have reached this point you should already have purchased a park pass. If not, the fee will be collected here.

Visitor Centers

Lake Louise Visitor Centre

403/522-3833; 9am-7pm daily early June-Aug., 9am-5pm daily rest of year

Lake Louise Visitor Centre is beside Samson Mall on Village Road in the heart of Lake Louise Village. This excellent Parks Canada facility has interpretive exhibits, slide and video displays, and staff on hand to answer questions, recommend hikes suited to your ability, and issue camping passes to those heading out into the backcountry.

Icefield Centre Information Desk

780/852-6288; 10am-5pm daily early May-late Sept.

At the Icefield Centre, opposite the Columbia Icefield along the Icefields Parkway, Parks Canada operates an information desk where you can learn about trail conditions in the immediate area.

Jasper Visitor Centre

Connaught Dr., Jasper; 780/852-6176; 9am-7pm daily mid-May-mid-Sept., 10am-5pm Wed.-Sun. the rest of the year, closed Nov.

The residence of Jasper's first superintendent, this beautiful old stone building dating to 1913 is now used by Parks Canada as the Jasper Visitor Centre. The staff provides general information on the park and can direct you to hikes in the immediate vicinity. **Tourism Jasper** (780/852-6236; www.jasper.travel) also has a desk in the building, and the friendly staff never seem to tire of explaining that all the rooms in town are full. As well as providing general information on the town, they have a large collection of brochures on activities, shopping, and restaurants. Also in the building is the **Friends of Jasper National Park** outlet (780/852-4767), selling maps, books, bear spray, and thoughtful souvenirs. Look for notices posted out front with the day's interpretive programs.

TRANSPORTATION
Getting There
From Banff National Park

The Icefields Parkway branches north from the Trans-Canada Highway 3.2 km (2 mi) north of Lake Louise and 58 km (36 mi) north of the town of Banff.

From Jasper National Park

Follow Connaught Drive west through downtown Jasper, then veer south at the edge of town, cross under the railway line, and your journey on the Icefields Parkway has begun.

Gas and Charging Stations
Along the Icefields Parkway, gas is available mid-April to mid-October at Saskatchewan River Crossing. There are currently no charging stations along the route; the closest are in Banff, Lake Louise, and Jasper.

Driving Tips
The Icefields Parkway is paved the entire length and has a wide shoulder, making driving easy. That said, you should always be aware of wildlife and other drivers. Often, when wildlife appears beside the road there will be a "bear jam" of vehicles. Slow down, be aware of your surroundings, and pull onto the shoulder if you want to view an animal.

Buses and Shuttles
Pursuit (866/756-1904; www.banffjaspercollection.com) operates a shuttle between Calgary International Airport and Jasper (C$183 one way) once daily May-October, with pickups in Banff and Lake Louise. Pursuit also operates all services at the Columbia Icefield, so there are options to break up the trip with an Icefield tour or to stay overnight at Glacier View Lodge. Between December and April, **Sun Dog Tours** (780/852-4056 or 888/786-3641, www.sundogtours.com) operates a winter shuttle between Calgary and Jasper once daily in each direction, with a stop in Banff.

Athabasca River

JASPER
NATIONAL PARK

Vast ice fields, beautiful glacial lakes, soothing hot springs, thundering rivers, and the most extensive backcountry trail system of any Canadian national park make Jasper a stunning counterpart to its sister park, Banff.

Encompassing 10,900 sq km (4,208 square mi), Jasper is a haven for wildlife; much of its wilderness is traveled only by wolves and grizzlies.

The park's most spectacular natural landmarks can be admired from two major roads. The Yellowhead Highway (Highway 16) runs east-west from Edmonton through the park. The Icefields Parkway runs north-south, connecting Jasper to Banff. At the junction of these two highways is the park's main service center—the town of Jasper. It has half the population of Banff, and its setting—at the confluence of the Athabasca and Miette Rivers, surrounded by rugged, snowcapped peaks—is a little less dramatic, though still beautiful. But the town is also less commercialized than Banff and its streets a little quieter—a major plus for those looking to get away from it all. Hiking is the number one attraction, but downhill skiing and rafting are also popular.

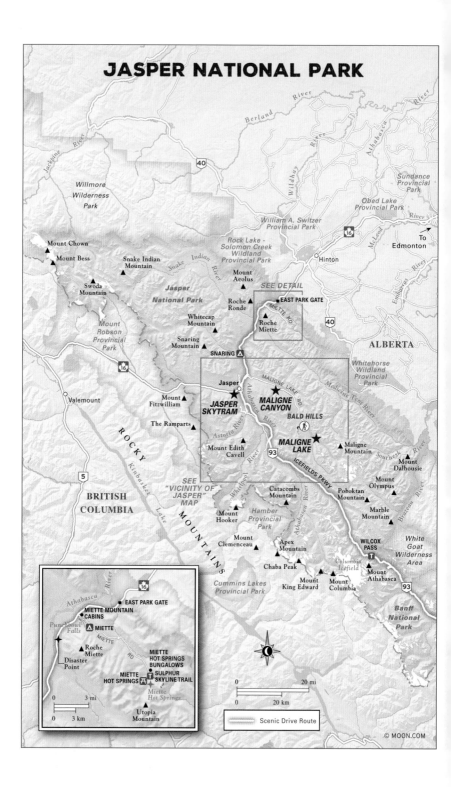

JASPER NATIONAL PARK

Berland River

Lackpine River

Snake Indian River

40

Willmore Wilderness Park

Wildhay River

Obed Lake Provincial Park

Sundance Provincial Park

William A. Switzer Provincial Park

16

○ Hinton

To Edmonton →

McLeod River

▲ Mount Chown
▲ Mount Bess

▲ Snake Indian Mountain

Rock Lake - Solomon Creek Wildland Provincial Park

▲ Mount Aeolus

SEE DETAIL

EAST PARK GATE ■

MIETTE RD.

40

Swoda Mountain ▲

Jasper National Park

Roche ▲ Ronde

Roche ▲ Miette

Embarras River

ALBERTA

Mount Robson Provincial Park

▲ Whitecap Mountain

▲ Snaring Mountain

SNARING ⊼

Whitehorse Wildland Provincial Park

16

Jasper ○

Athabasca River

MALIGNE LAKE RD.

★ **MALIGNE CANYON**

Medicine Tent River

○ Valemount

Mount ▲ Fitzwilliam

★ **JASPER SKYTRAM**

BALD HILLS 🥾

The Ramparts ▲

Astoria River

Maligne River

MALIGNE LAKE ★

▲ Maligne Mountain

▲ Mount Dalhousie

Southesk River

5

Kinbasket Lake

Mount Edith ▲ Cavell

93

ICEFIELDS PKWY.

Poboktan ▲ Mountain

▲ Mount Olympus

Brazeau River

BRITISH COLUMBIA

SEE "VICINITY OF JASPER" MAP

Whirlpool River

Catacombs ▲ Mountain

Athabasca River

Marble ▲ Mountain

ROCKY

Mount ▲ Hooker

Hamber Provincial Park

White Goat Wilderness Area

MOUNTAINS

Mount ▲ Clemenceau

Apex ▲ Mountain

WILCOX PASS �︎

Columbia Icefield

Cummins Lakes Provincial Park

Chaba Peak ▲

▲ Mount King Edward

▲ Mount Columbia

▲ Mount Athabasca

93

Banff National Park

Inset (lower left)

Athabasca River

16

EAST PARK GATE ■

MIETTE MOUNTAIN CABINS ●

⊼ **MIETTE**

MIETTE RD.

Punchbowl Falls

▲ Roche Miette

Disaster Point

MIETTE HOT SPRINGS BUNGALOWS ■

MIETTE HOT SPRINGS ♨

🚻 **SULPHUR SKYLINE TRAIL**

Miette Hot Springs

0   3 mi
0   3 km

▲ Utopia Mountain

0   20 mi
0   20 km

▭▭▭▭ Scenic Drive Route

© MOON.COM

TOP 3

★ **1. JASPER SKYTRAM:** Rise high above the valley floor to take in panoramic views, and then extend the adventure with the easy walk to an even higher vantage point (page 230).

★ **2. MALIGNE CANYON:** One of the Canadian Rockies' most spectacular chasms is carved from limestone bedrock and surrounded by viewpoints (page 234).

★ **3. MALIGNE LAKE:** This is the most famous body of water in Jasper National Park, and for good reason—it's simply stunning (page 234).

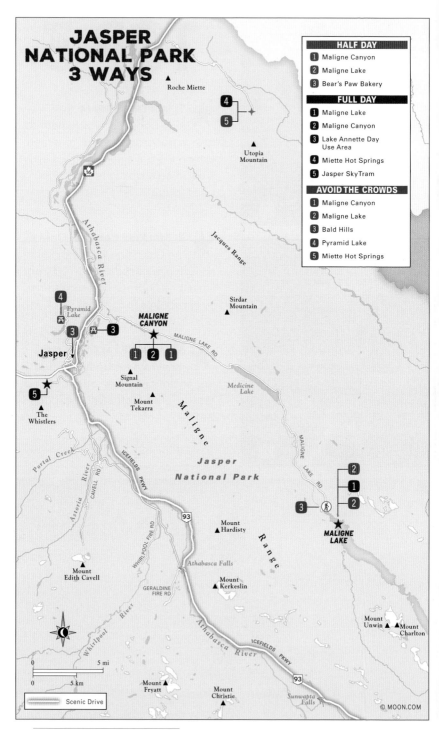

JASPER NATIONAL PARK 3 WAYS

HALF DAY
1. Maligne Canyon
2. Maligne Lake
3. Bear's Paw Bakery

FULL DAY
1. Maligne Lake
2. Maligne Canyon
3. Lake Annette Day Use Area
4. Miette Hot Springs
5. Jasper SkyTram

AVOID THE CROWDS
1. Maligne Canyon
2. Maligne Lake
3. Bald Hills
4. Pyramid Lake
5. Miette Hot Springs

Roche Miette

Utopia Mountain

Jacques Range

Pyramid Lake

Sirdar Mountain

MALIGNE CANYON

MALIGNE LAKE RD

Jasper

Signal Mountain

Mount Tekarra

Medicine Lake

Maligne

The Whistlers

Portal Creek

Astoria River

CAVELL RD

ICEFIELDS PKWY

Jasper National Park

Range

MALIGNE LAKE RD

MALIGNE LAKE

Mount Hardisty

Mount Edith Cavell

WHIRLPOOL FIRE RD

93

Athabasca Falls

GERALDINE FIRE RD

Mount Kerkeslin

Whirlpool River

Mount Unwin

Mount Charlton

0   5 mi

0   5 km

Mount Fryatt

Mount Christie

Athabasca River

ICEFIELDS PKWY

93

Sunwapta Falls

Scenic Drive

© MOON.COM

JASPER NATIONAL PARK 3 WAYS

HALF DAY

1 Visit **Maligne Canyon** and walk the shorter loop option down and across this geological wonder.

2 Drive farther down Maligne Lake Road to **Maligne Lake** itself. Take a boat tour on the lake to Spirit Island.

3 Head back to the town of Jasper and wander along the downtown streets, which are lined with interesting stores. Grab lunch at the **Bear's Paw Bakery.**

FULL DAY

It's possible to hit the major highlights of Jasper in just one day, with around 161 km (100 mi) of driving, starting and ending in the town of Jasper.

1 Leave Jasper to arrive at **Maligne Lake** in time for the first tour boat departure at 9am.

2 On the way back into town, stop at **Maligne Canyon** and marvel at the forces of nature at work.

3 For lunch, have a picnic at the **Lake Annette Day Use Area.** Stroll around Lake Annette before or after you eat.

4 Head out to **Miette Hot Springs** for a relaxing soak.

5 Return to Jasper and ride the **Jasper SkyTram** up to the summit of The Whistlers, where the restaurant is an outstanding destination for dinner.

Alternatively, if you want to visit or revisit parts of the Icefields Parkway, skip Miette Hot Springs and head south to **Athabasca Falls** and the **Columbia Icefield** for around 300 km (186 mi) of driving.

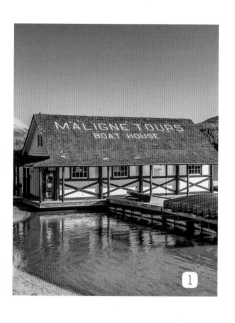

AVOID THE CROWDS

The best way to avoid the crowds in Jasper is to start your day early. As a bonus, early morning offers you the best chance of seeing wildlife—which is why heading down Maligne Lake Road at the beginning of your day is ideal.

1 Rise early and drive down Maligne Lake Road, stopping briefly at **Maligne Canyon.**

2 At **Maligne Lake,** rent a canoe and go for a paddle.

3 The hiking trail through the **Bald Hills** is one of the best ways in Jasper to experience an alpine environment with minimal effort.

4 Spend the remainder of the afternoon exploring the streets of downtown Jasper or relaxing along the shore of **Pyramid Lake.**

5 Wind down after your day by taking a dip in the warm waters at **Miette Hot Springs.**

HIGHLIGHTS

TOWN OF JASPER
Jasper-Yellowhead Museum and Archives

400 Bonhomme St.; 780/852-3013; 10am-5pm daily mid-May-Oct., 10am-5pm Thurs.-Sun. the rest of the year; adult C$8, senior and child C$7

At the back of the town of Jasper is the excellent Jasper-Yellowhead Museum and Archives, as unstuffy as any museum could possibly be and well worth a visit even for non-museum types. The main gallery features colorful, modern picture boards with exhibits that take visitors along a timeline of Jasper's human history through the fur trade, the coming of the railway, and the creation of the park. Documentaries are shown on demand in a small television room. The museum also features extensive archives, including hundreds of historical photos, manuscripts, documents, maps, and videos.

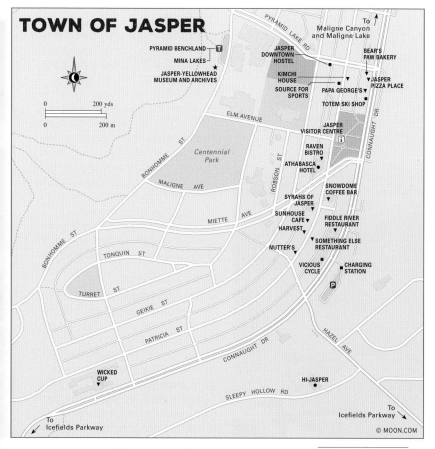

TOWN OF JASPER

★ Jasper SkyTram

780/852-3093; 8am-9pm daily in summer, shorter hours late Mar.-June and Sept.-Oct., closed the rest of the year; adult C$60, child 6-15 C$33

The Jasper SkyTram climbs more than 1,000 vertical m (3,280 vertical ft) up the steep north face of **The Whistlers,** named for the hoary marmots that live on the summit. Jasper SkyTram operates two 30-passenger cars that take seven minutes to reach the upper terminal, during which time the conductor gives a lecture about the mountain and its environment. From the upper terminal, a 1.4-km (0.9-mi) trail leads to the 2,470-m (8,104-ft) true summit. The view is breathtaking; to the south is the Columbia Icefield, and on a clear day you can see Mount Robson (3,954 m/12,970 ft)—the highest peak in the Canadian Rockies—to the northwest. Free two-hour guided hikes leave the upper terminal for the true summit at 10am, 11am, 2pm,

and 3pm daily. You should allow two hours on top and, on a clear summer's day, two more hours in line at the bottom. Jasper SkyTram is 3.1 km (1.9 mi) south of town on Highway 93 (Icefields Parkway), and then a similar distance up Whistlers Road.

VICINITY OF JASPER
Patricia and Pyramid Lakes

A winding road heads through the hills at the back of town to these two picturesque lakes, formed when glacial moraines dammed shallow valleys. The first, to the left, is Patricia; the second, farther along the road, is Pyramid, backed by **Pyramid Mountain** (2,765 m/9,072 ft). Both lakes are popular spots for picnicking, fishing, and boating. Boat rentals are available at **Pyramid Lake Boat Rentals** (780/852-4900; 9am-7pm daily in summer), across the road from the lake at Pyramid Lake Resort. Canoes, rowboats, paddleboats, paddleboards, and kayaks are C$45-80 per hour. The resort also rents electric motorboats that seat up to seven people for C$150 per hour. From the resort, the road continues around the lake to a bridge that leads to an island popular with picnickers. The road ends at the quieter end of the lake.

Lake Edith and Lake Annette

These two lakes along the road to the Fairmont Jasper Park Lodge—across the Athabasca River from town—are perfect for a picnic, swim, or pleasant walk. They are remnants of a much larger lake that once covered the entire valley floor. The lakes are relatively shallow; therefore, the sun warms the water to a bearable

Jasper SkyTram

Lake Annette

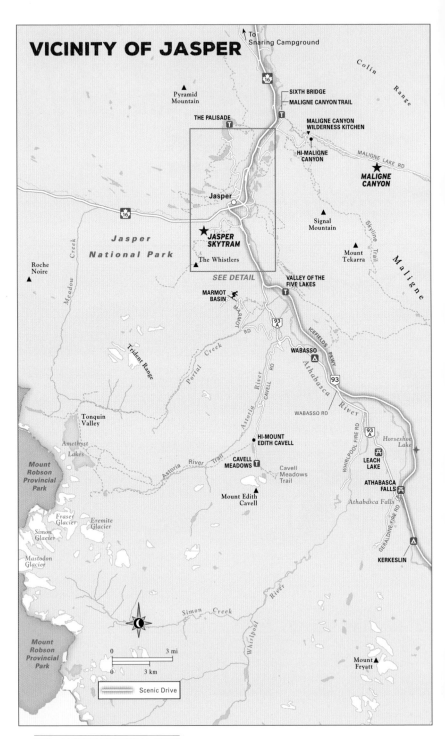

VICINITY OF JASPER

To Snaring Campground

Colin Range

16

SIXTH BRIDGE
MALIGNE CANYON TRAIL

THE PALISADE

Pyramid Mountain

MALIGNE CANYON WILDERNESS KITCHEN

HI-MALIGNE CANYON

MALIGNE LAKE RD

MALIGNE CANYON

16

Jasper

JASPER SKYTRAM

Signal Mountain

Skyline Trail

Maligne

Jasper National Park

Meadow Creek

Roche Noire

The Whistlers

Mount Tekarra

SEE DETAIL

VALLEY OF THE FIVE LAKES

MARMOT BASIN

MARMOT RD

93 A

ICEFIELDS PKWY

WABASSO

Trident Range

Portal Creek

Astoria River

CAVELL RD

Athabasca River

93

Tonquin Valley

Amethyst Lakes

WABASSO RD

HI-MOUNT EDITH CAVELL

CAVELL MEADOWS

Cavell Meadows Trail

Astoria River Trail

WHIRLPOOL FIRE RD

93 A

Horseshoe Lake

LEACH LAKE

Mount Robson Provincial Park

Mount Edith Cavell

ATHABASCA FALLS

Athabasca Falls

Fraser Glacier

Eremite Glacier

Simon Glacier

Mastodon Glacier

GERALDINE FIRE RD

KERKESLIN

Simon Creek

Whirlpool River

Mount Robson Provincial Park

0   3 mi
0   3 km

Scenic Drive

Mount Fryatt

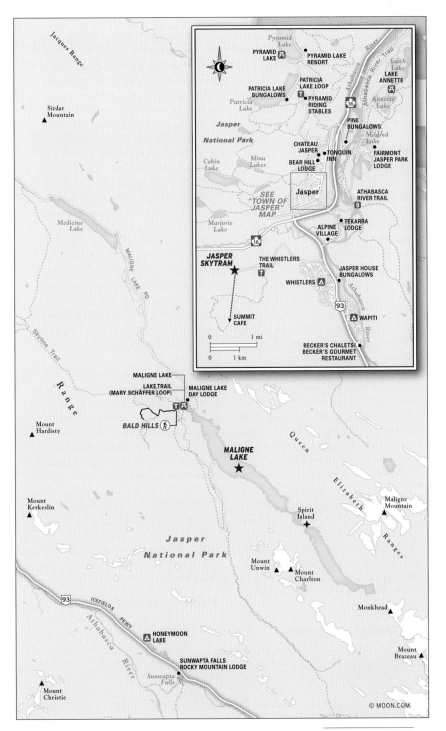

Jacques Range

Sirdar
Mountain ▲

Medicine
Lake

MALIGNE LAKE RD.

Skyline Trail

R a n g e

Mount
Hardisty ▲

Mount
Kerkeslin ▲

Jasper

National Park

93

ICEFIELDS PKWY

Athabasca River

Mount
Christie ▲

HONEYMOON
LAKE ⌂

SUNWAPTA FALLS
ROCKY MOUNTAIN LODGE

Sunwapta
Falls

MALIGNE LAKE
LAKE TRAIL
(MARY SCHÄFFER LOOP)
MALIGNE LAKE
DAY LODGE

BALD HILLS 🚶

MALIGNE
LAKE ★

Queen

Spirit
Island ✦

Mount
Unwin ▲

Mount
Charlton ▲

Elizabeth Ranges

Maligne
Mountain ▲

Monkhead ▲

Mount
Brazeau ▲

Inset map (SEE "TOWN OF JASPER" MAP):

Pyramid
Lake

PYRAMID
LAKE 🏕

PYRAMID LAKE
RESORT

PATRICIA LAKE
BUNGALOWS

PATRICIA
LAKE LOOP

Patricia
Lake

PYRAMID
RIDING
STABLES

Jasper

National Park

Cabin
Lake

Mina
Lakes

CHATEAU
JASPER

BEAR HILL
LODGE

TONQUIN
INN

SEE
"TOWN OF
JASPER"
MAP

Jasper

PINE
BUNGALOWS

Mildred
Lake

FAIRMONT
JASPER PARK
LODGE

ATHABASCA
RIVER TRAIL
🅱

Athabasca River

Athabasca River Trail

Edith
Lake

LAKE
ANNETTE

Annette
Lake

16

Marjorie
Lake

16

JASPER
SKYTRAM ★

THE WHISTLERS
TRAIL 🚻

SUMMIT
CAFE

ALPINE
VILLAGE

TEKARRA
LODGE

WHISTLERS ⌂

JASPER HOUSE
BUNGALOWS

93

WAPITI ⌂

Athabasca River

BECKER'S CHALETS/
BECKER'S GOURMET
RESTAURANT

0   1 mi
0   1 km

© MOON.COM

temperature for swimming. In fact, they have the warmest waters of any lakes in the park. The 2.6-km (1.6-mi) **Lake Annette Loop** encircles Lake Annette and is wheelchair accessible. In a forested area between the two lakes is a large day-use area with a playground.

MALIGNE VALLEY

Maligne Lake, one of the world's most photographed lakes, lies 48 km (30 mi) southeast of Jasper. It's the source of the **Maligne River,** which flows northward to **Medicine Lake** and then disappears underground, eventually emerging downstream of Maligne Canyon. The river was known to the Indigenous people as Chaba Imne (River of the Great Beaver), but the name by which we know it today was coined by a missionary. After his horses were swept away by its swift-flowing waters in 1846, he described the river as being *"la traverse maligne,"* (wicked crossing). Driving up the Maligne River Valley to the lake is a lesson in 600 million years of geology that can be appreciated by anyone.

To get to Maligne Valley, head northeast from Jasper along Highway 16 for 4 km (2.5 mi) and turn south (right) on Maligne Lake Road. The access road to Maligne Canyon veers left off Maligne Lake Road 10.9 km (6.8 mi) from Jasper. Maligne Lake is at the end of Maligne Lake Road, 48 km (30 mi) from Jasper.

★ Maligne Canyon

As the Maligne River drops into the Athabasca River Valley, its gradient is particularly steep. The fast-flowing water has eroded a deep canyon out of the easily dissolved limestone bedrock. The canyon is up to 50 m (165 ft) deep, yet so narrow that squirrels often jump across.

An interpretive trail winds down from the parking lot at the upper end of the canyon, crossing the canyon six times. The most spectacular sections of the canyon can be seen from the first two bridges, at the upper end of the trail. A **restaurant** operates at the top of the canyon. In front of the restaurant, you'll see large potholes in the riverbed. These potholes are created when rocks and pebbles become trapped in what begins as a shallow depression; under the force of the rushing water, they carve jug-shaped hollows into the soft bedrock.

To avoid the crowds at the upper end of the canyon, an alternative would be to park at **Sixth Bridge,** near the confluence of the Maligne and Athabasca Rivers, and walk *up* the canyon.

By late December, the torrent that is the Maligne River has frozen solid. Where it cascades down through Maligne Canyon, the river is temporarily stalled for the winter, creating remarkable formations through the deep limestone canyon. **Jasper Adventure Centre** (414 Connaught Dr.; 780/852-4056; adult C$85, child C$42.50) offers intriguing three-hour guided tours into the depths of the canyon daily throughout winter. These guided tours of the frozen canyon are an experience you'll never forget.

★ Maligne Lake

At the end of Maligne Lake Road, 48 km (30 mi) from town, is Maligne Lake, the largest glacier-fed lake in the Canadian Rockies and second largest in the world. The first paying visitors were brought to the lake in the 1920s, and it has been a destination

Maligne Canyon

for camera-toting tourists from around the world ever since. Once at the lake, activities are plentiful. But other than taking in the spectacular vistas, the only thing you won't need your wallet for is hiking one of the numerous trails in the area.

The most popular tourist activity at the lake is a 90-minute narrated **cruise** (10am-5pm daily June to early Oct.; adult C$85, child C$45, reservations recommended) on a glass-enclosed boat up the lake to oft-photographed **Spirit Island.** Rowboats, double kayaks, and canoes can be rented at the **Boat House** (9am-5pm daily June-mid-Sept.), a provincial historic site dating to 1929, from C$65 per hour or C$190 per day. The lake also has excellent lake trout fishing; guided fishing tours are available.

All commercial operations to and around the lake are operated by **Pursuit** (866/606-6700; www.banffjaspercollection.com). At the lake itself, in addition to the cruises and boat rentals, Pursuit operates **Maligne Lake Lodge,** a day-use facility that includes a souvenir shop and the **View Restaurant** (11:30am-6pm daily late June-Sept.; lunches $17-37), with a huge area of tiered outdoor seating overlooking the lake.

MIETTE HOT SPRINGS
780/866-3939; 10:30am-9pm daily mid-May-mid-Oct., extended to 8:30am-10:30pm daily in summer; day pass adult C$16.50, seniors and children C$14.25

Miette Hot Springs Road branches south from Highway 16 43 km (27 mi) northeast of Jasper. After curving, swerving, rising, and falling many times, Miette Hot Springs Road ends 17.7 km (11 mi) from Highway 16 at the warmest springs in the Canadian Rockies, Miette Hot Springs. In the early 1900s, these springs were one of the park's biggest attractions. In 1910, a packhorse trail was built up the valley, and the government constructed a bathhouse. The original hand-hewn log structure was replaced in the 1930s with pools that remained in use until new facilities were built in 1985. The water that flows into the pools is artificially cooled from 54°C (128°F) to a soothing 39°C (100°F). A newer addition to the complex is a smaller, cool plunge pool.

Many hiking trails begin from the hot springs complex; the shortest is from the day-use area to the source of the springs (allow five minutes each way) while the most strenuous is to the summit of Sulphur Skyline. Overlooking the pools is a café, while lodging is just down the hill.

Jasper Lake, Highway 16 (left); Roche Miette (right)

SCENIC DRIVES

ATHABASCA RIVER (HIGHWAY 16)
DRIVING DISTANCE: 50 km (31 mi) one-way
DRIVING TIME: 1 hour one-way
START: Jasper
END: East Park Gate

From Jasper, it's 50 km (31 mi) to the park's eastern boundary along Highway 16, following the Athabasca River the entire way. Beyond the turnoff to **Maligne Lake,** Highway 16 enters a wide valley flanked to the west by The Palisade ridge and to the east by the Colin Range. The valley is a classic montane environment, with open meadows and forests of Douglas fir and lodgepole pine. After crossing the Athabasca River, 20 km (12.4 mi) from Jasper, the highway parallels **Jasper Lake,** which is lined by sand dunes along its southern edge. At the highway, a plaque marks the location of **Jasper House** (the actual site is on the opposite side of the river). The next worthwhile stop is **Disaster Point,** 4 km (2.5 mi) farther north. This is a great spot for viewing bighorn sheep, which gather at a mineral lick, an area of exposed mineral salts. Disaster Point is on the lower slopes of **Roche Miette,** a distinctive 2,316-m-high (7,600-ft) peak that juts out into the Athabasca River Valley. Across the highway, the braided Athabasca River is flanked by wetlands alive with migrating birds in the spring and fall.

The junction with Miette Hot Springs Road (43 km/27 mi east of Jasper) marks the site of **Pocahontas,** a coal-mining town in existence between 1910 and 1921. The mine itself was high above the township, with coal transported to the valley floor by cable car. Most buildings have long since been removed, but a short interpretive walk leads through the remaining foundations. About 1 km (0.6 mi) along Miette Hot Springs Road, a short trail leads to photogenic **Punchbowl Falls.** Here Mountain Creek cascades through a narrow crevice in a cliff to a pool of turbulent water. From Pocahontas, the **East Park Gate** of Jasper National Park is 7 km (4.3 mi) away.

BEST HIKES

TOWN OF JASPER AND VICINITY
Pyramid Benchland
LENGTH: 7 km (4.3 mi) round-trip
DURATION: 2 hours round-trip
ELEVATION GAIN: 120 m (400 ft)
RATING: easy
TRAILHEAD: Jasper-Yellowhead Museum, 400 Bonhomme Street

Numerous official and unofficial hiking trails weave across the benchland immediately west of the town of Jasper. From the far corner of the parking lot beside the museum, a well-marked trail climbs onto the benchland. Keep right, crossing Pyramid Lake Road, and you'll emerge on a bluff overlooking the Athabasca River Valley. Bighorn sheep can often be seen grazing here. If you return to the trailhead from here, you will have hiked 7 km (4.3 mi). The trail continues north, disappearing into the montane forest until arriving at Pyramid Lake. You can return the way you came or take one of the various other trails in the area, such as Mina Lakes, to get back to town. Pick up a map at the park information center before setting out on the trail.

Mina Lakes
LENGTH: 2.5 km (1.6 mi) one-way
DURATION: 50 minutes one-way
ELEVATION GAIN: 70 m (230 ft)
RATING: easy
TRAILHEAD: Jasper-Yellowhead Museum, 400 Bonhomme Street

Lower and Upper Mina Lakes lie on the benchland immediately west of the town of Jasper. The trailhead is the same as for Pyramid Benchland, except instead of keeping right,

you'll need to take the first left fork (signposted as Route 8 to Cabin Creek West), which climbs up onto the bench and then crosses a treeless 100-m-wide (328-ft) corridor, cleared to act as a firebreak for the town. Cabin Lake Road passes along the firebreak, leading west (left) to artificial Cabin Lake and east (right) to Pyramid Lake Road. Continuing straight ahead, the trail climbs gradually through a typical montane forest of lodgepole pine, Douglas fir, and poplar before emerging at Lower Mina Lake. After 500 m (0.3 mi) more and just beyond the end of Lower Mina Lake, the upper lake is reached. The distance given above is to this point, but with a map from the park information center in hand, it's possible to continue along the shore of the upper lake to a fork in the trail—looping back to the trailhead via Cabin Lake to the left and Riley Lake to the right.

Patricia Lake Loop
DISTANCE: 5 km (3.1 mi) round-trip
DURATION: 1.5 hours round-trip
ELEVATION GAIN: minimal
EFFORT: easy
TRAIL SURFACE: unpaved
TRAILHEAD: 1.9 km (1.2 mi) along Pyramid Lake Road

This trail begins across the road from the riding stables on Pyramid Lake Road. It traverses a mixed forest of aspen and lodgepole pine—prime habitat for larger mammals such as elk, deer, and moose. The second half of the trail skirts **Cottonwood Slough,** where you'll see several beaver ponds. Unlike the name suggests, this trail doesn't encircle Patricia Lake but instead just passes along a portion of its southern shoreline.

The Palisade

DISTANCE: 10.9 km (6.8 mi) one-way
DURATION: 4 hours one-way
ELEVATION GAIN: 850 m (2,790 ft)
EFFORT: difficult
TRAIL SURFACE: unpaved
TRAILHEAD: the end of Pyramid Lake Road, 5 mi (8 km) from town

The destination of this strenuous hike is the site of an old fire lookout tower atop a high ridge between the Athabasca River Valley and Pyramid Mountain. From the locked gate at the end of Pyramid Lake Road, the trail crosses Pyramid Creek after 1 km (0.6 mi), then climbs steadily for the entire distance along a forest-enclosed fire road (take the right fork at the 7.5-km/4.7-mi mark). Once at the end of the trail, it's easy to see why this site was chosen for the lookout; the panorama extends down the valley and across Jasper Lake to Roche Miette (2,316 m/7,600 ft).

The Whistlers

DISTANCE: 8 km (5 mi) one-way
DURATION: 3 hours one-way
ELEVATION GAIN: 1,220 m (4,000 ft)
EFFORT: difficult
TRAIL SURFACE: unpaved
TRAILHEAD: 3.1 km (1.9 mi) along Whistlers Road from Highway 93

This steep ascent, the park's most arduous day hike, is unique in that it passes through three distinct vegetation zones in a relatively short distance. For the less adventurous, **Jasper SkyTram** (780/852-3093) ends at the same destination described here. From the trailhead on Whistlers Road, immediately below the hostel, the trail begins climbing and doesn't let up until you merge with the crowds getting off the tramway at the top. The trail begins in a montane forest of aspen and white birch, climbs through a subalpine forest of Engelmann spruce and alpine fir, and then emerges onto the open, treeless tundra, which is inhabited by pikas, hoary marmots,

Cottonwood Slough, Patricia Lake Loop

TOP HIKE
BALD HILLS

DISTANCE: 5.2 km (3.2 mi) one-way
DURATION: 2 hours one-way
ELEVATION GAIN: 495 m (1,620 ft)
EFFORT: moderate-strenuous
TRAIL SURFACE: unpaved
TRAILHEAD: day use area at the end of Maligne Lake Road

This trail follows an old road for its entire distance to the site of a fire lookout that has long since been removed. It is well worth continuing on a network of trails through alpine meadows to higher elevations, where sweeping views take in the jade-green waters of Maligne Lake, the Queen Elizabeth Ranges, and the twin peaks of Mount Unwin and Mount Charlton. The Bald Hills extend for 7 km (4.3 mi), their highest summit not exceeding 2,600

m (8,530 ft). It's well worth continuing beyond the fire lookout site, where options include climbing the bald knolls for which the trail was named or continuing southward through treeless meadows. On the return journey, make the short detour to **Moose Lake.**

and a few hardy plants. Carry water with you, because none is available before the upper Jasper SkyTram terminal.

MALIGNE VALLEY
Maligne Canyon

DISTANCE: 3.7 km (2.3 mi) one-way
DURATION: 90 minutes one-way
ELEVATION GAIN: 125 m (410 ft)
EFFORT: moderate
TRAIL SURFACE: unpaved
TRAILHEAD: turnoff to Sixth Bridge, 2.6 km (1.6 mi) along Maligne Lake Road from Highway 16

Maligne Canyon is one of the busiest places in the park, yet few visitors hike the entire length of the canyon trail. By beginning from the lower end of the canyon, at the confluence of the Maligne and Athabasca Rivers, you'll avoid starting your hike alongside the masses, and you'll get to hike downhill on your return (when you're tired). To access the lower end of the canyon, follow the

1-km (0.6-mi) spur off Maligne Lake Road to Sixth Bridge. Crowds will be minimal for the first 3.1 km (1.9 mi) to Fourth Bridge, where the trail starts climbing. By the time you get to Third Bridge, you start encountering adventurous hikers coming down the canyon, and soon thereafter you'll meet the real crowds—high heels, bear bells, and all. Upstream of here the canyon is deepest and most spectacular.

Lake Trail (Mary Schäffer Loop)

DISTANCE: 3.2-km (2-mi) loop
DURATION: 1 hour round-trip
ELEVATION GAIN: minimal
EFFORT: easy
TRAIL SURFACE: paved
TRAILHEAD: Boat House, Maligne Lake

This easy, pleasant walk begins from beside the Boat House, following the eastern shore of Maligne Lake through an open area of lakeside picnic tables to a point known as **Schäffer Viewpoint,** named for the first white person to see the valley. Across the lake are the aptly named Bald Hills, the Maligne Range, and, to the southwest, the distinctive twin peaks of Mount Unwin (3,268 m/10,720 ft) and Mount Charlton (3,217 m/10,550 ft). After dragging yourself away from the spectacular panorama, continue along a shallow bay before following the trail into a forest of spruce and subalpine fir, then looping back to the middle parking lot.

Third Bridge over Maligne Canyon

Sulphur Skyline

DISTANCE: 4 km (2.5 mi) one-way
DURATION: 1.5 hours one-way
ELEVATION GAIN: 700 m (2,300 ft)
EFFORT: difficult
TRAIL SURFACE: unpaved
TRAILHEAD: Miette Hot Springs, 43 km (27 mi) northeast of Jasper on Hwy 16, then 17.7 km (11 mi) south on Miette Road

The trail to the summit of Sulphur Ridge is the most strenuous hike in the vicinity of Miette Hot Springs. The ridge overlooks several remote wilderness valleys—the most prominent being Fiddle River, which snakes away to the southwest for over 15 mi (24 km) to its headwaters on Whitehorse Pass. This hike is particularly nice in late spring and early summer when Front Range wildflowers are in bloom, and you may see bighorn sheep on the way. But be sure to pack water—this is a steep, dry hike.

BACKPACKING

With 1,200 km (745 mi) of hiking trails, Jasper National Park has an extensive system of interconnecting backcountry trails that, for experienced hikers, can provide a wilderness adventure rivaled by few areas on the face of the earth. The most popular trails for extended backcountry trips are the **Skyline Trail** (44.5 km/27.6 mi; 3 days each way), between Maligne Lake and Maligne Lake Road; the extremely difficult **Athabasca Pass Trail** (50 km/31 mi; 3 days each way), which was used by fur traders for 40 years as the main route across the Canadian Rockies; and the **South Boundary Trail** (121 km/75 mi; 6-8 days each way), which traverses a remote section of the front ranges into Banff National Park.

Before setting off on any hikes, whatever the length, go to the **Jasper Visitor Centre** in downtown Jasper for waterproof Gem Trek hiking maps, trail conditions, and trail closures, or to purchase a copy of the *Canadian Rockies Trail Guide* by Brian Patton and Bart Robinson.

BIKING

Biking in the park continues to grow in popularity. In addition to the paved roads, many designated unpaved bicycle trails radiate from the town. Cyclists are particularly prone to sudden bear encounters; make noise when passing through heavily wooded areas. The brochure *Mountain Biking Trail Guide* listing designated trails is available from the information center and all local sport shops.

ATHABASCA RIVER TRAIL

One of the most popular biking routes is the Athabasca River Trail. It begins at the base of **Old Fort Point,** a distinctive knoll above the Athabasca River to the south of town, and follows the river to a point below Maligne Canyon, for a distance of 8 km (5 mi) one-way.

RENTALS

Expect bike rentals to run C$35-50 per hour or C$80-130 for any 24-hour period.

SOURCE FOR SPORTS
406 Patricia St., Jasper; 780/852-3654; 10am-8pm daily

VICIOUS CYCLE
630 Connaught Dr., Jasper; 780/852-1111; 10am-6pm Sun.-Thurs., 10am-7pm Fri.-Sat.

RAFTING

Within the park, the Athabasca and Sunwapta Rivers are run by a half-dozen outfitters.

ATHABASCA RIVER

On the Athabasca River, the **Mile 5 Run** is an easy two-hour float that appeals to all ages. Farther upstream, some operators offer a trip that begins from below **Athabasca Falls,** on a stretch of the river that passes through a narrow canyon; this run takes three hours.

SUNWAPTA RIVER

The boulder-strewn rapids of the Sunwapta River offer more thrills and spills—these trips are for the more adventurous and last 3-4 hours.

OUTFITTERS

Most companies offer a choice of rivers and provide transportation to and from downtown hotels. Expect to pay C$100 for trips on the Athabasca and C$120-140 for the Sunwapta. The following companies run on at least one of the rivers mid-May-September.

MALIGNE RAFTING
780/852-3331 or 844/808-7177; www.raftjasper.com

JASPER RAFT TOURS
780/852-2665 or 888/553-5628; www.jasperrafttours.com

JASPER'S WHITEWATER RAFTING
780/852-7238 or 800/557-7238; www.whitewaterraftingjasper.com

WINTER SPORTS

Winter is certainly a quiet time in the park, but that doesn't mean there's a lack of things to do. Downhill enthusiasts gravitate to the slopes of Marmot Basin, while many snow-covered hiking trails are groomed for cross-country skiing.

DOWNHILL SKIING
Marmot Basin

780/852-3816 or 866/952-3816; www.skimarmot.com; Dec.-Apr.; lift tickets adult C$115, senior and youth C$95

The skiing at Marmot Basin is highly underrated. The resort has nine lifts servicing 680 ha (1,675 ac) of terrain with a vertical rise of 900 m (2,940 ft). The longest run is 5.6 km (3.5 mi). A huge injection of cash in recent years has improved the facilities, and the resort's Canadian Rockies Express is the longest detachable quad in Alberta. Lifts take skiers and boarders into Charlie's Basin, a massive powder-filled bowl, and to the summit of Eagle Ridge, which accesses open bowls and lightly treed glades of two other mountain faces. Marmot doesn't get the crowds of the three alpine resorts in Banff National Park, so lift lines are uncommon. The season runs early December-late April.

CROSS-COUNTRY SKIING

For many people, traveling Jasper's hiking trails on skis is just as exhilarating as traversing them on foot. An extensive network of 300 km (185 mi) of summer hiking trails is designated for skiers, with around 100 km (62 mi) groomed.

The four main areas of trails are along **Pyramid Lake Road,** around **Maligne Lake,** in the **Athabasca Falls** area, and at **Whistlers Campground.** A booklet available at the park information center details each trail and its difficulty. Weather forecasts and avalanche-hazard reports are also posted here.

RENTALS

SOURCE FOR SPORTS
406 Patricia St., Jasper; 780/852-3654; 8am-6pm Mon.-Fri., 8am-8pm Sat.-Sun.

TOTEM SKI SHOP
408 Connaught Dr., Jasper; 780/852-3078; 8am-6pm Mon.-Fri., 8am-9pm Sat.-Sun.

rafting on the Athabasca River

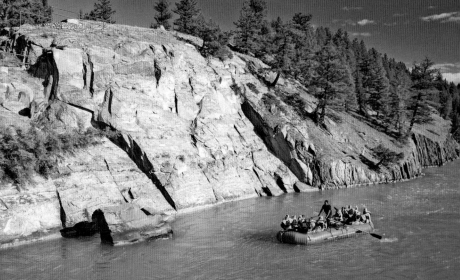

JASPER NATIONAL PARK FOOD

NAME	ADDRESS	TYPE
TOWN OF JASPER		
Bear's Paw Bakery	4 Pyramid Lake Rd., Jasper	café
SnowDome Coffee Bar	607 Patricia St., Jasper	café
★ **Wicked Cup**	Maligne Lodge, 912 Connaught Dr., Jasper	café
Nutter's	622 Patricia St., Jasper	groceries
Sunhouse Cafe	610 Patricia St., Jasper	café
Jasper Pizza Place	402 Connaught Dr., Jasper	sit-down restaurant
Papa George's	Astoria Hotel, 406 Connaught Dr., Jasper	sit-down restaurant
★ **Harvest**	616 Patricia St., Jasper	sit-down restaurant
Fiddle River Restaurant	620 Connaught Dr. (upstairs), Jasper	sit-down restaurant
Something Else	621 Patricia St., Jasper	sit-down restaurant
Raven Bistro	504 Patricia St., Jasper	sit-down restaurant
Syrahs of Jasper	606 Patricia St., Jasper	sit-down restaurant
Kimchi House	407 Patricia St., Jasper	sit-down and takeout
VICINITY OF JASPER		
Orso Trattoria	Fairmont Jasper Park Lodge	sit-down restaurant
★ **Great Hall**	Fairmont Jasper Park Lodge	sit-down restaurant
Tekarra Restaurant	Tekkara Lodge, Hwy 93A	sit-down restaurant
Summit Cafe	Jasper SkyTram upper terminal	sit-down restaurant
★ **Becker's Gourmet Restaurant**	6 km (3.7 mi) south of Jasper on Icefields Parkway	sit-down restaurant
MALIGNE VALLEY		
Maligne Canyon Wilderness Kitchen	Maligne Lake Road	sit-down restaurant

FOOD	PRICE	HOURS
coffee and baked goods	budget	6am-6pm daily
coffee and baked goods	budget	7am-8pm daily
coffee and baked goods	budget	7am-7pm daily
bulk foods	budget	9am-8pm daily in summer, shorter hours the rest of the year
breakfast and lunch	budget	8am-3pm daily
pizza	moderate	11am-11pm daily
casual Canadian	moderate	7:30am-2pm and 5-10pm daily
casual Canadian	moderate	10am-9pm daily
seafood	moderate	5-9pm daily
European	moderate	11am-10pm daily
European	moderate	11am-10pm daily
European	splurge	5-9pm daily
Korean	budget	noon-9pm daily
Italian	splurge	5:30-9:30pm daily
Canadian	splurge	7am-11pm daily
Canadian	splurge	7:30-10:30am and 5-9pm daily mid-May-Sept.
Canadian	budget	10:30am-4:30pm daily Apr.-mid-Oct.
Canadian	splurge	8-11am and 5:30-9pm daily mid-May-early Oct.
contemporary Canadian	moderate	11am-9pm daily summer, 9am-4pm Thurs.-Mon. only rest of year

FOOD

It's easy to get a good, or even great, meal in Jasper. Connaught Drive and Patricia Street are lined with cafés and restaurants. Considering this is a national park, menus are reasonably well priced. You should expect hearty fare, with lots of beef, game, and a surprisingly good selection of seafood.

STANDOUTS
Town of Jasper
WICKED CUP
Maligne Lodge, 912 Connaught Dr.; 780/852-1942; 7am-7pm daily; lunches C$11-14
Well worth searching out is Wicked Cup, on the west side of downtown. Seating is inside or out on a heated deck, and the café is far enough from downtown that it is usually crowd-free. The selection of coffee drinks and teas is extensive, and the food made to order and delicious, including lots of healthy breakfast choices.

HARVEST
616 Patricia St.; 780/852-9676; 10am-9pm daily; breakfasts C$28-42
Harvest is a casual, contemporary restaurant that serves up excellent food at reasonable prices. Breakfasts include mashed avocado on toast, Belgian waffles, and a delicious kale and potato hash topped with a poached egg and hollandaise sauce. The dinner menu is loaded with tapas-style choices designed for sharing—think a cheese board, fish tacos, cauliflower bravas, and fondue. Ingredients are fresh and simply prepared, making for a tasty dining experience.

Vicinity of Jasper
GREAT HALL
Fairmont Jasper Park Lodge, 1 Old Lodge Rd.; 780/852-3301; 7am-11pm daily; C$23-57
The resort's Great Hall takes pride of place in the expansive lobby of the main building. Table settings of various configurations are spread throughout the room while also sprawling out and along an outdoor promenade, from where views over picturesque Lac Beauvert to distant mountains are uninterrupted. Breakfast is served from 7am, while the all-day menu features a wide range of choices, including a fried chicken sandwich, flatbread pizza, and braised elk pie.

BECKER'S GOURMET RESTAURANT
780/852-3535; 8am-11am and 5:30pm-9pm daily mid-May-early Oct.; C$24-45
One of Jasper's best restaurants, Becker's Gourmet Restaurant is 3.7 mi (6 km) south of town along the Icefields Parkway, but well worth the short drive. From this cozy dining room, where the atmosphere is intimate, or the adjacent enclosed conservatory, the views of Mount Kerkeslin and the Athabasca River are inspiring. This restaurant is a throwback, with an ever-changing menu of seasonal game and produce that includes a wild game platter. A menu staple is the pesto-crusted rack of lamb. For dessert, the strawberry shortcake is a delight. Breakfast is also notable, especially the smoothies, and certainly worth a trip from town.

BEST PICNIC SPOTS
Pyramid Lake Day Use Area
Pyramid Lake Rd., 6.1 km (3.8 mi) north of the town of Jasper
With good paddling and swimming, the day-use areas along the west shore of Pyramid Lake are the perfect place to base yourself on a warm summer's day.

Lake Annette Day Use Area
Off Maligne Lake Rd., 7 km (4.3 mi) northeast of the town of Jasper
Picnic tables are spread through a forested area between Lakes Annette and Edith, providing easy access to two lakes, a playground, and changing rooms.

Maligne Lake Day Use Area
Maligne Lake Rd., 48 km (30 mi) north then southeast of the town of Jasper
At the very end of Maligne Lake Road, picnic tables are spread along the shore of Jasper's largest lake—the perfect place to relax after hiking up into the adjacent Bald Hills.

Miette Hot Springs Day Use Area
Miette Hot Springs Rd., 63 km (39 mi) north of the town of Jasper
Best known for hot springs, the end of Miette Hot Springs Road also has picnic tables with raised fire grills.

CAMPING

Campgrounds in Jasper begin opening in May, and all but Wapiti are closed by mid-October. All campsites have a picnic table and fire ring, with a fire permit costing C$9 (includes unlimited firewood).

Unlike neighboring Banff National Park, Jasper's 10 campgrounds can handle all but the busiest summer nights. And on the rare occasion all campsites fill, campers are directed to overflow areas. These are glorified parking lots with no designated sites, but fees are reduced (C$12 per unit).

Reservations
Sites in the most popular campgrounds—**Whistlers, Wapiti,** and **Miette**—can be reserved through **Parks Canada Reservation Service** (877-737-3783; https://reservation.pc.gc.ca) for C$12.

Tips
If you're traveling in June through September and know which dates you'll be in Jasper, it is strongly advised to take advantage of the reservation service above. Whistlers, Wapiti, and Wabasso are the only three campgrounds in the park with powered sites, and therefore they're in great demand.

STANDOUTS
Whistlers Campground
May-mid-Oct.; C$24-50
Whistlers Campground, 3.1 km (1.9 mi) south of Jasper, has 781 sites, making it the largest campground in either Banff or Jasper National Parks. It is divided into four sections, and prices vary with the services available: walk-in tent sites C$24, unserviced sites C$32, powered sites C$38, full hookups C$50. Washrooms and streetlights are spread

JASPER NATIONAL PARK CAMPGROUNDS

NAME	LOCATION	SEASON
★ Whistlers Campground	3.1 km (1.9 mi) south of Jasper on Icefields Parkway	May-mid-Oct.
★ Wapiti Campground	5 km (3.1 mi) south of Jasper on Icefields Parkway	year-round
Snaring Campground	Snaring Rd., 17 km (10.6 mi) north of Jasper, off Highway 16	mid-May-late Sept.
Miette Campground	45 km (28 mi) north of Jasper, off Highway 16	mid-June-early Sept.

throughout, while each section has showers, playgrounds, and a nightly interpretive program.

Wapiti Campground
year-round; C$34.50-39
About 1.2 mi (1.9 km) farther south of Whistlers Campground along the Icefields Parkway is Wapiti Campground, where 86 of the 363 sites have power hookups. Some sites are close to the Athabasca River; facilities include heated bathrooms and showers. Wapiti is also open throughout winter (mid-Oct.-early May) with fewer sites and no dump station.

LODGING

In summer, motel and hotel rooms here are expensive. Most of the motels and lodges are within walking distance of the town of Jasper and have indoor pools and restaurants. Luckily, alternatives to staying in C$400-plus hotel rooms do exist. The best of these are the lodges scattered around the edge of town, where rates are mostly similar, but

SITES AND AMENITIES	RV LIMIT	PRICE	RESERVATIONS
781 tent and RV sites, drinking water, flush toilets, showers, dump station, electrical hookups	no limit	C$24-50	yes
363 tent and RV sites, drinking water, flush toilets, showers, dump station, electrical hookups	no limit	C$34.50-39	yes
62 tent and RV sites, drinking water, pit toilets	8 m (27 ft)	C$26	no
140 tent and RV sites, drinking water, flush toilets	8 m (27 ft)	C$32.50	yes

the experience authentic. Open in summer only, each offers a rustic yet distinct style of accommodation in keeping with the theme of staying in a national park. Additionally, many private residences have rooms for rent in summer, and three hostels are close to town.

Rates quoted are for a standard room in summer. Outside the busy June-September period, most lodgings reduce rates drastically (ask also about ski packages during winter). Rooms have en suite bathrooms, unless otherwise indicated.

Reservations

Book as far in advance as possible, especially in July and August. Contact nonbranded properties directly.

Tips

If you are looking to save money, consider renting a room in a private residence. Unlike traditional bed-and-breakfasts, many of these properties are offering room-only, often with a private entrance. For listings, check out the **Jasper Home Accommodation Association** website (http://stayinjasper.com).

JASPER NATIONAL PARK LODGING

NAME	LOCATION
TOWN OF JASPER	
Jasper Downtown Hostel	400 Patricia St., Jasper
HI-Jasper	708 Sleepy Hollow Rd., Jasper
Athabasca Hotel	510 Patricia St., Jasper
★ **Bear Hill Lodge**	100 Bonhomme St., Jasper
Tonquin Inn	100 Juniper St., Jasper
Chateau Jasper	96 Geikie St., Jasper
VICINITY OF JASPER	
★ **Fairmont Jasper Park Lodge**	1 Old Lodge Rd., Jasper
Pine Bungalows	Northern entrance to town of Jasper
Patricia Lake Bungalows	Pyramid Lake Rd., Jasper
Pyramid Lake Resort	Pyramid Lake Rd., Jasper
Tekarra Lodge	Hwy 93A
★ **Alpine Village**	Hwy 93A at Icefields Parkway
Jasper House Bungalows	4 km (2.5 mi) south of Jasper on Icefields Parkway
★ **Becker's Chalets**	6 km (3.7 mi) south of Jasper on Icefields Parkway

SEASON	OPTIONS	PRICE
year-round	dormitory rooms with 2-8 beds; private rooms with en suite bathrooms	dorm beds C$80, private rooms C$260-300
year-round	dormitory rooms with 1-4 beds (some women-only rooms); private rooms with en suite bathroom	nonmember dorm C$72, private rooms starting at C$220
year-round	hotel rooms, some with shared bathrooms	from C$160 s or d
year-round	cabins; suites with kitchens	cabins starting at C$350
year-round	hotel rooms	rooms starting at C$480
year-round	hotel rooms	rooms starting at C$540
year-round	hotel rooms; suites; historic cabins starting from C$1,500 per night	rooms starting at C$850, cabins starting at C$1,300
May-mid-Oct.	cabins with kitchens	cabins starting at C$400
May-mid-Oct.	cottages with kitchens; suite-style units	cottages starting at C$440
year-round	motel rooms	rooms starting at C$650
mid-May-early Oct.	cabins with kitchenettes	rooms and cabins starting at C$370
late Apr.-mid-Oct.	cabins; suites	cabins starting at C$350
mid-May-mid-Oct.	cabins; motel-style units	motel-style units starting at C$340
May-mid-Oct.	hotel rooms; chalets with kitchenette; duplexes that sleep up to 8	rooms and chalets starting at C$195

JASPER NATIONAL PARK LODGING (CONT.)

NAME	LOCATION
MALIGNE VALLEY	
HI-Maligne Canyon	Maligne Lake Road
MIETTE HOT SPRINGS	
Miette Mountain Cabins	Miette Hot Springs Rd., 43 km (27 mi) north of Jasper on Hwy 16
Miette Hot Springs Bungalows	Miette Hot Springs Road, 17.7 km (11 mi) off Hwy 16

STANDOUTS
Bear Hill Lodge
100 Bonhomme St.; 780/852-3209; www.bearhilllodge.com; starting at C$350-900 s or d
With a variety of cabin layouts and a central location, Bear Hill Lodge makes a great base camp for travelers who want the cabin experience within walking distance of downtown services. The original cabins are basic, but each has a TV, bathroom, gas fireplace, and coffeemaking facilities. Chalet Rooms are larger and more modern, and each has a wood-burning fireplace but no kitchen. The Homestead suites are more spacious still; each sleeps up to eight adults in private bedrooms and includes a full kitchen. Amenities include a sauna, barbecue area, and laundry facilities.

Fairmont Jasper Park Lodge
1 Old Lodge Rd.; 780/852-3301 or 800/257-7544; www.fairmont.com; starting at C$850 s or d
The Fairmont Jasper Park Lodge lies along the shore of **Lac Beauvert** across the Athabasca River from downtown.

This is the park's original resort and its most famous. It's a sprawling property offering plenty of activities. The best known of these is the golf course, but guests also enjoy walking trails, horseback riding, canoeing, tennis, and swimming in an outdoor heated pool that remains open year-round. The main lodge features stone floors, carved wooden pillars, and a high ceiling. This building contains multiple restaurants and lounges, an activity booking desk, a fitness room, a game room, and Jasper's only covered shopping arcade. The 441 rooms vary in configuration and are linked by paths and green space. All have coffeemakers, TVs, telephones, and internet access. Starting from C$1,500 per night, the various historic cabins provide the Fairmont Jasper Park Lodge's premier accommodations and are among the most exclusive guest rooms in all of Canada, having hosted Queen Elizabeth and Marilyn Monroe, among others. Outside of summer, the Fairmont Jasper Park Lodge becomes a bargain, with rooms with lake views

SEASON	OPTIONS	PRICE
June-Sept.	dormitory beds in two cabins	nonmembers C$42
May-Sept.	cabins, some with kitchenette or full kitchen	cabins starting at C$220-600
May-Sept.	motel units; bungalows cabins	motel units starting at C$210 d

(remember, it'll be frozen in winter) for less than C$400.

Alpine Village
780/852-3285; www. alpinevillagejasper.com; late Apr.-mid-Oct.; C$350-880 s or d
At the junction of Highway 93A and the Icefields Parkway 3.1 km (1.9 mi) from town is Alpine Village. This resort is laid out across well-manicured lawns, and all buildings are surrounded by colorful gardens of geraniums and petunias. After a day exploring the park, guests can soak away their cares in the outdoor hot pool or kick back on a row of Adirondack chairs scattered along the Athabasca River, directly opposite the resort. The older sleeping cabins have been renovated (C$350 s or d, C$420 with a kitchen and fireplace), while the Deluxe Bedroom Suites feature open plans, stone fireplaces, luxurious bathrooms, and decks with private forested views. The Deluxe Family Cabins sleep up to five, with two beds in an upstairs loft, along with a fireplace and a full kitchen.

The Whistler cabins, with vaulted ceilings, full kitchens, and king beds, are my lodging of choice here.

Becker's Chalets
780/852-3779; www.beckerschalets. com; May-mid-Oct.; C$195-680 s or d
Becker's Chalets extend along a picturesque bend of the Athabasca River, 6 km (3.7 mi) south of town. This historic lodging took in its first guests more than 70 years ago and continues to be a park favorite for many who make staying here an annual ritual. Moderately priced chalets, each with a kitchenette, gas fireplace, and double bed, are an excellent deal (C$300, or C$340 for those on the riverfront). Deluxe log duplexes featuring all the modern conveniences, including color TV, start at a reasonable C$360 s or d and go up to C$680 for a unit that sleeps eight. Also available are a few one-bed sleeping rooms (C$195). Becker's also boasts one of the park's finest restaurants.

Pyramid Lake

INFORMATION AND SERVICES

Service Hubs

Jasper

The town of Jasper is the service center of Jasper National Park, and despite being within a national park, it has all the facilities of a regular town.

Entrance Gate

The **East Park Gate** is a tollbooth 50 km (31 mi) northeast of the town of Jasper. It is open 24 hours daily year-round to collect the entrance fee. Approaching Jasper from the south along the Icefields Parkway, the park boundary is marked by a sign at Sunwapta Pass, but there is no tollbooth.

Visitor Centers

Jasper Visitor Centre

Connaught Dr., Jasper; 780/852-6176; https://parks.canada.ca/jasper; 9am-7pm daily mid-May-Sept., 9am-5pm daily the rest of the year

The residence of Jasper's first superintendent, this beautiful old stone building dating to 1913 is now used by Parks Canada as the Jasper Park Visitor Centre. The staff provides general information on the park and can direct you to hikes in the immediate vicinity. **Tourism Jasper** (780/852-6236; www.jasper.travel) also has a desk in the building, and the friendly staff never seem to tire of explaining that all the rooms in town are full. As well as providing general information on the town, they have a large collection of brochures on activities, shopping, and restaurants. Also in the building is the **Friends of Jasper National Park** outlet (780/852-4767), selling maps, books, bear spray, and thoughtful souvenirs. Look for notices posted out front with the day's interpretive programs.

TRANSPORTATION

Getting There

Jasper is linked to the outside world by road and rail. Alberta's capital, Edmonton, is 364 km (226 mi) to the east along the wide, mostly twinned Highway 16. Heading south along the Icefields Parkway and east on the Trans-Canada Highway, Banff is 286 km (178 mi; 4 hours) and Calgary is 406 km (252 mi; 5 hours). From Vancouver, Jasper is 782 km (486 mi) to the northeast via Highways 1, 5, and 16; allow at least nine hours.

Air

The closest airport handling domestic and international flights is at Edmonton, a four-hour drive to the east. Edmonton International Airport is south of the provincial capital. From the airport, head north on Highway 2 and take Anthony Henday Drive to bypass downtown Edmonton. From the west side of the city, it's easy driving on a divided Highway 16 to Hinton and the park's east entrance.

From Banff National Park

To get from the town of Banff to Jasper, it's a minimum four-hour drive (286 km/178 mi) north along the Trans-Canada Highway and Icefields Parkway. Driving times can vary given the speed restrictions and often heavy traffic on this route; allow five or six hours for the drive in midsummer.

Gas and Charging Stations

Gas stations are spread along Connaught Drive through downtown Jasper. Electric vehicle charging stations are located at some hotels and downtown beside the railway station at 611 Connaught Drive.

Parking

Public paid parking lots are spread out in the town of Jasper between the rail line and Connaught Drive as they loop around the edge of downtown. RV parking is allowed along this stretch, or in the designated RV parking lot across the railway line on Hazel Avenue.

Shuttles

Pursuit (403/762-6700 or 866/606-6700; www.banffjaspercollection.com) provides a shuttle between downtown Jasper and Maligne Lake for those who have tour boat reservations.

bighorn sheep

WILDLIFE-WATCHING

One of the biggest attractions of Glacier, Banff, and Jasper National Parks is the abundance of wildlife, especially large mammals such as elk, moose, bighorn sheep, and bears, which are all widespread. Glacier National Park has even been designated a Biosphere Reserve by UNESCO due to its breadth of local wildlife. Be sure to bring binoculars in order to appreciate these creatures from a distance.

BEARS

Two bear species roam the mountains in Glacier, Banff, and Jasper: **black bears** and **grizzly bears.** They can be differentiated by size and shape. The second largest of eight recognized species of bears worldwide (only polar bears are larger), grizzlies are larger than black bears and have a flatter, dish-shaped face and a distinctive hump of muscle behind their neck. Color is not a reliable way to tell them apart. Black bears are not always black. They can be brown or cinnamon, causing them to be confused with the brown-colored grizzly. If you spot a bear feeding beside the road, chances are it's a black bear. Grizzlies are only occasionally seen by casual observers; most sightings occur in alpine and subalpine zones, although sightings at lower elevations are not unusual, especially when snow falls early or late.

Omnivores and opportunistic feeders, bears will eat anything that is easy pickings. Intent on gaining 100-150 lbs. (45-68 kg) before winter, bears feed on a diet heavy in plant matter: bulbs, roots, berries, shoots, and flowers. Ants, insects, carrion, and ground squirrels fill in proteins. Contrary to popular opinion, humans are not on their menu of favorite foods.

Bears don't actually hibernate, as their respiration and pulse remain close to normal. Instead, they enter a deep sleep in which the body temperature drops slightly. Bears emerge in the spring ravenously hungry, heading straight for avalanche chutes to rummage for snow-buried carcasses.

black bear cub in Glacier (top); grizzly sow and two cubs in Many Glacier (middle); black bear along the Icefields Parkway (bottom)

Safety

Food is the biggest bear attractant. Proper use, storage, and handling of food and garbage prevent bears from being conditioned and turning aggressive. Pick up any food you drop and pack out all your garbage. All national parks have strict food and garbage rules, which have minimized aggressive bear encounters, attacks, and both human and bear deaths.

Camp Safely: Use low-odor foods, keep food and cooking gear out of sleeping sites in the backcountry, and store them inside your vehicle in front-country campgrounds. Check park websites (www.nps.gov/glac, https://parks.canada.ca/banff, https://parks.canada.ca/jasper) for useful information on camping in bear country.

Hike Safely: Making noise, especially human voices, best prevents surprising a bear, so talk, sing, hoot, and holler. You may feel silly at first, but everyone does it.

Most hikers carry **pepper spray.** Its capsicum derivative deters bear attacks without injuring the bears or humans. Unlike insect repellents, do not use bear sprays on your body, in tents, or on gear; it is to be sprayed directly into a bear's face, aiming for the eyes and nose. Wind and rain may reduce its effectiveness. Small purse-size pepper sprays are too small to deter bears; buy an 8-ounce (237-ml) can. Practice how to use it, but still make noise on the trail. Carry it on the front of your pack where it is easily reached. Pepper spray is not allowed on airplanes unless it's in checked luggage.

Where to See Them (From a Distance)

GLACIER NATIONAL PARK

- Many Glacier (page 68)
- Granite Park Chalet (page 108)

BANFF AND LAKE LOUISE

- Bow Valley Parkway (page 134)
- Lake Louise Sightseeing Gondola (page 142)

JASPER NATIONAL PARK

- Maligne Valley (page 234)

WOLVES

Wolves weigh up to 132 lbs. (60 kg), stand up to 3 ft (1 m) high at the shoulder, and resemble large huskies or German shepherds. Their color ranges from snow white to brown or black, but in this region, it's most often shades of gray. They usually form packs of up to eight members, traveling, hunting, and resting together, and adhering to a hierarchical social order. As individuals, they are complex and intriguing, capable of expressing happiness, humor, and loneliness. They depend solely on meat for survival, and their

wolf

bugling elk (left); moose (right)

hunting territories are immense, often 50 square mi (129 square km), but they can and do travel much farther.

Where to See Them
GLACIER NATIONAL PARK

- Lower Lake McDonald area (page 57)
- North Fork (page 73)

BANFF AND LAKE LOUISE

- Bow Valley Parkway (page 134)

MOOSE

The giant of the deer family is the moose, an awkward-looking mammal that appears to have been designed by a cartoonist. It has the largest antlers of any animal in the world, stands up to 6 ft (1.8 m) at the shoulder, and weighs up to 1,100 lbs. (500 kg). Its body is dark brown, and it has a prominent nose, long spindly legs, small eyes, big ears, and an odd flap of skin called a bell dangling beneath its chin. Each spring, the bull begins to grow palm-shaped antlers that by August will be fully grown. Moose are solitary animals preferring marshy areas and weedy lakes, but they are known to wander to higher elevations searching out open spaces in summer. They forage in and around ponds, streambeds, and lakes on willows, aspens, birches, grasses, and all aquatic vegetation. Although they may appear docile, moose will attack humans if they feel threatened.

Moose thrive in Glacier's high and low country, but they are not particularly common in Banff and Jasper.

Where to See Them
GLACIER NATIONAL PARK

- Many Glacier Road (page 70)
- Many Glacier Boat Tour (page 70)
- Grinnell Lake (page 84)

BANFF AND LAKE LOUISE

- Vermilion Lakes (page 132)

ICEFIELDS PARKWAY

- Upper Waterfowl Lake (page 192)

JASPER NATIONAL PARK

- Patricia Lake (page 230)
- Moose Lake (page 241)

ELK

The elk has a tan body with a dark brown neck, dark brown legs, and a white rump. This second-largest member of the deer family weighs 550-1,000 lbs. (250-450 kg) and stands 5 ft (1.5 m) at the shoulder. Beginning each spring, bulls grow an impressive set of antlers, covered in what is known as velvet. The velvet contains nutrients that stimulate antler growth. By fall, the antlers have reached their full size and the velvet is shed. Rutting season takes place between August and October; listen for the shrill bugles of the bulls serenading the females. During the rut, randy males will challenge anything with their antlers and can be dangerous. The bulls shed their antlers each spring, but don't relax too much: Also in spring, females protecting their young can be equally dangerous.

In Glacier, elk live throughout the park. Large herds of elk also live in and around the towns of Banff and Jasper, often nonchalantly wandering along streets and feeding on tasty plants in residential gardens.

Where to See Them
GLACIER NATIONAL PARK

- Many Glacier (page 68)
- Two Dog Flats (page 64)

BANFF AND LAKE LOUISE

- Town of Banff (page 128)
- Lake Minnewanka Road (page 132)
- Bow Valley Parkway (page 134)

JASPER NATIONAL PARK

- Town of Jasper (page 229)
- Highway 16 (page 237)

white-tailed deer (top); mountain goat in Banff (middle); bighorn males facing off against each other to establish dominance (bottom)

DEER

Mule deer and white-tailed deer are similar in size and appearance. Their color varies with the season, but is generally light brown in summer, turning dirty gray in winter. While both species are considerably smaller than elk, the mule deer is a little stockier than the white-tailed deer. The mule deer has a white rump, a white tail with a dark tip, and large mulelike ears. The white-tailed deer's tail is dark on top, but when the animal runs, it holds its tail erect, revealing an all-white underside. Both inhabit open forests along valley floors.

Where to See Them
GLACIER NATIONAL PARK

- Lake McDonald (page 57)
- Two Medicine (page 70)

BANFF AND LAKE LOUISE

- Town of Banff (page 128)
- Bow Valley Parkway (page 134)

JASPER NATIONAL PARK

- Town of Jasper (page 229)
- Patricia Lake (page 230)

MOUNTAIN GOATS

The remarkable rock-climbing ability of these nimble-footed creatures allows them to live on rocky ledges or near-vertical slopes, safe from predators. The goats stand 3 ft (1 m) at the shoulder and weigh 140-290 lbs. (65-130 kg). Both sexes possess a peculiar beard—or rather, goatee—and have horns. It is possible to determine the sex by the shape of the horns; those of the female grow straight up before curling slightly backward, whereas those of the male curl back in a single arch. The goats shed their thick coats each summer, making them look ragged, but by fall they regrow a fine, new white woolen coat.

Where to See Them
GLACIER NATIONAL PARK

- Logan Pass (page 61)
- Hidden Lake Overlook Trail (page 79)
- Highline Trail (page 82)

ICEFIELDS PARKWAY

- Goats and Glaciers Lookout, Jasper National Park (page 202)

BIGHORN SHEEP

Bighorn sheep are some of the most distinctive mammals seen in these parks. Easily recognized by their impressive horns, they are often spotted grazing on grassy mountain slopes or at salt licks beside the road. The color of their coat varies with the season; in summer, it's a brownish-gray with a cream-colored belly and rump, turning lighter in winter. Fully grown males can weigh up to 270 lbs. (120 kg), while females generally weigh around 180 lbs. (80 kg). Both sexes possess horns, rather than antlers like members of the deer family. Unlike antlers, horns are not shed each year and can grow to astounding sizes. The horns of rams are larger than those of ewes and curve up to 360 degrees. The spiraled horns of an older ram can measure longer than 3 ft (1 m) and weigh as much as 33 lbs. (15 kg). During the fall mating season, a hierarchy is established among the rams for the right to breed ewes. As the males face off against each other to establish dominance, their horns act as both a weapon and a buffer against the headbutting of other rams. The skull structure of the bighorn, rams in particular, has become adapted to these clashes, keeping the animals from being knocked unconscious.

Bighorn sheep are particularly tolerant of humans and often approach parked vehicles; although they are not especially dangerous, as with all mammals, you should not approach or feed them.

Where to See Them
GLACIER NATIONAL PARK

- Logan Pass (page 61)
- Hidden Lake Overlook Trail (page 79)
- Dawson-Pitamakin Loop (page 88)

BANFF AND LAKE LOUISE

- Banff Gondola (page 132)
- Lake Minnewanka (page 132)

ICEFIELDS PARKWAY

- Near Tangle Falls (page 201)

JASPER NATIONAL PARK

- Disaster Point, Highway 16 (page 237)

MARMOTS

High in the mountains, above the tree line, hoary marmots are often seen sunning themselves on boulders in rocky areas or meadows. They are stocky creatures, weighing 9-19 lbs. (4-9 kg) and resembling fat house cat-size fur balls. When danger approaches, these large rodents emit a shrill whistle to warn their colony. Marmots are active for only a few months each summer, spending up to nine months a year in hibernation.

Where to See Them
GLACIER NATIONAL PARK

- Cobalt Lake (page 87)
- Highline Trail (page 82)

ICEFIELDS PARKWAY

- Helen Lake, Banff National Park (page 190)
- Bow Summit, Banff National Park (page 192)

JASPER NATIONAL PARK

- Jasper SkyTram (page 230)
- Bald Hills (page 240)

hoary marmot in Glacier (left); pika in Banff (right)

SAFETY AROUND WILDLIFE

Spotting wildlife is one of the thrills of visiting these three parks. In order to maintain the health and safety of animals and humans alike, obey park rules and use common sense.

- **Keep your distance.** Although it's tempting to get close to wildlife for a better look or a photograph, it disturbs the animal and, in many cases, can be dangerous. Instead, use binoculars to get close-up views and telephoto or zoom lenses for photographing wildlife. Do not attempt to take selfies with wildlife. Stay at least 100 yd (100 m) from bears and wolves and 3 bus lengths from other large animals, such as deer, elk, moose, mountain goats, and bighorn sheep.

- **Do not feed the animals.** Many animals may seem tame, but feeding them endangers yourself, the animal, and other visitors, as animals become aggressive when looking for handouts (even the smallest critters, such as squirrels).

- **Store food safely.** When camping, keep food out of reach of animals, such as in your vehicle or in approved storage containers. Just leaving it in a cooler isn't good enough.

- **Drive carefully.** The most common cause of premature death for larger mammals is being hit by vehicles.

PIKAS

In subalpine country, a chorus of eeks, screams, and squeaks bounce through rockfalls. The noisemakers are pikas, which look like tailless mice. However, pikas are not rodents but rather lagomorphs (members of the rabbit family), which are distinguished by a double set of incisors in the upper jaw. The small, grayish pika is a neighbor to the marmot, living among the rubble and boulders of scree slopes above timberline. But unlike marmots, pikas do not hibernate. They spend their summers gathering flowers and greenery to dry under rocks as their winter food.

Where to See Them

GLACIER NATIONAL PARK

- Piegan Pass Trail (page 79)

BANFF AND LAKE LOUISE

- Bourgeau Lake (page 145)

JASPER NATIONAL PARK

- The Whistlers (page 239)

Grizzly bears often cause traffic jams.

glacier lilies in Logan Pass meadows, Glacier

WILDFLOWERS

Glacier, Banff, and Jasper National Park are all rich in floral diversity. Glacier is even a UNESCO Biosphere Reserve for its variety of wildflower niches. Forests, prairies, and peaks have different vegetation specific to elevation, habitat, and weather. The season for wildflower blooms is short—most reach their peak during varying points in July and early August.

VEGETATION ZONES

Botanists divide the mountains of Glacier, Banff, and Jasper into three distinct vegetation zones (also called biomes): montane, subalpine, and alpine. The boundaries of these zones are determined by several factors, the most important being elevation. Latitude and exposure are also factors, but less so. Typically, within any 4,920 ft (1,500 m) of elevation change, you'll pass through each of the three zones.

The **montane** zone occurs at low to middle elevations, below about 4,920 ft (1,500 m). Next is the **subalpine** zone, which is generally 4,920-7,220 ft (1,500-2,200 m) above sea level. The upper limit of the subalpine zone is the tree line.

The **alpine** zone extends from the tree line to mountain summits. Here, the land appears to be barren rock, but a host of miniature plants adapt to the harsh conditions of high winds, drying altitude, short summers, cold temperatures, and rocky soil that lacks organic matter. Hugging the ground, large areas of alpine meadows burst with color for a short period each summer.

LILIES

In Glacier's subalpine zone, early July brings on fields of **yellow glacier lilies** as they force their blooms through the snow. Recognize their flowers by their posture, hanging downward but with their six petals curving upward. Later in the summer, grizzly bears dig up their bulbs to eat, leaving swaths of meadows looking like they've been rototilled. In Banff and Jasper National Parks, **wood lilies** flower in late spring at lower elevations, while up in the alpine meadows of Banff, glacier and **avalanche lilies** bloom.

Where to See Them
GLACIER NATIONAL PARK

- Logan Pass (page 61)
- Granite Park Chalet (page 108)

BANFF AND LAKE LOUISE

- Sunshine Meadows (page 133)
- Johnson Lake (page 163)

JASPER NATIONAL PARK

- Patricia Lake (page 230)

MOSS CAMPION

Mats of moss campion are among the plants that fling their energy into tiny flowers amid the harsh alpine tundra. Their tiny pink flowers are about the size of your littlest fingertip. To survive the harsh winds and arid conditions, they hug the ground in green mats or cushions that often look mossy, hence the name. Some mats can be around 100 years old.

Where to See Them
GLACIER NATIONAL PARK

- Scenic Point Trail (page 86)
- Siyeh Pass Trail (page 79)

ICEFIELDS PARKWAY

- Bow Glacier Falls, Banff National Park (page 191)

JASPER NATIONAL PARK

- Bald Hills (page 240)

LUPINE

In mountain meadows, lupine blooms in shades of blue to purple with a hint of white on long showy stalks towering above palm-like leaf clusters. At lower elevations, they grow taller than at upper elevations. You can recognize the spent plant as a member of the pea family due to its pods. In Glacier, lupine thrive in aspen parklands of the montane zone on the east side of the park in July and early August. You may also see a much shorter variety in the alpine tundra zones. In Banff and Jasper, lupine are among the wildflowers that bloom in alpine meadows for a short period each summer.

Where to See Them
GLACIER NATIONAL PARK

- Many Glacier Road (page 70)
- Two Medicine Lake (page 72)

ICEFIELDS PARKWAY

- Bow Lake, Banff National Park (page 190)

JASPER NATIONAL PARK

- Bald Hills (page 240)

COW PARSNIP

At lower elevations, the large white heads of cow parsnip bloom alongside roads in late June and early July before continuing into higher elevations as summer progresses. Sometimes their bloom clusters are so big that they appear like inverted dinner plates. These plants, members of the celery family, are an important food source for grizzly bears. A few people have allergic reactions to cow parsnip with blistering, so you may want to avoid touching them.

Where to See Them
GLACIER NATIONAL PARK

- Lower elevations of Going-to-the-Sun Road (page 60)

BEAR GRASS

Between tree islands in the subalpine zone, lush mountain meadows bloom with a colorful array of plants,

glacier lily (top); moss campion (middle); lupine (bottom)

including bear grass. Some years, bear grass stalks bloom so thickly in July that subalpine hillsides look snow-covered. Their sturdy, stiff evergreen leaves form a low mound, while their stalks shoot up to 3 ft tall (1 m). The creamy star-like flowers bloom in a large cluster at the head of the stalk and are a favorite food for deer and elk.

Where to See Them
GLACIER NATIONAL PARK

- Highline Trail (page 82)
- Iceberg Lake Trail (page 86)

PAINTBRUSH

Paintbrush spew across the subalpine mountain meadows of Glacier National Park and the montane zone of Banff and Jasper in fields of yellow, red, fuchsia, white, salmon, scarlet, and orange. You can recognize paintbrush because it looks like an upended brush dipped in paint. At lower elevations, they often bloom in early July. In subalpine meadows, blooming peaks mid-July-mid-August.

Where to See Them
GLACIER NATIONAL PARK

- Logan Pass and Hidden Lake Overlook (page 61)
- Piegan Pass Trail (page 79)
- Going-to-the-Sun Road (page 60)

BANFF NATIONAL PARK

- Bow Valley Parkway (page 134)

ICEFIELDS PARKWAY

- Helen Lake, Banff National Park (page 190)

bear grass (top); red paintbrush (middle); shooting stars (bottom)

- Cavell Meadows, Jasper National Park (page 206)

JASPER NATIONAL PARK

- Maligne Valley (page 234)

SHOOTING STARS

Late May-early June brings tiny shooting stars to montane meadows and along lakeshores as far north as Saskatchewan River Crossing in Banff. The subalpine meadows won't bloom with them until July. The pink to lavender flowers with yellow centers and black stamens look as though the petals have been blown backward to form a rocket. They grow on short fragile stalks singly or with several flowers.

Where to See Them
GLACIER NATIONAL PARK

- Hidden Lake Overlook Trail (page 79)

- Many Glacier Road (page 70)

BANFF AND LAKE LOUISE

- Johnson Lake (page 163)

CAMAS

In Glacier, camas are among the flowers that thrive in open meadows. **Blue camas** grows on a long stalk in damp montane meadows. The bulbs of the plant provided food for early Indigenous people. The **mountain death camas,** a cluster of cream-colored flowers, covers a wider range from montane meadows to subalpine meadows. Contrary to the blue camas, all parts of the plant are poisonous to humans if ingested.

blue camas (top); columbine (middle); balsamroot (bottom)

Where to See Them
GLACIER NATIONAL PARK

- Mountain death camas: Highline Trail (page 82)
- Blue camas: Two Medicine Road (page 70)

COLUMBINE

Yellow columbine bloom between tree islands in the subalpine zone. This delicate flower blooms atop a spindly tall stalk with five conical petals surrounded by lighter sepals. Find it in July and early August. In the harsh alpine tundra, **Jones' columbine** grow low to the ground in early July. Their deep blue-purple flowers have the traditional columbine cone shapes, but on tiny stalks for protection.

Where to See Them
GLACIER NATIONAL PARK

- Yellow columbine: Grinnell Glacier Trail (page 81)
- Jones' columbine: Siyeh Pass Trail (page 79)

BANFF AND LAKE LOUISE

- Sunshine Meadows (page 133)

ICEFIELDS PARKWAY

- Helen Lake, Banff National Park (page 190)
- Cavell Meadows, Jasper National Park (page 206)

BALSAMROOT

In Glacier's drier eastside montane meadows between groves of aspen trees, arrowleaf balsamroot grows in more arid locales favored by the sunflower family. Recognize them by their big showy yellow flowers and large dusty green arrowhead-shaped leaves. These are early summer flowers, often seen in June and early July. Indigenous people used all parts of the plant for food, and deer munch on the flowers or leaves.

Where to See Them
GLACIER NATIONAL PARK

- Two Dog Flats (page 64)
- Many Glacier Road (page 70)

MONKEYFLOWER

In midsummer, wet streambeds are lined with monkeyflower in subalpine meadows. The fuchsia monkeyflower has tiny yellow spots and grows on long leafy stalks. On the contrary, the short yellow monkeyflower hugs the ground around water. Recognize the flower by its streamside locale and tubular shape; it acquired its name because of the monkey-like face in the flower.

Where to See Them
GLACIER NATIONAL PARK

- Hidden Lake Overlook Trail (page 79)
- Cobalt Lake Trail (page 87)

MOUNTAIN AVENS

Mountain avens are low-to-the-ground white wildflowers that bloom in meadows and rocky areas above the tree line for a short period each summer. They often grow in areas where glaciers have recently receded, gaining a foothold as a dense mat among the barren rocky till. Their white flowers face the sun as it moves, and they dry into fuzzy tufts in late summer.

pink monkeyflower in Glacier

mountain avens (left); alpine forget-me-nots (right)

Where to See Them
GLACIER NATIONAL PARK

- Scenic Point Trail (page 86)

- Siyeh Pass Trail (page 79)

BANFF AND LAKE LOUISE

- Sunshine Meadows (page 133)

ICEFIELDS PARKWAY

- Parker's Ridge, Banff National Park (page 195)

- Cavell Meadows, Jasper National Park (page 206)

- Wilcox Pass Trail, Jasper National Park (page 198)

ALPINE FORGET-ME-NOTS

Growing in seemingly barren mountain tundra and in alpine meadows throughout the region, these small but distinctive flowers are yellow- or pink-centered with blue petals. To survive, they limit their growth, staying low to the ground to escape drying winds.

Where to See Them
GLACIER NATIONAL PARK

- Scenic Point Trail (page 86)

- Dawson-Pitamakin Loop (page 88)

BANFF AND LAKE LOUISE

- Sunshine Meadows (page 133)

ICEFIELDS PARKWAY

- Parker's Ridge, Banff National Park (page 195)

- Cavell Meadows, Jasper National Park (page 206)

HEATHER

Heather with tiny pink bell-like flowers blooms in Glacier's subalpine meadows during late July. In addition to pink heather, white and yellow heather grows in alpine meadows of Banff and Jasper, flowering between mid-July and mid-August.

Where to See Them
GLACIER NATIONAL PARK

- Hidden Lake Overlook Trail (page 79)

- Iceberg Lake Trail (page 86)

BANFF AND LAKE LOUISE

- Sunshine Meadows (page 133)

ICEFIELDS PARKWAY

- Parker's Ridge, Banff National Park (page 195)
- Cavell Meadows, Jasper National Park (page 206)

WILD ROSES

This large pink flower is common throughout montane forests in Banff and Jasper between late May and July.

Where to See Them
BANFF AND LAKE LOUISE

- Bow Valley Parkway (page 134)
- Johnson Lake (page 163)

JASPER NATIONAL PARK

- Cottonwood Slough (page 238)
- Maligne Valley (page 234)

FIREWEED

Tall and showy, these pink flowers thrive along roadsides and in areas where wildfire has swept through.

Where to See Them
GLACIER NATIONAL PARK

- North Fork (page 73)

BANFF AND LAKE LOUISE

- Bow Valley Parkway (page 134)

ICEFIELDS PARKWAY

- Saskatchewan River Crossing, Banff National Park (page 194)

JASPER NATIONAL PARK

- Medicine Lake (page 234)

heather (top); wild rose (middle); fireweed (bottom)

Goats and Glaciers Lookout

ESSENTIALS

FAST FACTS

GLACIER

- **Established:** 1910
- **Visitation in 2022:** 2,900,000
- **Area:** 1,583 square mi (4,100 square km)

BANFF

- **Established:** 1885
- **Visitation in 2022:** 4,200,000
- **Area:** 6,641 square km (2,564 square mi)

JASPER

- **Established:** 1907
- **Visitation in 2022:** 2,200,000
- **Area:** 11,228 square km (4,335 square mi)

GETTING THERE
AIR

Located closest to Banff, Calgary International Airport is the best airport for visiting all three parks. There are also other airports closer to Glacier and Jasper.

Calgary International Airport

YYC; 403/735-1200; www.calgaryairport.com
DRIVING TIME TO GLACIER:
4 hours to Many Glacier and St. Mary (border crossing at Carway-Piegan open 7am-11pm daily year-round)
DRIVING TIME TO BANFF: 90 minutes to the town of Banff
DRIVING TIME TO JASPER:
5-6 hours to the town of Jasper

Glacier National Park
GLACIER PARK INTERNATIONAL AIRPORT

FCA; Kalispell, Montana; www.iflyglacier.com
DRIVING TIME TO GLACIER: 35 minutes to West Glacier Entrance; 2.5-3 hours to St. Mary and Many Glacier

GREAT FALLS INTERNATIONAL AIRPORT

GTF; Great Falls, Montana; www.gtfairport.com
DRIVING TIME TO GLACIER:
2.5 hours to Two Medicine; 3 hours to St. Mary and Many Glacier

LETHBRIDGE AIRPORT

YQL; Lethbridge, Alberta; www.lethbridgeairport.ca; Westjet (www.westjet.com) only
DRIVING TIME TO GLACIER:
2 hours to St. Mary and Many Glacier

Jasper National Park
EDMONTON INTERNATIONAL AIRPORT

YEG; Edmonton, Alberta; https://flyeia.com

DRIVING TIME TO JASPER: 4 hours to the town of Jasper

CAR

Most visitors to Glacier, Banff, and Jasper arrive by car after landing at one of the area airports. Driving to the parks from other metropolitan areas can take 8 hours or more.

Driving Times

All driving times are for dry roads in summer.

VANCOUVER, BRITISH COLUMBIA

- **Driving Time to Glacier:** 11.5 hours
- **Driving Time to Banff:** 10 hours
- **Driving Time to Jasper:** 9 hours

SEATTLE, WASHINGTON

- **Driving Time to Glacier:** 9 hours
- **Driving Time to Banff:** 11 hours
- **Driving Time to Jasper:** 10 hours

SALT LAKE CITY, UTAH

- **Driving Time to Glacier:** 10 hours
- **Driving Time to Banff:** 14 hours
- **Driving Time to Jasper:** 17 hours

Road Rules
UNITED STATES

Driver's licenses from other countries are valid in Montana for 12 months, but you may also need an International Driver Permit for other states. Proof of insurance is also required (bring paperwork or insurance card). Drivers and passengers are required to wear seat belts. Highway signs post distances in **miles** and speeds in **miles per hour** (mph). The speed limits inside the park vary 25-45 mph (40-72 kph) but outside the park are 55-65 mph (89-105 kph) on highways.

CANADA

Driver's licenses from all countries are valid in Canada for up to three months.

You should also carry vehicle registration papers or rental contracts. Proof of insurance must also be carried, and you must wear seat belts. All highway signs in Canada give distances in **kilometers** and speeds in **kilometers per hour** (kph). Within Canadian national parks, the speed limit is 90 kph (56 mph), reduced even further on some roads, such as the Bow Valley Parkway.

Border Crossing

Driving between Glacier and Banff or Jasper involves crossing the U.S.-Canada border. Most drivers will pass through the border at **Roosville** (BC 93/US 93; 24 hours daily year-round) or **Carway-Piegan** (AB 2/US 89; 7am-11pm daily year-round). On Chief Mountain Highway, a seasonal port of entry at the **Chief Mountain border crossing** is open daily mid-May to mid-October: 9am-6pm May 15-30, 7am-10pm June 1-September 4, 9am-6pm September 5-30, closed October-May 15. Passports are required for crossing.

ENTERING CANADA

International travelers entering Canada must have passports and a valid visa, if required. The one exception is travelers from the United States, who may use NEXUS (entry by air or land) or FAST (land only) cards instead. Visas are not required for visitors from about 50 countries, including the United States. All others must apply for visas. Find the list of visa-exempt countries and visa requirements at www.cic.gc.ca.

ENTERING THE UNITED STATES

International travelers entering the United States must have passports. One exception applies to travelers from Canada and countries in the Western Hemisphere Travel Initiative, who may use passport cards, NEXUS cards, or enhanced driver's licenses. Visas are not required for visitors from Canada and many other countries. Find the list of visa-exempt countries and visa requirements at https://travel.state.gov/. All others must apply for visas.

passenger train in Banff National Park

CUSTOMS

In general, Canada and the United States have similar customs laws: no plants, drugs, firewood, or live bait can cross the border. Some fresh meats, poultry products, fruits, and vegetables are restricted. Pets are permitted to cross the border with a certificate of rabies vaccination dated within 30 days prior to crossing.

Be aware of two major differences in customs rules between the countries. While **marijuana** is legal in Canada and in certain states in the United States, it is illegal federally in the United States and therefore considered criminal to bring it across the border. Second, most firearms are illegal in Canada, including **pepper sprays.** Bear sprays are considered firearms in Canada; they must have a U.S. Environmental Protection Agency-approved label to go across the border.

To find out what can and can't go across the border into Canada or the United States, consult the following:

Canada Border Services Agency (CBSA; www.cbsa-asfc.gc.ca) or **U.S. Customs and Border Protection** (CBP; www.cbp.gov/travel).

TRAIN
Glacier National Park
AMTRAK EMPIRE BUILDER
800/872-7245; www.amtrak.com
In the United States, Glacier is one of the rare national parks serviced by train. Traveling east from Seattle or Portland and west from Chicago, Amtrak's daily *Empire Builder* stops at West Glacier year-round and also at East Glacier in the summer. Seattle/Portland to West Glacier takes a little more than 15 hours; Chicago to East Glacier takes 30 hours or more.

Banff and Jasper National Parks
VIA RAIL CANADIAN
416/366-8411 or 888/842-7245; www. viarail.ca
Government-run **VIA Rail** provides passenger-train service right across Canada. The *Canadian* is a service between Toronto and Vancouver with stops at Edmonton and Jasper.

ROCKY MOUNTAINEER
604/606-7245 or 877/460-3200; www.rockymountaineer.com; starting at C$2,300 per person d
This luxurious rail trip runs between Vancouver and Banff or Jasper and passes through the spectacular interior mountain ranges of British Columbia. Travel is during daylight hours only, so you don't miss anything. Trains depart in either direction in the morning (every second or third day throughout summer), overnighting at Kamloops.

GETTING AROUND
DRIVING
Glacier National Park

To get around Glacier, most visitors opt to drive themselves, allowing for more freedom in scheduling, although some parking lots fill early in the morning.

Driving in Glacier National Park is not easy. Narrow roads built for cars in the 1930s barely fit today's SUVs, much less RVs and trailers. With no shoulders and sharp curves, roads require reduced speeds and shifting into second gear on extended descents to avoid burning brakes. Smaller cars are easier to drive because of the narrow roads, and you do not need a 4WD.

Two paved two-lane roads go west-east across the Continental Divide: **Going-to-the-Sun Road** (mid-June–mid-Oct.) bisects the park, while **US 2** (year-round) hugs Glacier's southern border. The seasonal Going-to-the-Sun Road is the more difficult drive, climbing 1,500 ft (457 m) higher on a skinnier, curvier road than US 2. Between Avalanche and Rising Sun, the Sun Road does not permit RVs or trailer-combos over 21 ft (6.4 m) long, 10 ft (3.1 m) tall, and 8 ft (2.4 m) wide, including side mirrors.

Paved two-lane roads lead to Two Medicine, St. Mary, Many Glacier, and Waterton, but just because roads are paved doesn't mean that they are smooth. The North Fork has rough dirt and gravel roads, and the Inside North Fork Road does not allow RVs over 21 ft (6.4 m) nor trailers.

Find the status of roads in Glacier online (www.nps.gov/glac) or on the NPS app. The St. Mary and Apgar Visitor Centers have updates on road closures for weather, construction, or congestion. You can also receive text alerts about roads; send 333-111 the message "GNPROADS" to get alerts on closures, openings, and temporary restrictions.

GAS AND CHARGING STATIONS

Gas up before you head into Glacier, and make sure your car is in good condition. There are no gas stations inside the park. Find gas in the towns of West Glacier, East Glacier, St. Mary, Babb, and Waterton, but few of the stations can repair severely broken-down vehicles. Apgar Visitor Center parking lot has one charging station.

RESERVATIONS

Due to overcrowding, four roads require vehicle ticket reservations (www.recreation.gov; $2/vehicle) during peak season daily 6am-3pm. West-side accesses (Polebridge Entrance of the North Fork and West Glacier or Camas Entrance for Going-to-the-Sun Road) require tickets late May through mid-September. East-side accesses (Many Glacier, Two Medicine, and Rising Sun on Going-to-the-Sun Road from St. Mary) require tickets July-mid-September. Tickets are released online in one-month blocks four months in advance, and additional tickets are released one day in advance; they are not sold in the park. Going-to-the-Sun Road tickets are valid for three days; all other vehicle tickets are valid for one day. Check in advance online (www.nps.gov/glac) for potential adjustments.

Banff and Jasper National Parks

For most of the year, driving in Banff and Jasper National Parks is easy and enjoyable. All roads are paved, and aside from snow in winter, there are no major concerns. In summer, roads into major attractions get very busy and occasionally close when parking lots are full. This includes parking lots around the Lake Minnewanka loop, Johnston Canyon, and Lake Louise. Moraine Lake is closed to public vehicles. These destinations are monitored by traffic control personnel on the busiest days. The best advice is to arrive early. Gas is available year-round in Banff, Lake Louise, and Jasper. Between mid-April and mid-October, gas is also available along the Icefields Parkway at Saskatchewan River Crossing. Charging stations are located in the towns of Banff and Jasper.

TRAVELING BY RV

RVing is a great way to travel, but in Glacier it has its limitations. Roads are narrow, curvy, and shoulderless, and many inside-park campsites cannot fit larger RVs and do not have hookups. Most of all, RVs are restricted on Going-to-the-Sun Road to under 21 ft (6.4 m) long. RVs over 21 ft (6.4 m) and all trailers are prohibited on the Inside North Fork Road. Six campgrounds inside Glacier have disposal stations: Apgar, Fish Creek, Many Glacier, Rising Sun, St. Mary, and Two Medicine.

Conversely, camper vans, recreational vehicles, and travel trailers are a great way to get around Banff and Jasper. The only road with any restriction is Cavell Road in Jasper, where RVs and trailers are not allowed. The most difficult places to navigate larger vehicles are the towns of Banff and Jasper, but both have designated RV parking lots. For Banff, check https://banffparking.ca for information on where to park. At least one campground near the towns of Banff and Jasper and the village of Lake Louise have sites suitable for the longest RVs, with hookups and dump stations, although you will need reservations well in advance.

BUSES AND SHUTTLES
Glacier National Park
BUS

Inside Glacier, the National Park Service runs free **Going-to-the-Sun Road shuttles** July-Labor Day and more limited in September. These are shuttles, not guided tours. Between Apgar and St. Mary, they stop at lodges, trailheads, campgrounds, and Logan Pass. Get on or off at any of the stops denoted by interpretive signs. No tickets are needed, and no reservations are taken. Departing every 15-30 minutes, these extremely popular shuttles enable point-to-point hiking on some of Glacier's most spectacular trails. Check schedules and routes online (www.nps.gov/glac).

Two companies operate fee-based shuttles on Glacier's east side. For hikers and backpackers, these aid in doing point-to-point trails, and for travelers without vehicles, they help connect with the Sun Road shuttles. **Pursuit Glacier Park Collection** (844/868-7474; www.glacierparkcollection.com) runs van service daily early June-late September north-south between East Glacier, Two Medicine, and St. Mary. **Xanterra** (855/733-4522; www.glaciernationalparklodges.com) operates daily shuttles July-Labor Day from Many Glacier to St. Mary.

BOAT

Hikers and backpackers also use tour boats as shuttles to reduce foot miles. In Glacier, **Glacier Park Boat Company** (406/257-2426; https://glacierparkboats.com; June-Sept.) carts hikers across Two Medicine Lake and in Many Glacier across Swiftcurrent Lake and Lake Josephine. Both add early morning Hiker Express shuttles July-August. Get advance reservations online for round-trip shuttles and one-way return trips.

In Waterton, **Waterton Shoreline Cruises** (403/859-2362; www.watertoncruise.com) runs boat shuttles to the Crypt Lake trailhead late May-early October, and the tour boat to Goat Haunt functions as a hiker shuttle June-mid-September for round-trip or one-way rides. Buy tickets at least a day in advance.

Banff National Park
BUS

In summer and fall, Parks Canada operates buses from the **Lake Louise Ski Resort** (www.reservation.pc.gc.ca; round-trip adult C$10, senior or child C$5) to Lake Louise and Moraine Lake. Shuttles operate continuously 8am-6pm, with earlier departures at the busiest times of year.

Roam Transit (https://roamtransit.com; C$2-10 per sector) operates bus service along two routes through the town of Banff: one from the Banff Gondola north along Banff Avenue, the other from the Fairmont Banff Springs to the Tunnel Mountain campgrounds.

Roam buses also run to Canmore, Lake Louise, and Moraine Lake.

Jasper National Park
BUS
Pursuit (403/762-6700 or 866/606-6700; www.banffjaspercollection.com) provides a complimentary shuttle between downtown Jasper and Maligne Lake for those who have tour boat reservations.

NEARBY TOWNS
NEAR GLACIER NATIONAL PARK
Small seasonal towns cling to the boundaries of Glacier. Going-to-the-Sun Road has West Glacier on its west end and St. Mary on its east end. East Glacier is a small town located outside the southeastern corner of the park, near the Two Medicine Entrance. Farther afield, the Flathead Valley is a year-round recreation hub about 35 minutes outside the West Entrance of Glacier National Park. It offers the most options for food and lodging near the park as well as the closest airport to the park. Columbia Falls, Whitefish, and Kalispell are all located in the Flathead Valley.

West Glacier
Only 2 mi (3.2 km) from Lake McDonald, West Glacier sits just outside the park's West Entrance and makes a good base. It's convenient for hopping on the train, going river rafting or fishing, and heading off on guided backpacking trips. Most services are open mid-May-September.

FOOD
West Glacier offers a range of dining options to supplement the limited dining inside the park. Seasonal restaurants cater to summer visitors; hours can shorten in spring or fall, and only a few remain open in winter. There are also two seasonal stores (May-Sept.) that carry convenience foods, beer, wine, camping items, ice, and firewood.

LODGING
The limited inside-park lodgings at Apgar are extremely popular, so West Glacier options often serve as backup for both hotels and campgrounds. During midsummer, most West Glacier lodgings fill nightly; reservations are advised. Lower rates are available in spring and fall. Additional food and accommodations options are also available in Coram, 5 mi (8 km) west of West Glacier.

INFORMATION
Two visitor centers offer information on things to do surrounding Glacier. Located in Belton Train Depot, the **West Glacier Visitor Information Center** (junction of Going-to-the-Sun Rd. and US 2; 406/892-3250; http://glacier.org; 9am-5pm daily summer) has the main Glacier Conservancy bookstore and information for the Flathead Valley. The **Crown of the Continent Discovery Center** (12000 US 2 E.; 406/387-4405; www.crowndiscoverycenter.com; 10am-7pm daily early May-mid-Oct.) has regional planning information, hands-on displays, and brochures on geotourism activities that includes national parks, national forests, World Heritage Sites, and wilderness areas in Montana and Canada.

St. Mary
St. Mary is the eastern portal to Going-to-the-Sun Road, located 21 mi (34 km) southeast of Many Glacier. At the junction of the Sun Road and the Blackfeet Highway (US 89), the town clusters at the park boundary along the highway. Only the visitor center and St. Mary Campground are within the park; the town, restaurants, grocery stores, lodging, and commercial campgrounds are on the Blackfeet Reservation. St. Mary is convenient for exploring Going-to-the-Sun Road, and it works as a home base for day trips to Waterton, Many Glacier, and Two Medicine, plus it's a good place to stay before heading up to Banff. It is a seasonal town with most

services open mid-May-September, but otherwise everything closes.

FOOD

St. Mary has several eateries, which include options at the lodge in St. Mary Village and family-run cafés. There are also two summer-only (daily June-Sept.) grocery stores on US 89. Restaurants and grocery stores in St. Mary do not serve alcohol during North American Indian Days, a reservation-wide four-day celebration beginning the second Thursday in July. Alcohol sales are also prohibited on other selected days, such as graduation in June.

LODGING

Amenities at St. Mary accommodations are limited, especially internet access. In most locations, Wi-Fi is slow and usually only available in lobbies. The St. Mary Village complex has several different options ranging from value rooms to upscale accommodations. Other properties in St. Mary offer cabin accommodations.

INFORMATION

Located at the St. Mary entrance to Glacier National Park, the **St. Mary Visitor Center** (406/888-7800; www.nps.gov/glac; 8am-5pm daily mid-June-early Oct., 8:30am-5pm late May-June) provides information on the park but not on the town of St. Mary.

East Glacier

Outside the park boundary on the Blackfeet Reservation, East Glacier caters to tourists with multiple restaurants, motels, cabins, a lodge, and hostels, many of which are only open mid-May-September. East Glacier sits about 7 mi (11.3 km) from the Two Medicine park entrance.

FOOD

Most visitors hit East Glacier to dine out. The casual eateries include cafés, bakeries, and a Mexican restaurant. During special days on the Blackfeet Reservation, such as graduation and North American Indian Days, none of the restaurants, groceries, or bars serve alcohol, including East Glacier. The four-day celebration is usually scheduled beginning the second Thursday in July. Given the small size of the town, you'll be able to walk to most of the restaurants from your accommodations.

LODGING

On the west side of the railroad tracks, historic Glacier Park Lodge is on MT 49 along with a compact strip of motels—think very rustic, not a highway megastrip. On the east side of the tracks along US 2, East Glacier has several motels within a few blocks of restaurants. All fill completely in midsummer, so reservations are strongly advised.

Columbia Falls

Sprawling along the highway, Columbia Falls is the closest Flathead Valley town to Glacier and Glacier Park International Airport. The town is 18 minutes from West Glacier and 12 minutes from the airport. The gateway to Glacier, Columbia Falls never had a waterfall of its own until the town built one. A recent boom in restaurants has upgraded the quality of dining. In summer, it has a public outdoor swimming pool, Big Sky Waterpark, and a Thursday night farmers market with music, food, and family fun.

FOOD

New restaurateurs have ushered in fresh tastes, including a brewery, catapulting the cuisine beyond the fast-food enterprises along the highway.

LODGING

The town has a lodge and a couple of small independent motels located on US 2 for those on a budget. Surrounding Columbia Falls, cabins and vacation homes are scattered in the woods and along the Flathead River. Locate properties rented by their owners via **VRBO** (www.vrbo.com) and **Airbnb** (www.airbnb.com). Summer rates are highest, but you can find lower rates and deals during the rest of the year.

INFORMATION
The **Flathead Valley Convention and Visitors Bureau** (406/756-9091 or 800/543-3105; www.fcvb.org) and **Columbia Falls Chamber of Commerce** (406/892-2072; www.columbiafallschamber.org) provide mostly online information.

Whitefish
Whitefish is a resort town. It is 15-20 minutes west of US 2 and Glacier Park International Airport (on US 2) and 45 minutes west of Glacier National Park. It garners the most visitors in the Flathead. Whitefish boasts shops, boutiques, restaurants, bars, art galleries, and theaters. In the summer, downtown streets crowd with shopping tourists, especially during the Tuesday evening farmers market. In winter, its ski town heritage emerges in early February with the Winter Carnival. The town also serves as a springboard for boating, paddling, golfing, hiking, mountain biking, and skiing. One of its biggest summer attractions is the scenic chairlift ride at **Whitefish Mountain Resort** (406-862-2900; www.skiwhitefish.com) to see the panorama of Glacier's peaks.

FOOD
As a resort town, Whitefish is overloaded with outstanding restaurants, from casual to fine dining. Because of the crowds, make reservations to avoid long waits in summer or winter. In spring and fall, a few restaurants alter their hours.

LODGING
Whitefish is the only Flathead Valley town that offers luxury lodging, but it also has a myriad of less-pricey options, including chains and independent hotels. Find a full listing at https://explorewhitefish.com. You can also locate vacation homes and cabins to rent through **Lakeshore Rentals** (406/863-9337 or 877/817-3012; www.lakeshorerentals.us). Reservations in town are mandatory in summer, but when town books out, rooms are usually still available at Whitefish Mountain Resort. In town, summer has the highest rates, with the second-highest rates in winter.

INFORMATION
The **Flathead Valley Convention and Visitors Bureau** (406/756-9091 or 800/543-3105; www.fcvb.org) and **Whitefish Convention and Visitors Bureau** (877/862-3548; https://explore-whitefish.com) provide mostly online information.

Kalispell
Built at highway crossroads, Kalispell is the Flathead Valley's largest town. Most of the hotels and restaurants are located 15 minutes south of Glacier Park International Airport (on US 2), the opposite direction from Glacier National Park, and almost 1 hour from West Glacier.

FOOD
Kalispell has common national chain restaurants along US 93 and several large grocery markets for those wanting to get supplies.

LODGING
Kalispell has several chain hotels sprawled on the outskirts of downtown, including hotels around the mall and strip mall areas. You can find them online (https://kalispellchamber.com). Other than chain hotels, the pickings are slim. Rates will be highest in summer, with lower prices in fall, winter, and spring.

INFORMATION
The **Flathead Valley Convention and Visitors Bureau** (406/756-9091 or 800/543-3105; www.fcvb.org) and **Kalispell Chamber of Commerce** (406/758-2800; kalispellchamber.com) provide mostly online information.

NEAR BANFF NATIONAL PARK

The town of Banff, which is located within the national park, is a commercial center in its own right, with a range of restaurants, accommodations, and services available. Canmore and Calgary are two larger population centers near the park.

Canmore

Canmore lies in the Bow Valley, 27 km (17 mi) southeast of Banff and just a 20-minute drive to the park. With a range of excellent restaurants and a choice of comparatively well-priced accommodations, the town can make a good base for your trip to Banff.

FOOD

Canmore offers a range of food options. You can get inexpensive meals at the many cafés; other choices run the gamut, from the lively atmosphere of dining in the front yard of a converted residence to top-notch Alberta beef.

LODGING

Most of Canmore's newer lodgings are on Bow Valley Trail (Highway 1A). Although hotel pricing in Canmore may be high, it is definitely cheaper than nearby Banff, so much of the local business is overflow from the adjacent park. As with all resort towns in the Canadian Rockies, reservations should be made as far in advance as possible in summer.

More than 40 bed-and-breakfasts operate in Canmore as well as hundreds of vacation rentals. For a full list of B&Bs, check the website of the Canmore/Bow Valley Bed and Breakfast Association (www.bbcanmore.com) for one that suits your needs.

INFORMATION

The best source of pretrip information is **Tourism Canmore Kananaskis** (www.explorecanmore.ca). A **Travel Alberta Information Centre** (2801 Bow Valley Trail; 403/678-5277; 8am-8pm daily May-Sept., 9am-6pm daily Oct.), just off the Trans-Canada Highway on the west side of town, provides plenty of information about Canmore—and other destinations throughout the province.

Calgary

Located 90 minutes east of Banff and with an international airport, Calgary is the entry point for the vast majority of those arriving by air to visit these parks. A city of more than one million residents, Calgary is a major center for the oil and gas industry. Calgary is also the closest large city to Glacier National Park; it's a 4-hour drive to the east-side entrances of Many Glacier and St. Mary.

FOOD

Calgary has many reasonably priced restaurants, as well as a wide variety of choices. The area southwest of downtown, along 17th Avenue and 4th Street, has become a focal point for Calgary's restaurant scene, with cuisine to suit all tastes.

LODGING

Accommodations in Calgary vary from campgrounds, a hostel, and budget motels to a broad selection of high-quality hotels catering to top-end travelers and business conventions. Most downtown hotels offer reduced rates on weekends—Friday and Saturday nights might be half the regular room rate. During Stampede Week, a 10-day early July celebration of everything cowboy, prices are higher than the rest of the year, and accommodations are booked months in advance.

INFORMATION

Tourism Calgary (403/263-8510 or 800/661-1678; www.visitcalgary.com) operates a Visitor Information Centre at Calgary International Airport (403/735-1234; 7am-midnight daily) that greets visitors arriving by air across from Carousel 4.

NEAR JASPER NATIONAL PARK

Jasper is relatively remote, but it has all the services needed for visitors. The closest town outside the park boundary is Hinton to the east.

Hinton

On the south bank of the Athabasca River and surrounded in total wilderness, Hinton is just outside the Jasper National Park boundary 81 km (50 mi) east of the town of Jasper. Although mostly a forestry town, it is a gateway to interesting parks north and south of town, and the motels and restaurants have prices you'll appreciate after pricing out Jasper.

FOOD

The main strip through Hinton has all the usual fast-food and family restaurants, but you can also find local cafés and an array of Asian restaurants dotted through downtown. If Hinton is your last stop before Jasper, it's a good place to stock up on groceries at reasonable prices.

LODGING

Highway 16 through Hinton is lined with midpriced motels, including many in the Wyndham and Choice chains, a Holiday Inn, and a few lower-priced independents. Hotel rates vary greatly with demand; in summer, expect to pay upward of C$200 per night, but the rest of the year, many rooms are under C$100.

INFORMATION

The **Hinton Visitor Information Centre** (309 Gregg Ave.; 780/865-7000; https://explorehinton.org; 9am-5pm daily) is on the main highway through town. Here you can purchase park and attraction passes for Jasper, take advantage of free coffee and Wi-Fi, and find out about opportunities to explore the surrounding region.

RECREATION
HIKING
Glacier National Park

Conditions on Glacier's trails vary significantly depending on the season, elevation, recent severe weather, and bear closures. Swinging and plank bridges across rivers and creeks are installed in late May-June. Some years, bridges are installed and then removed a few weeks later to wait for rivers swollen with runoff to subside. Most years, higher passes are snowbound until mid-July, including the steep snowfields that close the Highline Trail. Ptarmigan Tunnel's doors are usually open mid-July-early October. Several backcountry campsites are snowbound until August. To find out about trail conditions before hiking, stop at ranger stations or visitor centers for updates, or consult trail status reports June-September online (www.nps.gov/glac). Bear or fire closures are also listed online. Before you leave home, text 333-111 the message "GNPTRAILS" for alerts on trail closures, reopenings, and postings/unpostings for bears frequenting.

Banff National Park

Banff National Park holds a great variety of trails. Here you can find anything from short interpretive trails with little elevation gain to strenuous slogs up to high alpine passes. Trailheads for some of the best hikes are accessible on foot from the town of Banff. Those farther north begin at higher elevations, from which access to the tree line is less arduous. Although lower elevation trails begin opening in May, the main hiking season July-September. The park's website (https://parks.canada.ca/banff) lists all trail conditions, including closures.

Jasper National Park

The trails in Jasper National Park are oriented more toward the experienced backpacker, offering plentiful routes for long backcountry trips. Locals often hit the trails around the town of Jasper as early as April, but the main hiking season is July-September. This is also the busiest time of year in the park, so plan on heading out early in the day to avoid crowds. For trail reports, check the park's website (https://parks.canada.

ca/jasper), which lists trail conditions and closures.

BACKPACKING
Glacier National Park
Wilderness permits are required (adults $7 pp/night) for backpacking. Starting mid-March, **advance reservations** (www.recreation.gov, $10 per permit) for backpacking trips mid-June through September are available for 1-4 people. Reservations are mandatory if your heart is set on a specific route in July-August as 70 percent of the campsites are in the reservation system. You'll still need to pick up the physical permit the day before your trip. If you don't have an advance reservation, 30 percent of the permits are available in person 24 hours prior to a trip. Year-round, permits are available 24 hours in advance in person during and outside the reservation season. Current availability is updated frequently online (www.recreation.gov or www.nps.gov/glac).

Get permits in person at the **Apgar Backcountry Permit Office** (406/888-7859 May-Oct., 406/888-7800 Nov.-Apr.; 7:30am-5pm daily June-Sept., 8am-4pm daily May and Oct.) or **St. Mary Visitor Center** (406/888-7800; backcountry permit desk 7:30am-5pm daily late May-late Sept.). You can also get permits at **Many Glacier Ranger Station, Two Medicine Ranger Station,** and **Polebridge Ranger Station.** All permits must be picked up by 4:30pm. Trip-planning maps, reservations, and the permits use three-letter codes to denote assigned camps, but specific campsites are first-come, first-served. Outside the reservation season (mid-June-Sept.), permits are only issued in person. During winter, permits are available at park headquarters by appointment (406/888-7800; Nov.-Apr.).

Each backcountry campground has 2-7 sites, with four people allowed per site. All wilderness campgrounds have pit toilets (some with great views), community cook sites, and separate tent sites. Store all food, garbage, toiletries, and cookware on the provided bear pole or hanging bar or in the bear-proof food storage boxes, not in tent sites. Many backcountry campsites do not allow fires; carry a lightweight stove for cooking. Take low-odor foods to avoid attracting bears, and practice Leave No Trace principles religiously.

Banff and Jasper National Parks
Staying overnight in the backcountry of Banff or Jasper offers many rewards. Some effort is involved in preparing for a backcountry trip, such as gathering the necessary gear, but you'll be traveling through country inaccessible to the casual day hiker, well away from the crowds and far from any road. Banff and Jasper National Parks also have backcountry lodges. Another option for backcountry accommodations is offered by the **Alpine Club of Canada** (403/678-3200; www.alpineclubofcanada.ca). The club maintains a series of huts, each generally a full-day hike from the nearest road, in these parks.

Gear
Bring backpacking gear (tent, sleeping bag, pad, clothing, rain gear, topographic maps, compass or GPS device, first-aid kit, insect repellent, sunscreen, fuel, cooking gear, and stove) plus a 25-ft (7.6-m) rope for hanging food, a small screen or strainer for sifting food particles out of gray water, a one-micron or smaller filter for purifying water (tablets and boiling can also do the job), and a small trowel for emergency human waste disposal when a pit toilet is unavailable.

BIKING
Glacier National Park is a tough place to cycle. There are no shoulders, roads are narrow and curvy, and drivers gawk at scenery instead of the road, all putting cyclists in precarious positions. Spring, when roads are closed to cars for plowing, is a good season for biking. All manner of bikes (roadies, mountain

bikes, kiddie trailers, tagalongs, tot striders, and even tricycles) hit Going-to-the-Sun Road on sunny spring days. Riding starts in mid-April and goes until the roads open to cars, which can be May-mid-July. You can ride as far as plowing operations and avalanche closures permit. Do not ride beyond closure signs.

Banff and Jasper National Parks are perfect for both road biking and mountain biking. On-road cyclists will appreciate the wide shoulders on all main highways. Mountain biking is allowed on designated trails throughout the national parks. Park information centers hand out brochures detailing these trails and giving them ratings.

PADDLING AND RAFTING

Glacier National Park has instituted strict boating and paddling guidelines in order to protect its pristine waters from invasive aquatic species. The lakes are only open in summer and only available by permit to boaters and paddlers who have passed an inspection. Permitting requirements make bringing a power-boat from home impractical for most short-term visitors. River rafting is a big activity outside the park in West Glacier, which is near two rivers that run along the park boundaries.

In Banff and Jasper, canoeing, kayaking, and stand-up paddleboarding are great ways to explore the waterways of the mountains that are otherwise inaccessible—such as Vermilion Lakes in Banff National Park, where a great variety of birds can be appreciated from water level. In Jasper, river rafting offers a chance to get out on the water. To help stop the spread of invasive aquatic species, watercraft inspection stations are set up along major highways leading in and out of the Canadian Rockies.

WINTER SPORTS

In Glacier National Park, some roads and trails in the park make for prime cross-country skiing and snowshoeing routes. For route descriptions, pick up

Skiing and Snowshoeing in the visitor centers or online (www.nps.gov/glac). Skiers and snowshoers should be well equipped and versed in winter travel safety before venturing out.

Although cross-country skiing and snowshoeing can be done in Banff National Park, it's well known as a world-class downhill skiing destination, with three winter resorts, including Lake Louise, the second largest in all of Canada. Jasper has one downhill skiing resort, as well as 300 km (185 mi) of cross-country skiing trails. Most resorts open in early December and close in May.

INTERPRETIVE PROGRAMS
GLACIER NATIONAL PARK

Ranger programs in Glacier National Park include guided walks, astronomy programs, and even amphitheater presentations. Find program schedules at park visitor centers or in the park newspaper handed out at entrance stations.

Evening Programs

Rangers lead free 45-minute park naturalist evening programs on wildlife, fires, and natural phenomena at the following locations in summer.

- Lake McDonald Lodge
- Fish Creek Campground Amphitheater
- Apgar Campground Amphitheater
- Rising Sun Amphitheater
- Many Glacier Hotel
- Many Glacier Campground Amphitheater
- St. Mary Campground Amphitheater
- St. Mary Visitor Center
- Two Medicine Campground Amphitheater

DARK SKIES

GLACIER NATIONAL PARK

With minimal light pollution, Waterton-Glacier has been designated the first transboundary International Dark Sky Park in the world. When weather cooperates, you can experience thousands of stars, the Milky Way, the Perseid meteor shower in August, and the aurora borealis in spring and fall.

Skywatching Spots

- Logan Pass
- Two Medicine Campground
- Dusty Star Observatory at St. Mary Visitor Center

view of the Milky Way from Logan Pass

BANFF NATIONAL PARK

Once you leave the bright lights of the town of Banff behind, the wonders of the night sky can be appreciated from many places.

Skywatching Spots

- Vermilion Lakes
- Lake Minnewanka

ICEFIELDS PARKWAY

Skywatching Spots

- Bow Lake
- Columbia Icefield

JASPER NATIONAL PARK

Jasper is officially a Dark Sky Park (https://jasperdarksky.travel), which is celebrated with a festival in mid-October.

Skywatching Spots

- Old Fort Point
- Maligne Lake

Native America Speaks

Since 1982, Glacier's naturalist programs have included the acclaimed Native America Speaks in summer. Look for shows in park lodges, St. Mary Visitor Center, and at campground amphitheaters. Free 45-minute evening campground amphitheater programs feature members of the Blackfeet, Salish, and Kootenai people who use storytelling, humor, and music to share their culture and heritage. Check the park newspaper or online for the current schedules and location of presentations.

Two specialty programs occur throughout the summer. Jack Gladstone, a Grammy-nominated Blackfeet musician, presents Triple Divide: Heritage and Legacy (www.jackgladstone.com; check current schedule at www.nps.gov/glac), which blends storytelling and music into a one-hour multimedia walk through Glacier's history from the Blackfeet perspective. At the St. Mary Visitor Center's auditorium, the Two Medicine Lake Singers and Dancers draw standing-room-only crowds for demonstrating Blackfeet dances in full traditional regalia. Tickets (adults $5, kids 12 and under free; check current schedule at www.nps.gov/glac) go on sale the Monday before a performance for the 90-minute show, and they sell out quickly.

Kid-Friendly Programs

Kids can earn a Junior Ranger badge by completing self-guided activities in the *Junior Ranger Activity Guide,* available at all visitor centers. Most activities target ages 6-12 and coincide with a trip over Going-to-the-Sun Road. When kids return the completed newspaper to a visitor center, they are sworn in as Junior Rangers and receive Glacier National Park badges. Waterton has a comparable program with the Parks Canada Xplorers Program.

BANFF AND JASPER NATIONAL PARKS

Parks Canada offers a number of different interpretive programs, including guided walks, campground presentations, and wildlife talks. Program schedules are posted at visitor centers and campgrounds.

CELL SERVICE AND INTERNET

Glacier has very limited cell service reception and public Wi-Fi. Plan to download the apps, maps, podcasts, and PDFs you will need for your travels before you arrive. Limited public Wi-Fi is available at two visitor centers and for guests in lodge lobbies. Cell and internet service is available in towns surrounding Glacier, but is limited in St. Mary and East Glacier.

Cell service and internet access are available in and around the towns of Banff and Jasper, as well as in the village of Lake Louise. Beyond these population centers, there is no access, including along the Icefields Parkway (except at the Icefield Centre).

ACCESSIBILITY

The website www.wheelchairtraveling.com offers a wide range of tips on accessible travel, as well as firsthand stories of travel. The Society for Accessible Travel and Hospitality (212/447-7284; www.sath.org) supplies information on tour operators, vehicle rentals, specific destinations, and companion services. For frequent travelers, the membership fee ($49 per year) is well worth it. **Emerging Horizons** (www.emerginghorizons.com) is an online magazine dedicated to travelers with special needs.

GLACIER NATIONAL PARK

Visitors with mobility, hearing, and vision disabilities should consult Glacier's accessibility page (www.nps.gov/glac/planyourvisit/accessibility.htm) for resources. The park's *Accessible Facilities and Services* brochure, which contains the same information, is available at visitor centers. The **Disabled Traveler's Companion** (www.

tdtcompanion.com) also gives comprehensive information for traveling in Glacier.

Blind or permanently disabled U.S. citizens or permanent residents can get a free lifetime National Parks and Federal Recreational Lands Access Pass for all national parks and other federal sites. The pass admits the pass holder plus three other adults in the same vehicle; children under age 16 are free. Pass holders also get 50 percent discounts on federally run tours and campgrounds. Get these passes in person at entrance stations with proof of medical disability or eligibility for receiving federal benefits.

Five campgrounds in Glacier reserve a couple of sites each for wheelchair needs: Apgar, Fish Creek, Rising Sun, Sprague Creek, and Two Medicine. Picnic areas at Apgar, Rising Sun, and Sun Point also have wheelchair access, as do all lodges within the park boundaries, although they have a limited number of guest rooms that conform to Americans with Disabilities Act accessibility guidelines. Most parking lots offer designated parking.

Other wheelchair-accessible sites include **boat docks** at Lake McDonald, Many Glacier, and Two Medicine as well as **evening naturalist programs** in Apgar Amphitheater, Lake McDonald Lodge Auditorium, Many Glacier Hotel Auditorium, Rising Sun Campground, and Two Medicine Campground. Shuttles on the Sun Road have wheelchair ramps or lifts, and each can take one wheelchair.

While pet dogs are not permitted on Glacier's backcountry trails, service dogs are allowed. But due to bears, they are discouraged. With service dogs, be safe by sticking to well-traveled trails around midday.

BANFF AND JASPER NATIONAL PARKS

The best source for pretrip planning information for visitors with disabilities is the Banff Lake Louise Tourism website (www.banfflakelouise.com/

accessibility). Throughout both parks, some trails are paved and wheelchair accessible, shuttles have wheelchair ramps, and all but the remotest accommodations are accessible. Both commercial hot springs have water-accessible wheelchairs.

TRAVELING WITH PETS

If traveling with your pet to all three parks, which requires crossing the U.S.-Canada border, you will need to have a certificate of rabies vaccination dated within 30 days prior to crossing the border.

GLACIER NATIONAL PARK

Pets are allowed in Glacier National Park, but only in limited areas: campgrounds, parking lots, and roadsides. They are not allowed on trails, beaches, off-trail in the backcountry, or at any park lodges or motor inns. When outside a vehicle or in a campground, pets must be on a leash.

Protection of fragile vegetation and prevention of conflicts with wildlife are two main reasons pets are not allowed on Glacier National Park trails. For pooch-walking purposes, go to the paved Apgar Bike Trail (2 mi/3.2 km), which allows pedestrians as well as pets on leashes. Contrary to Glacier, Waterton permits dogs on leashes on some of its trails.

Be considerate of wildlife and other visitors by keeping your pet under control and disposing of waste in garbage cans.

BANFF AND JASPER NATIONAL PARKS

Pets are permitted in both national parks but must be on leash and under control at all times (the exception is off-leash parks in the towns of Banff and Jasper). Some hotels are pet-friendly, and all campgrounds allow pets. Although dogs are allowed on hiking trails, there may be restrictions if wildlife is present.

HEALTH AND SAFETY

For traveling in the United States, you should have health insurance, as health care needs are up to individuals to cover financially. Be sure your health insurance plan will cover doctors, emergency clinics, and hospitals in the United States.

It's a good idea to have health insurance or some form of coverage before heading to Canada; check that your plan covers foreign services. Some hospitals impose a surcharge for nonresidents.

EMERGENCY SERVICES

Glacier National Park

For emergencies inside the park, call 911. All hospitals are located outside the park.

- **Logan Medical Center:** 310 Sunny View Ln., Kalispell; 406/752-5111; 35 minutes from West Glacier

- **Logan Health-Whitefish:** 1600 Hospital Way, Whitefish; 406/863-3500; 35 minutes from West Glacier

- **Blackfeet Community Hospital:** 760 Blackweasel Rd., Browning; 406/338-6100; 1 hour from St. Mary

Banff and Jasper National Parks

Call 911 for all emergencies within the two parks. There are hospitals inside the parks, each in their respective towns.

- **Mineral Springs Hospital:** 301 Lynx St., Banff; 403/762-2222

- **Seton-Jasper Healthcare Centre:** 518 Robson St., Jasper; 780/852-3344

WATER HAZARDS

Be extremely cautious around lakes, fast-moving streams, and waterfalls, where slick moss and algae cover the rocks.

GIARDIA

Lakes and streams can carry parasites like *Giardia lamblia*. If ingested, it causes cramping, nausea, and severe diarrhea for up to six weeks. Avoid giardia by boiling water (for one minute, plus one minute for each 1,000 ft/305 m of elevation above sea level) or using a one-micron filter. Bleach also works (add two drops per quart and wait 30 minutes). Tap water in campgrounds, hotels, and picnic areas has been treated.

DEHYDRATION

Many first-time hikers to these parks are surprised to find they drink more water than at home. Wind, altitude, and lower humidity can add up to a fast case of dehydration. It manifests first as a headache. While hiking, drink lots of water, even more than you normally would. With children, monitor their fluid intake.

ALTITUDE

Some visitors from lower elevations feel the effects of altitude at high elevations like Logan Pass. Watch for light-headedness, headaches, or shortness of breath. To acclimatize, slow down the pace of hiking and drink lots of fluids. If symptoms spike, descend in elevation as soon as possible. Altitude also increases UV radiation exposure: To prevent sunburn, use a strong sunscreen and wear sunglasses and a hat.

ICE AND SNOW

While glacial ice often looks solid to step on, it harbors unseen caverns beneath. Buried crevasses (large vertical cracks) are difficult to see, and snow bridges can collapse as a person crosses. Be safe by staying off the ice; even tiny ice fields have caused fatalities. Steep-angled snowfields also pose a danger from falling. Use an ice ax and caution, or stay off them.

HYPOTHERMIA

Insidious and subtle, hypothermia is a risk for exhausted and physically unprepared hikers. The body's inner core loses heat, reducing mental and physical functions. Watch for uncontrolled shivering, incoherence, poor judgment, fumbling, mumbling, and slurred speech. Avoid becoming hypothermic by staying dry. Don rain gear and warm moisture-wicking layers, rather than cottons that won't dry and fail to retain heat. Get hypothermic hikers into dry clothing and shelter. Give warm non-alcoholic and noncaffeinated liquids. If the victim cannot regain body heat, get into a sleeping bag with the victim, both stripped for skin-to-skin contact.

HANTAVIRUS

Hantavirus infection, with flu-like symptoms, is contracted by inhaling dust from deer mice droppings. Avoid burrows and woodpiles thick with rodents. Store all food in rodent-proof containers. If you find rodent dust in your gear, disinfect it with water and bleach (1.5 cups bleach to 1 gallon water). If you contract the virus, get immediate medical attention.

MOSQUITOES AND TICKS

Bugs can carry diseases such as West Nile virus and Rocky Mountain spotted fever. Protect yourself by wearing long sleeves and pants as well as using insect repellent in spring-summer, when mosquitoes and ticks are common. If you are bitten by a tick, remove it, disinfect the bite, and see a doctor if lesions or a rash appears.

COVID-19

Glacier National Park

Currently Glacier has no COVID-related restrictions in place. However, lack of staff from the pandemic fallout still affects many businesses and park facilities with shorter hours, limited services, and closures. If COVID-19 transmission levels go high again in Flathead and Glacier Counties, then face masks may once again be required in federal buildings and visitor centers in Glacier regardless of vaccination status.

RESOURCES

- **Glacier National Park Status Update** (www.nps.gov/glac/planyourvisit/conditions.htm): This page lists the current alerts for Glacier.

- **COVID-19 Montana Response** (https://covid19.mt.gov): Find information on COVID-19 transmission in Flathead and Glacier Counties, which surround Glacier National Park.

- **Blackfeet Nation** (https://blackfeetnation.com/covid19): This page lists current regulations and resources regarding the Blackfeet reservation and COVID-19.

- **Flathead County Health Department** (https://flatheadhealth.org/novel-coronavirus-covid-19): Find information about current regulations regarding masks, current cases, and vaccines.

Banff and Jasper National Parks

There are no COVID-related restrictions or mitigation measures in Banff or Jasper National Parks. Traveling to both parks is now similar to the way it was before the pandemic.

RESOURCES
GLACIER
Glacier National Park
www.nps.gov/glac

The official website for Glacier National Park. It provides information on park conditions, roads, campsites, trails, history, and more. Six webcams are updated every few minutes. In addition to trip-planning information, the site includes downloadable maps, publications, and wilderness permit information as well as trail conditions.

Glacier National Park Conservancy
https://glacier.org

The best resource for books, maps, posters, and cards on Glacier Park. Proceeds from book sales are donated to the park to support education, preservation, and research.

National Park Service Reservation Center
www.recreation.gov

This service is for making reservations for Glacier's reserveable campgrounds and road vehicle reservations.

Xanterra
www.glaciernationalparklodges.com

This park concessionaire operates Many Glacier Hotel, Lake McDonald Lodge, Rising Sun Motor Inn, Swiftcurrent Motor Inn, and Apgar Village Inn, as well as tours and shuttles.

Pursuit Glacier Park Collection
www.glacierparkcollection.com

Pursuit operates Apgar Village Lodge and Motel Lake McDonald, as well as a shuttle on the east side of the park.

BANFF AND JASPER
Alberta Parks and BC Parks
https://albertaparks.ca
https://bcparks.ca

These departments oversee management of the provincial parks in Alberta and British Columbia. The websites detail facilities, fees, and seasonal openings of the parks.

Parks Canada
https://parks.canada.ca

Official website of the agency that manages Canada's national parks and national historic sites. The website has information on each park and historic site, including fees, camping, and wildlife.

Parks Canada Reservation Service
https://reservation.pc.gc.ca

Online reservation service for national park campgrounds, shuttles, and tours.

Citizenship and Immigration Canada
www.cic.gc.ca

Check this government website for anything related to entry into Canada.

Fairmont Hotels and Resorts
www.fairmont.com

Lodging chain that owns famous mountain resorts such as the Banff Springs, Chateau Lake Louise, and Jasper Park Lodge.

Pursuit
www.banffjaspercollection.com

Operator offering attractions, tours, airport shuttles, and accommodations in both parks.

INDEX

A

accessibility: 293–294
accommodations: *see* lodging
air travel: 280–281
alpine forget-me-nots: 276
Alpine Village: 255
altitude sickness: 295
Angel Glacier: 206
Apgar: 93–94, 95; map 57
Apgar Bike Trail: 92
Apgar Picnic Area: 57, 98–99
Apgar Visitor Center: 96, 112
Assiniboine people: 40
Athabasca Falls: 191, 202, 244, 245
Athabasca Falls Day Use Area: 210
Athabasca Glacier: 36, 38, 197, 199, 201
Athabasca Pass Trail: 243
Athabasca Pass Viewpoint: 206–207
Athabasca River: 244
Athabasca River Drive (Highway 16): 237
Athabasca River Trail: 243
auto travel: 281–282, 283
Avalanche: 61
Avalanche Campground: 95
Avalanche Creek Picnic Area: 99
Avalanche Gorge: 77
Avalanche Lake: 77

B

backpacking: general discussion 290; Banff 154–155; Glacier 88–90; Ice-fields Parkway 209; Jasper 243
Bald Hills: 34, 240–241; map 240
balsamroot: 274
Banff Canoe Club: 158
Banff Gondola: 15, 132
Banff Legacy Trail: 155
Banff National Park: 30, 117–176; backpacking 154–155; bicycling 155, 158; camping 164–167, 170; food 160–161, 162–164; highlights 121, 128–135, 136, 142–144; hiking 138, 140, 144–151; information and services 174–175; itineraries 123, 124; lodging 168–173; maps 118–119, 122, 127, 130–131; paddling 158; winter sports 158–159
Banff Sunshine Summer Gondola: 133

Banff, town of: 128–133, 144–145, 171–172; map 130–131
Banff Upper Hot Springs: 129, 132
Banff Visitor Centre: 174
beaches: 57
bear grass: 271–272
Bear Hill Lodge: 254
bears: 260–261
Bear Valley: 83
Becker's Chalets: 255
Becker's Gourmet Restaurant: 246
bicycling: general discussion 290–291; Banff 155, 158; Glacier 90–92; Ice-fields Parkway 209; Jasper 243–244
Big Beehive: 149, 150–151
Big Bend: 61, 195
bighorn sheep: 264–265
Bird Woman Falls: 61
Blackfeet Interpretive Loop: 41
Blackfeet Peaks: 73
Blackfeet people: 40
Blackfoot Glacier: 79
boat tours: Grinnell Lake 70; Lake McDonald 57; Lake Minnewanka 133; Maligne Lake 236; St. Mary Lake 68; Two Medicine Lake 73
boat travel: 284
border crossing: 281
Bourgeau Lake: 145
Bow Glacier Falls: 191–192
Bow Glacier Falls Trail: 42
Bow Lake: 42, 190–191
Bow Lake Day Use Area: 210
Bowman Lake: 77
Bow Peak: 189
Bow River: 15, 128, 158, 192
Bow River/Hoodoos: 144–145
Bow Summit: 192
Bow Valley Parkway: 121, 134–135, 147, 155, 172; map 134
Brewster's Mountain Lodge: 171
Bridal Veil Falls: 149
Bridal Veil Falls Viewpoint: 195
Buffalo Nations Luxton Museum: 41, 129
Bullhead Lake: 85
bus tours: 66, 68
bus travel: 219, 284–285

C

Calgary: 288
camas: 273–274
Camas Road: 95
Cameron Falls: 75
camping: Banff 164–167, 170; Glacier 100–105; Icefields Parkway 211–214; Jasper 249–251
Canmore: 288
car travel: 281–282, 283
Cascade Ponds Day Use Area: 163
Castle Junction: 135
Castle Lookout: 147
Castle Mountain: 135
Cataract Creek: 94
Cave and Basin National Historic Site: 129
Cavell Meadows: 206
cell service: 293
Chalet: 209
charging stations: 113, 175, 219, 257, 283
Chephren Lake: 194
Chief Mountain International Highway: 74
cirques: 39
Cirrus Mountain: 195
C Level Cirque: 145
Cliffhouse Bistro: 162–163
climate: 27–28
Cobalt Lake: 87
Coleman Creek Day Use Area: 210
Columbia Falls: 286–287
Columbia Icefield: 20, 195–201; map 196
Columbia Icefield Skywalk: 200–201
columbine: 274
Continental Divide: 61, 192, 194–195
Cottonwood Slough: 238
COVID-19: 296
cow parsnip: 271
cross-country skiing: 245
The Crossing Resort: 195
crowds, avoiding: 56, 126, 188, 228
Crowfoot Glacier: 42, 189–190
Crypt Lake: 75–76
customs regulations: 282

DE

dark skies: 292
Dawson-Pitamakin Loop: 88–89
deer: 264
dehydration: 295

disabilities, travelers with: 293–294
Disaster Point: 237
Dome Glacier: 197, 200
East Glacier: 286
East Park Gate: 237
East Side Tunnel: 64
Egypt Lake: 154
Elizabeth Lake: 90
elk: 263
Emerald Lake: 136, 138, 140
Emerald Lake Lodge: 141
emergency services: 295
Endless Range: 201
entrance fees: 30, 31
entrance stations/gates: 77, 111–112, 174, 218, 257

F

Fairmont Banff Springs: 171–172
Fairmont Chateau Lake Louise: 142, 173
Fairmont Jasper Park Lodge: 25, 254–255
Fairview Day Use Area: 164
Fifty Mountain: 83, 89–90
fireweed: 277
Fish Creek Campground: 95
Fish Creek Picnic Area: 57
Fishercap Lake: 85
Flattop Camp: 90
food: Banff 160–161, 162–164; Glacier 96–100; Icefields Parkway 209–211, 246; Jasper 246–249; nearby towns 285, 286, 287, 288, 289
forget-me-nots: 276

G

Garden Wall: 61
gas: 113, 175, 219, 257, 283
Geraldine Lakes: 202
giardia: 295
glacial lakes: 38–39
Glacier Gallery: 197
Glacier National Park: 30, 47–115; backpacking 88–90; bicycling 90–92; camping 100–105; food 96–100; highlights 51, 57, 60–77; hiking 77–88; information and services 111–115; itineraries 53–54; lodging 105–109; maps 48–49, 52; paddling 93–94; winter sports 94–96
glaciers: general discussion 38; Angel Glacier 206; Athabasca 36, 38, 197,

199, 201; Blackfoot 79; Crowfoot 42, 189–190; Dome Glacier 197, 200; Grinnell 34, 38, 51, 69, 70, 81, 84; Jackson 79; Piegan 79; Saskatchewan 38; Sexton 80; Sperry 79; Stanley 156; Stutfield 201; tours 200
Gladstone, Jack: 41
Glenns Lake: 90
Goat Haunt: 76, 83
Going-to-the-Sun Mountain: 64
Going-to-the-Sun Road: 11, 51, 60–68, 77–81, 90–92, 94–95, 99–100; map 62–63
Granite Park Chalet: 34, 83, 89, 90, 108; map 82
Great Hall: 246
Grinnell Glacier: 34, 38, 51, 69, 70, 81, 84
Grinnell Glacier Overlook: 83
Grinnell Lake: 39, 70, 84–85
Grizzly Lake: 133
Grizzly-Larix Lakes Loop: 34, 146–147; map 146
guides: bicycling 92; hiking 88; winter sports 95–96
Gunsight Lake: 89
Gunsight Pass: 89

H
hantavirus: 296
Harvest: 246
Haystack Falls: 61
Haystack Saddle: 83
health and safety: 261, 266, 295–296
heather: 276–277
Heavens Peak: 61
Hector Gorge: 156
Hector Lake Viewpoint: 189
Helen Lake: 18, 39, 42, 190
Herbert Lake: 42, 189
Hidden Lake Overlook: 11, 36, 61, 79
highlights: Banff 121, 128–135, 136, 142–144; Glacier 51, 57, 60–77; Icefields Parkway 181, 189–207; Jasper 223, 229–236
Highline Trail: 34, 61, 82–83
Highline Trail and Granite Park Chalet: 82–83; map 82
Highway 16 (Athabasca River): 237
Highway 93A (Wabasso Road): 202, 206
hiking: general discussion 34, 289–290; Banff 138, 140, 144–151; Glacier

75–76, 77–88; Icefields Parkway 190, 191, 194, 195, 198–199, 202, 206, 207; Jasper 238–243
Hinton: 289
Hole-in-the-Wall: 135
hoodoos: 144–145
Horseshoe Lake: 206
hospitals: 295
hotels: see lodging
hot springs: Banff 129, 132, 156; Miette Hot Springs 236; Radium Hot Springs 156
Howse Pass Viewpoint: 194
hypothermia: 296

I
ice and snow safety: 295
Iceberg Lake: 39, 86
Icefield Centre: 197, 209
Icefields Parkway: 42, 43, 177–219; backpacking 209; bicycling 209; camping 211–214; food 209–211, 246; highlights 181, 189–207; hiking 190, 191, 194, 195, 198–199, 202, 206, 207; information and services 218–219; itineraries 183–186; lodging 214–217; maps 43, 178–179, 184–185
Iceline Trail: 140
ice-skating: 159
Indigenous peoples: 40–41
information and services: Banff 174–175; Glacier 111–115; Icefields Parkway 218–219; Jasper 257; nearby towns 285, 286, 287, 288, 289
Ink Pots: 135
internet access: 112–113, 293
interpretive programs: 291, 293
itineraries: 9–25; Banff 123, 124; Glacier 53–54; Icefields Parkway 183–186; Jasper 225–226

J
Jackson Glacier: 79
Jackson Glacier Overlook: 64, 89
Jasper Adventure Centre: 234
Jasper House: 237
Jasper Lake: 237
Jasper National Park: 31, 221–257; backpacking 243; bicycling 243–244; camping 249–251; food 246–249; highlights 223, 229–236; hiking 238–243; information and services 257; itineraries 225–226;

lodging 250–255; maps 222, 224, 232–233; rafting 244; winter sports 244–245
Jasper SkyTram: 230, 239
Jasper, town of: 229–230, 238–239, 242, 246; map 229
Jasper, vicinity of: 230, 234; map 232–233
Jasper Visitor Centre: 209, 243
Jasper-Yellowhead Museum and Archives: 229
Johnson Lake Day Use Area: 163
Johnston Canyon: 135
Josephine Lake: 12

KL

Kalispell: 287
kid-friendly programs: 293
Kintla Lake: 77
Kootenai people: 40
Kootenay National Park: 156–157; map 157
Laggan's Mountain Bakery: 163
Lake Agnes: 34, 148–149; map 148
Lake Agnes Teahouse: 149
Lake Annette: 230, 234
Lake Annette Day Use Area: 249
Lake Annette Loop: 234
Lake Edith: 230, 234
Lake Ellen Wilson: 89
Lake Josephine: 84–85, 94
Lake Louise: 17, 39, 121, 135, 142–144, 147, 150–151, 159, 172–173; maps 142, 143
Lake Louise Campground: 165, 170
Lake Louise sightseeing gondola: 142, 144
Lake Louise Ski Resort: 36, 142, 159
Lake Louise Visitor Centre: 174
Lake McDonald: 10, 57, 61, 93–94, 98–99
Lake McDonald Lodge: 89, 107–108
Lake Minnewanka: 132–133, 155
Lake Minnewanka Day Use Area: 163
Lake O'Hara: 136, 138
Lake Trail (Mary Schäffer Loop): 242
Larch Valley: 151; map 150
Larix Lake: 133
Leach Lake Day Use Area: 210
Leave No Trace: 44
lilies: 270
Little Beehive: 149
Lodge at Bow Lake: 191, 215

Lodge of the Ten Peaks: 144
lodging: Banff 168–173; Glacier 105–109; Icefields Parkway 214–217; Jasper 250–255; nearby towns 285, 286–287, 288, 289; see also camping
Logan Pass: 61, 64, 83, 89
Logan Pass Visitor Center: 112
Lone Walker Mountain: 73
The Loop: 61, 83
Louise Lakeshore Trail: 147
Lower Sunwapta Falls: 201
Lower Waterfowl Lake: 39, 194
Lunch Creek: 64
lupine: 270–271

M

Maligne Canyon: 23, 234, 242
Maligne Lake: 24, 36, 39, 234, 236, 237, 245
Maligne Lake Day Use Area: 249
Maligne Lake Lodge: 236
Maligne River: 234
Maligne Valley: 234–236, 242–243
Many Glacier: 51, 68–70, 81, 83, 84–86, 90, 94, 100; maps 69, 85
Many Glacier Campground: 101
Many Glacier Entrance: 111
Many Glacier Hotel: 13, 36, 70, 80, 109
Many Glacier Picnic Area: 100
Many Glacier Road: 70
Marble Canyon: 156
Marmot Basin: 244–245
marmots: 265
Mary Schäffer Loop (Lake Trail): 242
Medicine Lake: 234
Miette Hot Springs: 236
Miette Hot Springs Day Use Area: 249
Mile 5 Run: 244
Mina Lakes: 238
Mirror Lake: 149
Mistaya Canyon: 42, 194
monkeyflower: 274
moose: 262
Moose Lake: 241
Moraine Lake: 16, 121, 144, 151; map 143
Morant's Curve: 135
Morning Star Lake: 89
mosquitoes: 296
moss campion: 270
mountain avens: 274, 276
mountain goats: 264

Mount Amery: 195
Mount Assiniboine: 133
Mount Athabasca: 197, 199, 200
Mount Burgess: 138
Mount Chephren: 195
Mount Clements: 79
Mount Edith Cavell: 202–203, 206;
    map 203
Mount Forbes: 194
Mount Hector: 189
Mount Kerkeslin: 202
Mount Kitchener: 201
Mount Murchison: 194, 195
Mount Outram: 194
Mount Patterson: 192
Mount Sarbach: 195
Mount Saskatchewan: 195
Mount Temple: 189
Mount Victoria: 142
Mount Wilson: 195
Muleshoe: 134–135

NO

Nakoda people: 40
Native America Speaks: 41, 293
No Name Lake: 89
Norquay: 158
North American Indian Days: 41
Northern Circle: 90
northern lights: 69
North Fork: 73, 77
Numa Falls: 156
Oberlin Bend Overlook: 61
Old Fort Point: 243
Old Man Lake: 89
Olive Lake: 156
Opabin Plateau Circuit: 140–141

P

Packer's Roost: 90
paddling: general discussion 291;
    Banff 158; Glacier 93–94
paintbrush: 272–273
Paint Pots: 156
The Palisade: 239
Paradise Lodge and Bungalows: 172–173
Park: 162
Parker's Ridge: 195
parking: 114, 175, 257
Path of the Glacier Trail: 206
Patricia Lake: 230
Patricia Lake Loop: 238–239
pets, traveling with: 294
Peyto Lake: 42

Peyto Lake Viewpoint: 192
picnic spots: Banff 163–164; Glacier
    98–100; Icefields Parkway 210;
    Jasper 249
Piegan Glacier: 79
Piegan Mountain: 64
Piegan Pass: 64, 79–80; map 80
Piegan Pass Trail: 80
pikas: 266
Plain of Six Glaciers: 147, 150
Plain of Six Glaciers Teahouse: 150
Pocahontas: 237
Polebridge Entrance: 77
Post Hotel: 172
Pray Lake: 94
Preston Park: 79
Prince of Wales Hotel: 75
Ptarmigan Dining Room: 96, 98
Punchbowl Falls: 237
Pyramid Benchland: 238
Pyramid Lake: 230
Pyramid Lake Day Use Area: 249
Pyramid Lake Road: 245
Pyramid Mountain: 230

QR

Radium Hot Springs: 156
rafting: 244, 291
rail travel: 282
ranger programs: 291, 293
recreation: see specific activity, place
Red Buses: 66, 68
Redrock Lake and Falls: 85
reservations: 283
resources: 297
restaurants: see food
Rising Sun: 64
Rising Sun Campground: 100–101
Rising Wolf Mountain: 72, 73
road rules: 281
Roche Miette: 237
Rock Isle Lake: 133
Rock Isle Lake Viewpoint: 146
Rockwell Falls: 87
Rocky Point: 95
roses, wild: 277
Rundle Patio: 162
Running Eagle Falls: 72
Russell's Fireside Dining Room: 96
RV travel: 284

S

safety: 295–296
Salish people: 40

Saskatchewan Glacier: 38
Saskatchewan River: 194–195
scenic drives: general discussion 42–43; Athabasca River (Highway 16) 237; Bow Valley Parkway 134–135; Chief Mountain International Highway 74; Going-to-the-Sun Road 61, 64–65; Icefields Parkway 189–207; Many Glacier Road 70; Wabasso Road (Highway 93A) 202, 206; Yoho Valley Road 138
Scenic Point: 86–87; map 87
Schäffer Viewpoint: 242
seasons: 27–28
service hubs: 218
Sexton Glacier: 80
Shadow Lake: 154
Shadow Lake Lodge: 154
Sherburne Reservoir: 70
shooting stars: 273
Shuswap people: 40
shuttles: 114–115, 175, 219, 257, 284
sightseeing gondola (Lake Louise): 142, 144
Sinopah Mountain: 73
Sixth Bridge: 234
Siyeh Bend: 64, 80
Siyeh Pass: 64, 79–80; map 80
Siyeh Pass Trail: 80
Ski Big3 Adventure Hub: 158
skiing/snowboarding: 158–159, 244–245, see also cross-country skiing
Skoki Lodge: 154
Skoki Valley: 154–155
Skyline Trail: 243
Snow Dome: 200
Snyder Lakes: 95
South Boundary Trail: 243
Sperry Chalet: 89, 108–109
Sperry Glacier: 79
Spirit Island: 236
Sprague Creek Picnic Area: 57
Spray River Loop: 155
Standish Chairlift: 133
Stanley Glacier: 156
stargazing: 292
St. Mary: 65, 68, 285–286
St. Mary Entrance: 111
St. Mary Falls: 81
St. Mary Lake: 64, 68
St. Mary Scenic Overlook: 41
St. Mary Scenic Overlook and Blackfeet Interpretive Loop: 68

St. Mary Visitor Center: 88, 112
Stoney people: 40
Stony Indian Lake: 90
Storm Mountain Lodge: 163, 172
Storm Mountain Viewpoint: 135
Storm Mountain Viewpoint Day Use Area: 164
Stutfield Glacier Viewpoint: 201
Sulphur Mountain: 36, 132
Sulphur Skyline: 243
Sundance Canyon: 155
Sun Point: 12, 64
Sun Point Picnic Area: 99–100
Sunrift Gorge: 80
Sunshine Meadows: 133–134, 146–147
Sunshine Village: 158–159
Sun Tours: 41, 66
Sunwapta Falls: 191, 201
Sunwapta Falls Rocky Mountain Lodge: 215
Sunwapta Lake: 200
Sunwapta Pass: 195
Sunwapta River: 200–201, 244
sustainable travel: 44
Swiftcurrent Lake: 12, 69, 94
Swiftcurrent Lookout: 83, 85
Swiftcurrent Pass: 85
Swiftcurrent Valley: 70

T
Takakkaw Falls: 136, 138
Tangle Falls: 191, 201
Tangle Ridge: 201
ticks: 296
Tonquin Valley: 209
Trail of the Cedars: 61, 77
train travel: 282
transportation: 58–59, 113–115, 174–175, 219, 257, 280–285
Triple Arches: 61
Truffle Pig Bistro: 141
Two Dog Flats: 64
Two Jack Lake Day Use Area: 163
Two Jack Lakeside Campground: 165
Two Medicine: 70, 72–73, 86–87, 94, 100; map 72
Two Medicine Campground: 89, 104
Two Medicine Entrance: 111–112
Two Medicine Lake: 72–73, 94
Two Medicine Lake Singers and Dancers: 41
Two Medicine Picnic Area: 100

U-Z

Upper Spiral Tunnel Viewpoint: 138
Upper Waterfowl Lake: 192
Valley of the Five Lakes: 207; map 207
vegetation zones: 270
Vermilion Lakes: 132
views, best: 36
Virginia Falls: 81
visitor centers: Banff 174; Glacier 112; Icefields Parkway 218–219; Jasper 257
Wabasso Campground: 214
Wabasso Road (Highway 93A): 202, 206
Wapiti Campground: 250
waterfalls: Athabasca Falls 191, 202, 244; Bird Woman Falls 61; Bow Glacier Falls 191–192; Bridal Veil Falls 149; Cameron Falls 75; Glacier Falls 61; Haystack Falls 61; Johnston Canyon 135; Numa Falls 156; Punchbowl Falls 237; Redrock Falls 85; Rockwell Falls 87; Running Eagle Falls 72; St. Mary Falls 81; Sunwapta Falls 191, 201; Takakkaw Falls 136; Tangle Falls 191, 201; Twin Falls 73; Virginia Falls 81; Weeping Wall (Banff) 191, 195; Weeping Wall (Glacier) 61
Waterfowl Lake: 42
Waterfowl Lakes Campground: 214
water hazards: 295
Waterton Lakes National Park: 74–76; map 75
weather: 27–28
Weeping Wall (Banff): 191, 195
Weeping Wall (Glacier): 61
West Glacier: 285
West Glacier Entrance: 111
West Side Tunnel: 61
The Whistlers: 230, 239, 242
Whistlers Campground: 245, 249–250
Whitefish: 287
Whitehorn Lodge: 144
Whyte Museum of the Canadian Rockies: 128–129
Wicked Cup: 246
Wilcox Pass: 22, 34, 198–199; map 198
wildflowers: 269–277
Wild Goose Island Overlook: 64
wildlife/wildlife-watching: 259–267
wild roses: 277
winter sports: general discussion 291; Banff 158–159; Glacier 94–96; Jasper 244–245
wolves: 261–262
Yoho National Park: 136–141; map 137
Yoho River: 138

LIST OF MAPS

Front Map
Glacier, Banff & Jasper National Parks:
   2-3

Welcome to Glacier, Banff & Jasper
Glacier, Banff & Jasper National Parks:
   29

Best of the Best
Icefields Parkway—South Section: 43

Glacier National Park
Glacier National Park: 48-49
Glacier National Park 3 Ways: 52
Apgar: 57
Going-to-the-Sun Road: 62-63
Many Glacier: 69
Two Medicine: 72
Waterton Lakes National Park: 75
Piegan Pass and Siyeh Pass: 80
Highline Trail and Granite Park Chalet:
   82
Many Glacier Trails: 85
Scenic Point: 87

Banff and Lake Louise
Banff and Lake Louise: 118-119

Banff and Lake Louise 3 Ways: 122
Banff National Park: 127
Vicinity of Banff: 130-131
Bow Valley Parkway: 134
Yoho National Park: 137
Lake Louise: 142
Lake Louise and Moraine Lake: 143
Grizzly-Larix Lakes Loop: 146
Lake Agnes: 148
Larch Valley: 150
Kootenay National Park: 157

Icefields Parkway
Icefields Parkway: 178-179
Icefields Parkway 3 Ways: 184-185
Columbia Icefield: 196
Wilcox Pass: 198
Mount Edith Cavell: 203
Valley of the Five Lakes: 207

Jasper National Park
Jasper National Park: 222
Jasper National Park 3 Ways: 224
Town of Jasper: 229
Vicinity of Jasper: 232-233
Bald Hills: 240

PHOTO CREDITS

National Parks Travel Guides from Moon

ACADIA
NATIONAL PARK
SEASIDE TOWNS · FALL FOLIAGE
CYCLING & PADDLING

HILARY NANGLE

ARCHES & CANYONLANDS
NATIONAL PARKS
HIKING · BIKING
SCENIC DRIVES

JUDY JEWELL & W. C. McRAE

BANFF
NATIONAL PARK
HIKE · CAMP
SEE WILDLIFE

ANDREW HEMPSTEAD

CANADIAN ROCKIES
WITH BANFF & JASPER NATIONAL PARKS
SCENIC DRIVES · WILDLIFE
HIKING & SKIING

ANDREW HEMPSTEAD

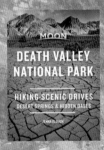

DEATH VALLEY
NATIONAL PARK
HIKING · SCENIC DRIVES
DESERT SPRINGS & HIDDEN OASES

JENNA BLOUGH

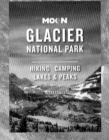

GLACIER
NATIONAL PARK
HIKING · CAMPING
LAKES & PEAKS

BECKY LOMAX

GRAND CANYON
HIKE · CAMP
RAFT THE
COLORADO RIVER

TIM HULL

GREAT SMOKY MOUNTAINS
NATIONAL PARK
HIKING · CAMPING
SCENIC DRIVES

JASON FRYE

JOSHUA TREE
& PALM SPRINGS
HIKING · SCENIC DRIVES
DESERT GETAWAYS

JENNA BLOUGH

ROCKY MOUNTAIN
NATIONAL PARK
HIKE · CAMP
SEE WILDLIFE

ERIN ENGLISH

SEQUOIA & KINGS CANYON
HIKING · CAMPING
WATERFALLS & BIG TREES

LEIGH BERMACCHI

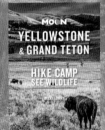

YELLOWSTONE
& GRAND TETON
HIKE · CAMP
SEE WILDLIFE

BECKY LOMAX

YOSEMITE SEQUOIA & KINGS CANYON
HIKING · CAMPING
WATERFALLS & BIG TREES

ANN MARIE BROWN

ZION & BRYCE
WITH ARCHES, CANYONLANDS, CAPITOL REEF,
GRAND STAIRCASE-ESCALANTE & MORE
HIKING & BIKING
STARGAZING · SCENIC DRIVES

MAYA SILVER

Get the bestselling all-parks guide, or check out Moon's new Best Of Parks series to make the most of a 1-3 day visit to top parks.

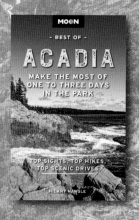

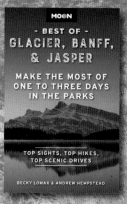

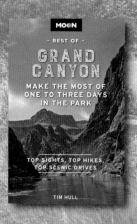

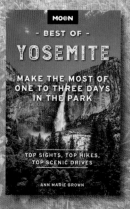

Get inspired for your next adventure

Follow **@moonguides** on Instagram or subscribe to our newsletter at **moon.com**

MAP SYMBOLS

═══	Highway	○	City/Town	P	Parking Area	🛆	Small Park
═══	Primary Road	◉	State Capital	T	Trailhead	▲	Mountain Peak
───	Secondary Road	⊛	National Capital	B	Bike Trailhead	✦	Unique Natural Feature
- - -	Unpaved Road	★	Top 3 Sight	△	Camping	✦	Unique Hydro Feature
----------	Trail	🚶	Top Hike	🎴	Picnic Area		
▬▬▬	Paved Trail	★	Highlight/Sight	M	Mass Transit	🦅	Waterfall
▦▦▦	Pedestrian Walkway	•	Accommodation	✈	Airport	🎿	Ski Area
············	Ferry	▼	Restaurant/Bar	✕	Airfield		
- - - -	Railroad	■	Other Site	🛆	Place of Worship	☁	Glacier

CONVERSION TABLES

$°C = (°F - 32) / 1.8$

$°F = (°C \times 1.8) + 32$

1 inch = 2.54 centimeters (cm)

1 foot = 0.304 meters (m)

1 yard = 0.914 meters

1 mile = 1.6093 kilometers (km)

1 km = 0.6214 miles

1 fathom = 1.8288 m

1 chain = 20.1168 m

1 furlong = 201.168 m

1 acre = 0.4047 hectares

1 sq km = 100 hectares

1 sq mile = 2.59 square km

1 ounce = 28.35 grams

1 pound = 0.4536 kilograms

1 short ton = 0.90718 metric ton

1 short ton = 2,000 pounds

1 long ton = 1.016 metric tons

1 long ton = 2,240 pounds

1 metric ton = 1,000 kilograms

1 quart = 0.94635 liters

1 US gallon = 3.7854 liters

1 Imperial gallon = 4.5459 liters

1 nautical mile = 1.852 km

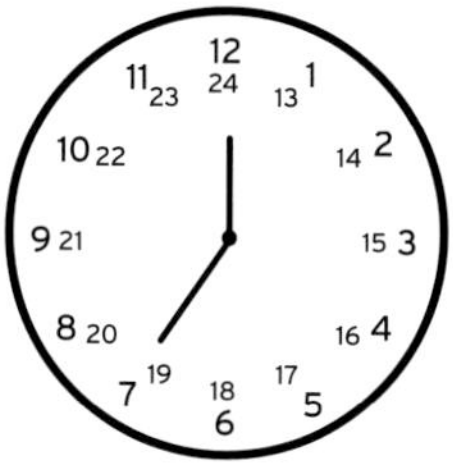

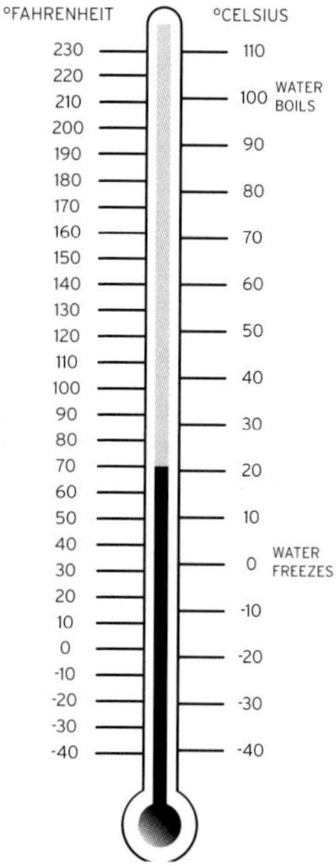

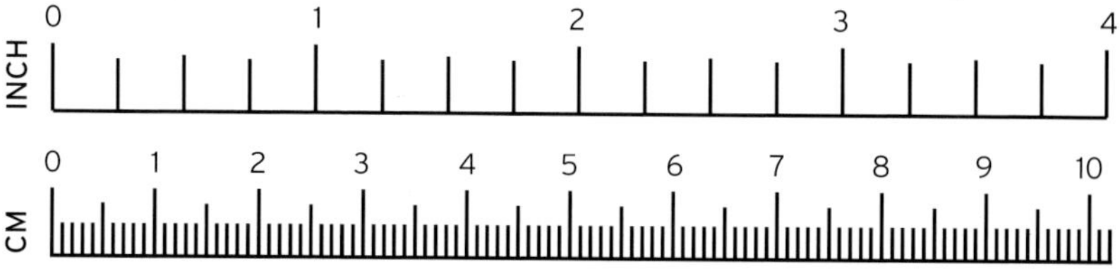

MOON BEST OF GLACIER, BANFF & JASPER

Avalon Travel
Hachette Book Group
1700 Fourth Street
Berkeley, CA 94710, USA
www.moon.com

Editor: Grace Fujimoto
Managing Editor: Hannah Brezack
Copy Editor: Ashley Benning
Graphics Coordinator: Ravina
  Schneider
Production Coordinator: Ravina
  Schneider
Cover Design: Marcie Lawrence
Interior Design: Tabitha Lahr
Map Editor: John Culp
Cartographers: John Culp, Karin Dahl,
  Albert Angulo
Proofreader: Callie Stoker-Graham
Indexer: Greg Jewett

ISBN-13: 979-8-88647-026-0

Printing History
1st Edition — 2021
2nd Edition — March 2024
5 4 3 2 1

Front cover photo: Banff © Kevin
Mueller | Unsplash.com

Back cover photo credits: Bow Lake
© Andrew Hempstead (top); St.
Mary Scenic Overlook & Blackfeet
Interpretive Loop © Becky Lomax
(middle); Dawson-Pitamakin Loop ©
Becky Lomax (bottom)

Interior back cover photo: Many
Glacier © NPS / Tim Rains

Printed in China by APS